Journal of Consciousness Studies
controversies in science & the humanities

Vol. 11, No. 3–4, March/April 2004

SPECIAL FEATURE ON 'ART AND THE BRAIN', PART III
Edited by Joseph A. Goguen and Erik Myin

Cover Illustration: Claire Harper

Published in the UK and USA by Imprint Academic, PO Box 200, Exeter EX5 5YX, UK

JCS is indexed and abstracted in: *Social Sciences Citation Index®*, *ISI Alerting Services* (includes *Research Alert®*), *Current Contents®: Social and Behavioral Sciences, Arts and Humanities Citation Index®*, *Current Contents®: Arts & Humanities Citation Index®*, *Social Scisearch®*, *PsycINFO®* and *The Philosopher's Index*.

Journal of Consciousness Studies ISSN 1355 8250

Art and the Brain, Vol.3 ISBN 0 907845 98 3

ABOUT AUTHORS

The Editors

Joseph Goguen is professor, and Director of the Meaning and Computation Lab, at the University of California, San Diego. He was previously at Oxford, SRI, UCLA, and Chicago, and is Editor in Chief of *JCS*. His interests include algebraic semantics, interface design, semiotics, fuzzy logic, databases, ethics, sociology of science, and music. More information can be found at http://www.cs.ucsd.edu/users/goguen.

Erik Myin teaches and does research at the Department of Philosophy of the Vrije Universiteit Brussel, Centre for Logic and Philosophy of Science. His work is focused on the philosophy of cognitive science, in particular on issues concerning perception, meaning and the (dis)unity of science. His webpage is at http://homepages.vub.ac.be/~emyin.

Other Contributors

Elvira Brattico graduated in philosophy at the University of Bari, and in piano performance at the Conservatory of Bari, Italy. She is currently pursuing her PhD degree in psychology at the University of Helsinki, under the supervision of professors. M. Tervaniemi and R. Näätänen. Her research interests concern the neural bases of musical sound perception investigated with electrophysiological and brain-imaging methods.

Neus Barrantes-Vidal is a psychologist working as a senior lecturer in clinical psychology at the Universitat Autònoma de Barcelona. Parallel to her academic career she obtained a clinical master's in adult psychotherapy in the Hospital Clínic de Barcelona. Her main research topic relates to psychosocial and biological risk factors for major mental disorders, but she also maintains the research line initiated with a master's thesis on the relationship between creativity and personality. She is also an amateur singer and general art lover.

David Borgo is a jazz saxophonist, improvisor, and ethnomusicologist, and an assistant professor in the Critical Studies and Experimental Practices program at the University of California, San Diego. He has a BM in jazz studies from Indiana University and a PhD in ethnomusicology from UCLA. Borgo's scholarly work appears in *Black Musical Research Journal*, *The Pacific Review of Ethnomusicology*, *The Open Space Magazine*, *The Society for American Music Bulletin*, and as a chapter in the forthcoming *Playing Changes* (Duke University Press). His recordings as both leader and collaborator appear on the Resurgent Music, Positone, Acoustic Levitation, and Circumvention Music labels. He is currently at work on a CD project dedicated to South African jazz pioneers and a book exploring the relationship between the emerging sciences of complexity and contemporary improvised music.

Ivar Hagendoorn is a freelance choreographer and researcher. He studied mathematical finance, philosophy and literature and before turning full-time to dance worked as a quantitative analyst with an investment bank. His research focuses on the cognitive and mathematical foundations of dance and choreography. In 2001 he was a visiting scientist and artist at the University of Southern California, Los Angeles. His latest project, an evening-long choreography for the Ballett Frankfurt, was premiered in January 2004.

Erich Harth is an emeritus professor of physics at Syracuse University, where he directed experimental research on the physics of elementary particles that resulted in many publications. In the mid-1960s his interests shifted to neuroscience. He and his students investigated processes involved in sensory (particularly visual) information processing, proposing neural mechanisms of top-down control, through which 'higher' level areas in the brain can cause feature-specific changes of primary sensory stimuli. Harth has written three books for the general reader and is currently completing another, titled *Chimps Don't Dance*, on the uinqueness of humans originating in the brain.

Amy Ione is an international lecturer, painter, and writer, and co-founder with Christopher Tyler of the Diatrope Institute. She has long explored the nature of creativity, cognition, and areas of convergence in innovative art and science practices. Her academic studies have been widely published in the books and journals of several disciplines, including an invited contribution to the *Encyclopedia of Creativity* (Academic Press, 1999). Her artwork has been commissioned by the City of San Francisco, exhibited internationally, and is found in many collections. More information about her art and academic research can be found at http://www.diatrope.com/ione.

Vijay Iyer is a New York-based pianist, composer, improvisor, and occasional scholar. His most recent recordings include *In What Language?* (2004, with poet/performer Mike Ladd), *Blood Sutra* (2003), and *Your Life Flashes* (2002, as the collective trio Fieldwork). Iyer has performed around the world as a leader and in collaboration with artists such as Roscoe Mitchell, Amiri Baraka, Steve Coleman, Miya Masaoka, Trichy Sankaran, George Lewis, Butch Morris, Will Power, and Burnt Sugar. He holds a BS. from Yale College and a PhD in Technology and the Arts from the University of California at Berkeley. He received the 2003 CalArts Alpert Award in the Arts.

Mari Tervaniemi is a researcher at the Cognitive Brain Research Unit in Helsinki, having received a PhD in psychology, with minor in musicology in 1997. In 2000 Tervaniemi held a twelve-month professorship in developmental neuropsychology, and in 2001 worked at Leipzig as a visiting researcher, hosted by the BioCog group at the Department of Allgemeine Psychologie, working in close collaboration with the researchers at the Max-Planck Institute for Cognitive Neuroscience.

Joseph A. Goguen & Erik Myin

Editorial Introduction

Music raises many problems for those who would understand it more deeply. It is rooted in time, yet timeless. It is pure form, yet conveys emotion. It is written, but performed, interpreted, improvised, transcribed, recorded, sampled, remixed, revised, rebroadcast, reinterpreted, and more. Music can be studied by philosophers, psychologists, sociologists, mathematicians, biologists, computer scientists, neuro-scientists, critics, politicians, promoters, and of course musicians. Moreover, no single perspective seems either sufficient or invalid. This situation is not so different from that of other arts, but perhaps more intense, due to the pervasiveness of pop, the inaccessability of much contemporary classical music, the strong cultural associations of many styles (e.g., hip hop, salsa, twelve tone, heavy metal), the infusions of technology, and the combination with lyrics.

Although this is a challenging situation for researchers, it is also exciting, and advances in experimental technique, such as fMRI, and in theory, such as metaphor and blending in cognitive linguistics, have made it more so, fueling a surge of interest, and mobilizing a very diverse set of ideas, approaches and methods, e.g. see Assayag *et al.* (2002); Benzon (2001); Spiro (2003); Zatorre & Peretz (2001); Zbikowski (2002). Certain aspects of the resulting positions can be visualized on a linear spectrum. At one end we find positions characterized as representational, modular, realist, reductionistic, or internalistic. At the other end are positions described as nonrepresentational, holistic, non-reductionistic, externalist, or embodiment-oriented. Of course, this crude projection onto a single dimension fails to capture many subtle distinctions; moreover, theoretical options that seem incompatible do get combined, and mixed positions are often vigorously defended. The difficulties of classification are amplified by a variety of other associated metaphorical oppositions, including western versus eastern, and context-free versus contextualized. It will be convenient to refer to the end points of this spectrum as east and west, without intending any religious or political connotations. On the other hand, this classification does reflect ancient, deep divisions within western culture, that remain very intense and productive to this day.

Correspondence:
J.A. Goguen, Dept of Computer Science & Engineering, University of California at San Diego, 9500 Gilman Drive, La Jolla, CA 92093-0114, USA. *Email: Goguen@cs.ucsd.edu*
Erik Myin, Center for Logic & Philosophy of Science, Vakgroep Wijsbegeerte, Vrije Universiteit Brussel, Pleinlaan 2, B 1050 Brussel, Belgium. *Email: emyin@vub.ac.be*

Journal of Consciousness Studies, **11**, No. 3–4, 2004, pp. 5–8

Hence, though we hope it is not completely misguided, the following attempt to place the papers of this volume on this spectrum should be taken with more than a grain of sceptical salt, or even regarded as merely rhetorical. With this caveat, we place the papers by Tervaniemi and Brattico and by Bruce Katz near the western end. Tervaniemo and Brattico apply cognitive neuroscience to music perception. From within a standard representational framework, they address questions such as whether musical perception requires attention, and whether and at what stage of neural processing, cultural knowledge comes into play. Two (among many) intriguing results reported, are that increased complexity of musical sound facilitates processing, and that musical knowledge gained from experience enters at early and often unattended levels of processing.

Katz's paper defines a numerical measure of musical preference based on the degree of synchrony of a neural net model of musical cognition. This measure is separately applied to harmonic, melodic, and rhythmic patterns abstracted from three bodies of data (for western popular and classical, and for Turkish art songs), and is shown consistent with some simple regularities noted by music theorists. A number of interesting differences among the three styles and three dimensions are also discussed.

The paper by Neus Barrantes-Vidal combines some of the perspectives discussed above. Its basic hypothesis is that underlying both madness and creativity is a constellation of personality traits that, in their advantageous manifestation, lead to creativity, while in their disadvantagous form, make a person vulnerable to psychosis. The author offers the additional conjecture that this possibility for beneficial expression, might be a factor in keeping what alternatively turns out to be a — possibly genetic — vulnerability for psychosis in the population. One innovative aspect of the paper is its break with traditional dichotomous thinking about personality traits and mental (dys)function.

Hagendoorn moves us further east, but not beyond the midpoint. This paper approaches dance from a neuro-cognitive perspective, and in particular, attempts to explain how emotion can be aroused by dance. Although it is not about music as such, it is intriguing how its themes of emotion, embodiment, and anticipation connect with other papers in this volume, e.g., those of Tervaniemo and Brattico, and of Goguen. This paper also contains an excellent review of relevant experimental evidence, and a fascinating treatment of dance, drawing on the author's experience as a choreographer.

Erich Harth's short paper is an elegant attempt to reconcile the scientific method of reduction with more cultural concerns, by appeal to an extension of reduction to include 'downward' causation as well as the traditional 'upward' causation.

Moving further eastward, the paper by Joseph Goguen presents its reflections on music as an alternative theory of qualia, in which, contrary to most other treatments, qualia are seen as deeply contextual and social. Throughout, the author sketches, sometimes in broad strokes, sometimes in considereable depth, how a future theory of musical experience could be articulated, using concepts and methods from phenomenology, cognitive linguistics, and non-linear dynamical systems theory. Although rigorous use of the latter might seem to place this paper far to the west, the author claims otherwise.

The paper by Amy Ione explores relationships between art and music in the work of the painters Vasily Kandinsky and Paul Klee. Both were pioneers in abstract expressionism, both worked at Bauhaus, and both were knowledgeable about and inspired by music. Kandinsky was (apparently) a synaesthete, as well as a mystic who aspired to a unified science of the arts, whereas Klee was less grand in his aspirations, creating what can be seen as small experiments in colour and arrangement.

Vijay Iyer, being both a theorist and a well-regarded composer/performer, provides a compelling case for music as an embodied and culturally embedded experience. Focusing on temporality, Iyer shows how in improvistation, music literally becomes 'the sound of human action', and he illustrates this with his own experiences of improvisation in ensembles led by Cecil Taylor and Roscoe Mitchell.

The paper of David Borgo is a brilliant exploration of relations among technical, cognitive, and social aspects of jazz improvisation. Both an ethnomusicologist and jazz improviser, Borgo also deploys blending and cross space mappings from cognitive linguistics, to describe how jazz musicians respond to social conditions and to prior landmark performances, emphasizing in particular the important notion of signifyin(g), and how it differs from signification. This takes us very near indeed to the eastern pole.

Some reasons to place music in the western area include its similarity to language, which has been a basis for strong claims (e.g. from Chomsky) about innateness and modularity of mind, as well as influences from theories such as neural reductionism and behaviourism. Some reasons to place music near the eastern pole include the inevitability of action whenever music becomes concrete, the importance of rhythm and its relatedness to processes of bodily coordination (e.g., in walking and dancing), the social aspects of musical performance, and the role of emotion in music. It may be that east is east and west is west and never the twain shall meet (as claimed by Rudyard Kipling); perhaps there are even good theoretical reasons for such a supposition, e.g., that musical phenomena are so inherently heterogeneous, that one method is more suited for some aspects, and another for other aspects.

But there are also reasons to suppose that the east/west dichotomy can be overcome. For example, something like Harth's proposal for downward causation or Searle's emergentism (Searle, 1997) might eventually become sufficiently developed as to constitute a viable method for the humanities. Further out is the late Heideggerian proclamation of the 'end of philosophy' (Heidegger, 1972), in which thinking time and Being overcome the long history of thinking beings 'in the manner of representational thinking which gives reasons', thus revitalizing pre-Socratic insights that transcend the traditional oppositions with which we have been playing in this introduction.

In any case, we can safely predict that music theory will remain far from equilibrium, in a dynamic instability and evolution that mirrors its subject, and we hope that this volume will play some role in that ongoing process.

References

Assayag, Gerard, Feichtinger, Hans & Rodrigues, Jose-Francisco (ed. 2002), *Mathematics and Music: A Diderot Mathematical Forum* (Berlin: Springer).

Benzon, William (2001), *Beethoven's Anvil* (New York: Basic Books).

Heidegger, Martin (1972), *On Time and Being*, trans. Joan Stambaugh (Chicago).

Searle, John (1997), *The Mystery of Consciousness* (New York Review of Books).

Spiro, John (ed. 2003), 'Focus on Music', Feature in *Nature Neuroscience*, **6** (7), pp. 661–95.

Zatorre, Robert & Peretz, Isabelle (ed. 2001), *The Biological Foundations of Music*, Annals of the New York Academy of Sciences, Vol. 930.

Zbikowski, Lawrence (2002), *Conceptualizing Music* (Oxford).

Mari Tervaniemi & Elvira Brattico

From Sounds to Music

Towards Understanding the Neurocognition of Musical Sound Perception

Abstract: *In this chapter we present a new approach to research in music perception allowing one to investigate how musical sound representations are formed in the human brain. By studying subjects' brain responses to unattended stimuli we can determine, for instance, whether neural circuits are more readily activated by musical sounds implicitly learned than by unfamiliar sounds even in non-musicians. Indeed, neuronal populations seem to respond more efficiently to pitch deviations within sound patterns following the rules of Western scale structure, rather than to deviations inside patterns artificially created. Moreover, neural circuits are selectively activated by mistunings inside tonal melodies or by out-of-key chords inside harmonic cadences even when attention is not directed towards the sounds. These data together suggest that incoming sounds are more efficiently processed when they match the neural templates derived from our musical culture. The existence of 'musical memories' in the auditory cortex that are effortlessly activated enabling us, e.g., to identify and recognize speech vs. music sounds can thus be postulated.*

I: Brain Researchers' Approach to the Study of Music Perception

1. Traditional approach

During the past three decades, researchers had the opportunity to investigate the neural foundation of cognitive functions in the brain with the help of sophisticated techniques. Among those, the averaging of the voltage or magnetic changes time-locked to stimuli in an electroencephalogram (EEG) or magnetoencephalogram (MEG) gave origin to the field of event-related potentials (ERPs) or event-related fields (ERFs). This technique permitted to study the dynamics of information processing in the brain with an accuracy of

Correspondence:
Mari Tervaniemi, Cognitive Brain Research Unit, Department of Psychology, P.O. Box 9, FIN-00014 University of Helsinki, Finland. *Email: mari.tervaniemi@helsinki.fi*

milliseconds. Additionally, techniques such as positron emission tomography (PET) and, more recently, functional magnetic resonance imaging (fMRI) helped visualizing the metabolic consumption in the brain related to the mental activity the subject is performing. Among the research topics of cognitive neuroscience, music perception has recently become an increasingly attractive field of interest.

Due to strict methodological constraints, the great majority of the studies investigating sound perception up to now used sinusoidal tones or, rarely, isolated harmonic sounds composed of few lowest partials. However, if we ask naïve or expert listeners whether a sine tone presented in isolation is musical their answer would be certainly negative. Thus, in order to study music perception, we need to use musical sounds and sound scenes as our experimental material, that is, sounds and sound sequences that are temporally, spectrally, and structurally complex. This sound complexity is the plastic material that composers creatively organize on the basis of specific intents and generative principles. First of all, sounds may be complex in their structure, so that they consist of harmonic or inharmonic partials. This spectral structure in part creates the timbre typical of the instruments used in music. Alternatively, sound sequences can be temporally complex, such as in a succession of several sine tones.

In particular, when sounds occur within a context, it is possible to attribute to them a specific pitch. The dimension of perceptual pitch is related to the physical frequency of the sound (which corresponds to the cycles of a periodic wave per second): when the frequency increases the pitch sounds 'higher'. Our exposure to Western tonal musical culture determines when the succession of sounds is more or less musical, according to the frequency relations between the tones involved. However, this estimation highly depends on the listeners' musical expertise and aptitude. Moreover, sounds presented serially are characterized not only by their pitch, but also by the contour they create with their succession, by the perceived loudness (which does not necessarily coincide with the physical intensity), their perceived duration, and by their timbre. This implies that the way those different features are processed is another important factor for unveiling the neural mechanisms of musical sound perception.

The first studies dealing with the brain correlates of music perception employed experimental paradigms in which the participants were asked to actively listen to some melodies and, for example, to evaluate the appropriateness of the ending sound as compared to the preceding musical context. The final sound was thus the target of the subject's behavioral response. These studies showed that the ending sounds having a pitch, rhythm or harmony discrepant from the preceding context elicit larger positive electric brain responses (the so-called P3) than less discrepant ones (Besson & Macar, 1987; Besson *et al.*, 1994; Besson & Faita, 1995). From such findings it was concluded that electrophysiological responses might reflect the musical structures processed in our brains. However, when compared with other auditory responses originating in the cerebral cortex (see below), those responses start relatively late after the onset of the unexpected sound (between 300 and 400 ms). This may result in a partial masking of the earlier neural correlates of faster processes permitting a speeded recognition of unexpected musical sound events (occurring between 100 and 250 ms). Moreover, taken into account the speed in which musical information is accumulated, it seems even less plausible that these attentional brain processes would be required in everyday music listening. Rather it may be relevant in music perception research to study how these attentional processes are initiated; in other words, whether earlier brain mechanisms triggering attention toward unexpected and interesting events in music may be identified.

Consequently, neurophysiological research on late attentive brain responses, though interesting in many aspects, still left it open whether conscious attention towards music is necessary for forming and activating musical neural mechanisms. In other words, it remained unsolved at which neuronal and attentional levels musical percepts and tonal hierarchies are generated. This is a crucial question since the effortless ability to encode and integrate sounds over time, even when we are not focusing our attention and mental resources on them, intuitively enables us to appreciate music. In other words, neural mechanisms underlying preattentive sound processing may trigger the attention switching towards musical events that might be of interest to the listener. Therefore, it is relevant to also focus on the neural processes that underlie any conscious musical experience. These processes can be divided into the following stages: (1) the encoding and temporal integration of each sound characterized by its specific acoustic and perceptual features (e.g., pitch, duration, timbre) into a brief neural memory trace; (2) the simultaneous maintenance and integration of the neural traces for acoustic features leading possibly to the memorization of musical motifs; and (3) the modulation of sound percepts by the memory of the previous sounds.

Experimental studies in which subjects' behavioral responses were measured first proposed that even nonmusicians may have implicit knowledge of many different aspects of music. The paradigm most commonly used was termed harmonic priming. It consisted of presenting subjects with a chord cadence and asking them to respond as quickly and accurately as possible to the spectral or timbral features of the last chord of the cadence. For instance, subjects had to judge the consonance or dissonance of the chord, or whether it was played with one of two possible timbres. In this task, no explicit judgment of the overall musical context was required. Results showed that this decision was faster and more accurate when the last chord was harmonically related to the preceding context than when the same chord was harmonically less related or completely extraneous to the previous musical context (Bharucha & Stoeckig, 1986, 1987; Bigand *et al.*, 1999; Bigand & Pineau, 1997). This then suggests that the perception and processing of sounds by subjects even without any musical training is unavoidably and unconsciously influenced by the preceding musical context.

A theoretical explanation of those behavioural results was provided by using a connectionist computational model (Bharucha, 1987; Tillmann *et al.*, 2000). In the model, the implicit musical knowledge of the listener is represented as a network of interconnected units organized in three layers. Each layer represents tones, chords and keys. When a musical piece is presented to the model, tone units are activated and this activation reverberates between layers until equilibrium is reached (rather than an activation flowing in a bottom-up manner from tone to chord to key units). The activation pattern emerging from the reverberation represents tonal and harmonic hierarchies of the key in which the musical piece was played. This means that units corresponding to harmonically related chords are activated more strongly than units corresponding to unrelated chords. In our review we will introduce studies aimed at finding neural correlates of the implicit and automatic aspects of music perception. These processes are automatic in the sense that the listeners' brain cannot encode the incoming sounds without taking into account the knowledge of the sounds preceding them in the near past and of all the sounds that have been listened since birth. Furthermore, the studies reviewed will show which processes may occur automatically in the brain even during inattentive listening. We will not go into detailed discussion of the neurophysiological mechanisms underlying those processes but rather will present some evidence concerning how temporally and spectrally complex sounds are automatically encoded in the auditory cortex and how this encoding might be affected by top-down processing.

2. *Complementary approach: MMN as an index to pre-attentive sound processing*

Inspired by literature on orienting reflex (Sokolov, 1963), Näätänen initially formulated his theory on auditory perception, cognition, and memory in late 1960s and initiated empirical brain research in mid 1970s (as evidenced in Näätänen *et al.*, 1978, reviewed, *e.g.*, in Näätänen & Winkler, 1999). Based on ideas originating from earlier work , intensive research on preattentive forms of auditory perception has been established. During recent years the neurocognition of musical sound has also been studied using these techniques.

Empirically, the research on preattentive sound processing is concretized in an experimental paradigm in which the subject is presented with sounds of two types, differing, for instance, in pitch. One pitch is frequent, and another infrequent, both presented while the subject is engaged in a task not related to the sounds, such as playing a computer game, watching a silent movie, reading a book. The infrequently presented (perceptually discriminable) sounds have consistently been shown to evoke the mismatch negativity (MMN; see Figure 1). The presence of the MMN implies that the invariant parameters of the standard sound were neurally encoded and differentiated from the parameters of the deviant sound.

Of particular theoretical and practical value is that the MMN can be recorded in such a situation in which the subject is performing a task unrelated to the stimulation under interest. Theoretically, the MMN allows us to study processes of sound encoding and storage without being masked by attentive processing or behavioral decisions. In fact, music perception and its linkage to previous musical knowledge can be largely automatic and occurs in a way that is unavoidable by the listener. Moreover, it is a very fast process. In electrophysiological brain

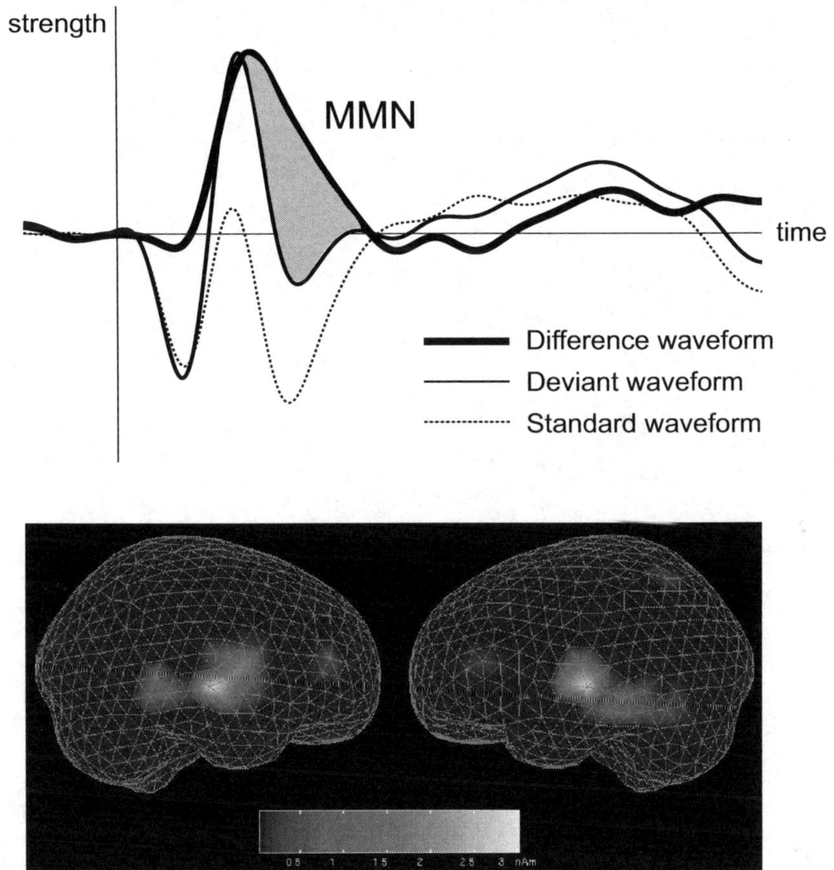

Figure 1. Schematic illustration of the mismatch negativity (MMN). Top, magnetic evoked field (ERF) waveforms recorded from a gradiometer over the temporal cortex in response to the standard (red line) and the deviant stimuli (blue line). These waveforms overlap with the difference waveform (black line) obtained by subtracting the standard stimulus waveform from that to the deviant stimulus. Bottom, source model (minimum L1 norm estimation) of the currents underlying the magnetic MMN generation, indicating the locus of MMN generator.

measurements, the attentive component, termed the P300 complex, occurs 300 milliseconds after the stimulus onset (Besson *et al.*, 1994; Besson & Faita, 1995). However, we may suppose that some neural representations of musical sounds and structures may be formed automatically and almost immediately after the presentation of the sounds. In fact, if our brain would need to wait 300 ms to detect a sound being discrepant in some of its physical or cognitive features from the precedent context in the complexity of the rapidly accumulating sound information during a music performance, we would not be able to understand and enjoy music at all.

The practical benefits of using the MMN paradigm are that it requires minimal participation from the subject's side and, in fact, has been employed even to study the functional state of the auditory cortex in comatose patients (Näätänen *et al.*, 2003) and in infants (Cheour *et al.*, 2000). From a musical perspective, it

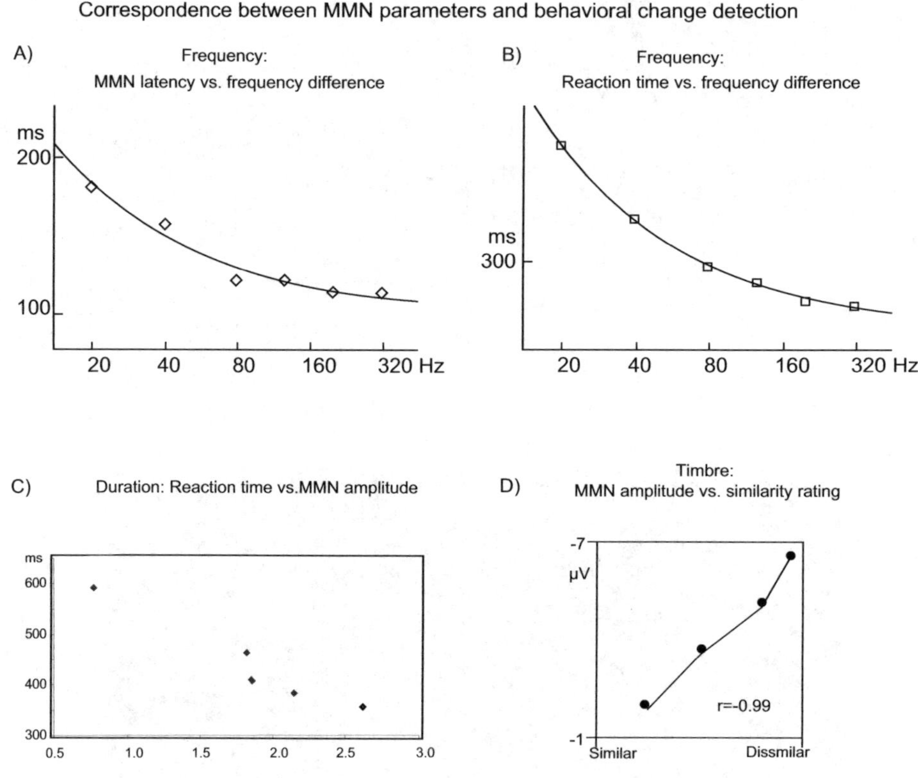

Figure 2. Graphs illustrating the correspondence between MMN parameters and behavioral measures of the accuracy in sound change discrimination [figure combined from Tiitinen *et al.* (1994): A and B panels; Jaramillo *et al.* (1999): C panel; Toiviainen *et al.* (1998): D panel].

would be of great interest to probe the development of auditory perception by using MMN responses in childhood. For instance, MMN experiments could help disentangling the role of learned knowledge and innate predispositions for our musical preferences.

Several sets of data indicate that the MMN parameters closely correlate to behavioral measures of the subjects' perceptual accuracy as determined in separate sessions. For instance, the MMN amplitude (indexing the extent of activity in the neural populations of the auditory cortex) and latency (the time of occurrence of such neural activity) reflect perceptual sound detection accuracy, as determined by musicality tests (Tervaniemi *et al.*, 1997) or by traditional indices of the psychoacoustical tradition such as hit rate and reaction time (Tiitinen *et al.*, 1994; Jaramillo *et al.*, 2000; Toiviainen *et al.*, 1998; Novitski *et al.*, in press). Some examples are illustrated in Figure 2.

It is of great importance that these experiments have used very diverse stimulation paradigms, such as sounds manipulated in their different acoustical parameters (frequency, duration, timbre), or in their informational content (speech vs. non-speech sounds). Time and frequency information is known to be encoded by different neural systems at several levels of the sound processing starting from the cochlea, ending up to the auditory cortex. Consequently, sounds differing in their duration by only a few milliseconds are analyzed and decomposed into their acoustic features by the neural centers preceding the auditory cortex. At the cortical processing stages, the feature traces are integrated in a unique neural auditory representation and the brain is thus able to detect the small modulations in sound pitch, duration, loudness, etc., by comparing the current auditory representation with the precedent ones — a process reflected by the MMN elicitation (Näätänen & Winkler, 1999). Consequently, we claim it is justified to conclude that the correlation between the MMN parameters and behavioral responses implies the central role of pre-attentive neural functions in determining the accuracy of the subsequent attentive processes.

Such a high correlation between behavioral and MMN measures thus renders the MMN an optimal tool for studying the neural bases of human auditory perception. For instance, in the field of cognitive neuroscience in general and of neuroscience of music in particular the question of possible modularity in auditory perception has been of longitudinal interest. The modularity hypothesis suggests the existence of separated mental modules for each sensory, motoric, or cognitive function, with their own procedures and knowledge base and possibly each associated to a separate neural structure (Fodor, 1983; Peretz & Coltheart, 2003). In the auditory system, those functions have been subdivided into smaller units, or submodules, such as the ones dedicated to music and to speech processing. These submodules serve for the analysis and processing of the acoustic or abstract features of the incoming auditory events, which can be objectively measured and localized. With Peretz & Coltheart (2003)'s words, 'to claim that there is a music processing module is to claim that there is a mental information processing system whose operations is specific to the processing of music. That system may contain smaller modules whose processing domains may also be restricted to particular aspects of music' (p. 688).

Interestingly, by means of the MMN we can look into the separate submodules examining with an optimal time resolution the dynamic stages of information processing, as well as their automaticity and possible top-down modulation (which may be determined, for example, by implicit or explicit knowledge of musical sounds). In particular, MMN is considered as an index of sensory memory: it can be elicited by a deviating sound only if a neural trace for a repeated sound was formed (Näätänen *et al.*, 2003). This trace is of a sensory nature since it disappears when the time interval between successive sounds is longer than about 10 sec (Sams *et al.*, 1993). Sensory memory is thus a first stage of processing during which a sound is integrated as a unified percept.

II: Automatic Discrimination of Music vs. Speech Sounds

Great interest in cognitive neuroscience resides in defining the neural counterparts of the mental modules for speech vs. music processing. This line of research is motivated by the similarities of music and speech information at several levels of processing: acoustically, both signals can be reduced to consist of variations of the air pressure as a function of time which are transformed to sound percepts in the brain. In parallel, both music and speech can form highly complex cognitive entities, both with syntactic properties, speech with semantic properties, and also music with some associative elements linking it to (at least) episodic memories.

Traditionally, these investigations were carried out in behavioural paradigms, either with healthy individuals or with brain-lesioned patients. Later on, non-invasive brain research methods were also utilized but, again, in paradigms in which subject's were to attentively listen to the sounds. These data gave support for the existence of the neuronal networks devoted specifically to music vs. speech processing (see reviews by Zatorre *et al.* 2002 and Tervaniemi & Hugdahl, 2003). Very generally, it can be summarized that the left hemisphere was found to be more involved in speech processing and that the right hemisphere was found to be more involved in music-sound processing. Alternatively, the conclusions can be formulated to evidence that the left hemisphere is more involved in processing fast temporal information (intrinsic to speech) and that the right hemisphere is more involved in processing tiny changes in pitch (intrinsic to music). However, since attentional processes are known to be unequally distributed between the hemispheres (the right hemisphere being dominant at least in directing spatial attention; Heilman & Van Den Abell, 1980) those data leave it open how much the roles of the hemispheres are specialized when pre-attentive processing is concerned.

MMN to changes in sinusoidal tones has been evidenced in the primary auditory cortex or in its immediate vicinity as shown by MEG, intracranial electrode recordings, and fMRI (Kropotov *et al.*, 1995; Alho, 1995; Opitz *et al.*, 2002) with right-hemispheric dominance. During recent years, several attempts were also made to differentiate the roles of the left and right auditory primary cortices in music vs. speech processing by recording MMN. In the first MEG and PET investigations using a MMN paradigm, it was shown that the chord discrimination (A major vs. A minor) evoked a stronger right- than left-hemispheric activity centered in the vicinities of the auditory cortices (Tervaniemi *et al.*, 1999; Tervaniemi *et al.*, 2000b). Thus, the previously obtained right-hemisphere dominance with pure tones as determined with electric recordings (with less certain localization of the neural generator: Giard *et al.*, 1990; Rinne *et al.*, 1999; Paavilainen *et al.*, 1991; Brattico *et al.*, 2001) was confirmed with MEG and PET when musically meaningful stimuli were used.

Moreover, the MEG data indicated that within each hemisphere, the MMN loci were located superiorly (that is, upper within the auditory cortex) for chord-MMN when compared with vowel-MMN (Tervaniemi, *et al.*, 1999). These data suggest that there are spatially distinct areas within both hemispheres representing sounds of different informational content (speech, music). However, prior to memory-related MMN elicitation, no indication of such spatial specialization between speech and music sound processing was found. This was evidenced by the lack of source separation between P1 evoked by speech vs. music sounds (P1m belonging to the family of so called exogenous ERP components which is modulated by acoustic sound features but not by cognitive processes). This dissociation between the generator loci of the acoustically and cognitively determined brain responses thus promotes the views on partial modularity of the auditory neurocognition.

To summarize, different neural networks specialized in processing speech vs. music sounds were demonstrated even when only simple items were presented during a performance of a task not related to the sounds. This indicates that neuronal populations in our brain are at least up to some extent affected by the stimulus informational content at relatively early stages of auditory processing.

III: Neural Representation of Complex Sound Features

According to some traditional views, the primary auditory areas are devoted to primary (sensory) analysis of the sound information while more cognitive, memory-related functions (especially those related to more complex acoustic signals) occur beyond those. However, recent MMN findings question those views. In these studies it was investigated which aspects of the musically relevant sounds or sound features are automatically processed, i.e., how complex sound features are processed within the primary auditory areas even when the subjects perform a parallel task outside the auditory modality.

When musically relevant sounds are considered, it was found, first of all, that the MMN is evoked by the sounds deviating from the majority of the tones in their timbre (e.g., Toiviainen *et al.*, 1998). This and related findings highlight the ability of the auditory cortex to encode sound according to a multidimensional sound attribute such as timbre which in acoustical terms is quite complex but which forms a common cue in our daily auditory scene to differentiate sounds even with same spatial origin and time course (see, e.g., Bregman, 1990). It was also found that the MMN elicited by a pitch change among harmonically rich sounds is stronger in amplitude and earlier in latency than that elicited by pure sinusoidal tones. These MMN findings were also reflected in a more accurate behavioral detection of the pitch change when sounds were harmonically rich as compared to pure tones (Tervaniemi *et al.*, 2000a). Thus, adding acoustical information into a sound signal seems to help its neural encoding rather than delaying or complicating it. This suggests a hard-wired facilitation to process spectrally complex, natural and familiar sound signals above artificially pure 'laboratory' sounds (see Rauschecker, 1998 for corroborating evidence in primates).

Additionally, it has been shown that multiple sound features can simultaneously be stored in sensory memory. This was evidenced through MMN elicitation by an infrequent combination of two repeated tone patterns (Brattico *et al.*, 2002). In this experiment, the subjects (who concentrated on watching a soundless subtitled movie) were presented with two short melody-like four-tone patterns with equal probability of 45%. Infrequently, a four-tone pattern of the third type was presented (10%), this tone pattern being a hybrid of the other patterns. The number of tones in each of the three pattern types was chosen as an example of a short musical motif, which in tonal compositions may consist of four to eight notes, i.e., of the amount of notes that can be sang with a single breath (Schönberg, 1967). Results showed that the infrequent four-tone pattern elicited an MMN like in previous studies in which much simpler sounds or sound patterns of only two types were presented (Tervaniemi *et al.*, 1999; Brattico *et al.*, 2000). This result implies that the four tones in each of the two patterns were automatically maintained into sensory memory as a unique Gestalt (Koffka, 1935), pointing at the immediate memory mechanisms that enable us to maintain several musical motifs while we listen (even without attentional effort) to music.

However, the MMN latencies were longer than when acoustic changes were introduced in sequences containing only two types of sounds. This suggests that the comparison between the multiple memory traces of the two patterns and the deviant one (each characterized by specific frequency and temporal tone successions) was more effortful for the auditory cortex than the easy comparison between two tones.

According to the present views, the memory system behind MMN elicitation encodes sound information far beyond the acoustical sound properties. In addition to previous examples, the direction of the pitch change within a tone pair (Saarinen *et al.*, 1992) or within a continuous pitch change such as a Shepard-tone sequence (Tervaniemi *et al.*, 1994) as well as the contour of transposed melody-like sound patterns (Tervaniemi *et al.*, 2001) are automatically encoded by the primary auditory cortex. Thus, these findings indicate that the human auditory cortex encodes, without the subject's attentional listening, relatively invariant, abstract sound information (Näätänen *et al.*, 2001). Consequently, such studies suggest that even abstract invariances such as the melodic, harmonic and rhythmic ones, may be extracted from the acoustic environment and encoded to a large extent without the listener being actively aware of them.

IV: Consonant and Dissonant Intervals

In some of the experiments described above, musical intervals, i.e., the relations between sounds played simultaneously or serially, were abstracted from the varying absolute frequencies and maintained as neural traces in the auditory cortex, suggesting that intervals are a basic feature for our auditory system.

Krumhansl (2000) pointed out that the musical interval has a special status and a central role for music perception. For example, a perfect octave interval is produced by any two tones having fundamental frequencies in a ratio of 2:1. Such link to integer numbers of the musical intervals and also of the harmonics in complex periodic sounds was first identified by Pythagoras (ca. 570-500 B.C.).

Stemming from this theory, it was proposed that when sounds are approximately in a simple integer ratio, they most likely would produce a pleasant, or consonant, percept. In contrast, when the sounds are in a complex integer ratio they will produce an unpleasant, or dissonant, percept. The acoustic basis of this phenomenon studied extensively by psychoacousticians and termed sensory dissonance (to be distinguished from musical dissonance; Plomp & Levelt, 1965; Kameoka & Kuriyagawa, 1969), is that when the frequency ratios between sinusoidal sounds are simple their phases coincide and do not interfere. When frequency ratios are more complex, the sound waves interfere producing beats, amplitude oscillations. Beats are unpleasant to our hearing when they fall in the critical bandwidth, which happens when sine tones are very close in frequency distance (Plomp & Levelt, 1965). Similarly, this also occurs with spectrally complex sounds, in which harmonics may interfere or not, producing a consonant or a dissonant percept.

Considering the special status of each interval in Western music and its automatic encoding by the auditory cortex, it is also of interest to study whether electrophysiological responses to musical intervals differ according to their dissonance and consonance (as music theory and psychoacoustics would suggest) or simply to the distance between their pitch components (as previous electrophysiological studies would suggest).

In a series of very recent studies (Brattico *et al.*, 2000, 2003), we investigated how the discrepancy in the perceptual quality, that is, dissonance vs. consonance, of musical intervals is preattentively discriminated. We showed that the MMN is affected by the context of the interval change. For instance, it was larger in amplitude to an infrequent dissonant interval (e.g., the major seventh) in a context of repeated consonant intervals (e.g., the major sixth) than to an infrequent consonant interval in a consonant context (e.g., the perfect octave replacing the major sixth). This result was obtained even if the pitch change between dissonant deviants and consonant standards was smaller in pitch distance than that between consonant deviants and consonant standards. This result thus contradicts the evidence that MMN increases its amplitude with acoustically larger pitch shifts (e.g., Tiitinen *et al.*, 1994). Thus, we demonstrated that the brain is more vigorously responding to the distance in dissonance between infrequent musical intervals and the repeated context than to the distance in pitch between their tone components.

V: Pitch Processing Facilitation in a Familiar Tuning Context

From listening studies we know that the presence of a tonal musical context facilitates pitch discrimination (e.g., Dewar *et al.*, 1977). In the previous paragraph we described experiments in which the tone context was formed by repeated consonant and dissonant intervals, this context significantly affecting the processing of dissimilar intervals. However, such repeated and monotonous events (which are appropriate for studying sensory dissonance) are rare in real music. Rather, a succession of different acoustic events in music forms the context needed by the listener to grasp any musical meaning. Similarly, in language the meaning of a spoken word is, for instance, better extracted in the context of such complex speech events than those occurring when uttering a sentence.

In the process of meaning extraction, familiarity plays an important role. Cognitive psychologists have emphasized that any stimulus is interpreted against prior knowledge, often called schemas, which is acquired through prior experience. In music, such schemas include, for example, tuning, keys, and tonality. As Krumhansl (2000, p. 159) points out, 'perceptual information is assimilated to these, facilitating the organization of the sounded events into patterns and generating expectations for future events'. However, only recently scientists have started unveiling the neural bases of these processes.

In a recent ERP experiment on the long-term effects of sound-context familiarity, we compared the pitch processing in single tones vs. patterns differing in tuning[1] familiarity in both professional musicians and non-musicians (Brattico *et al.*, 2001). The subjects, concentrating on reading a book, were presented with sound stimuli having a large infrequent pitch shift in three contexts: familiar major-minor pattern constructed according to the equal temperament tuning, unfamiliar pattern with arithmetically determined frequencies and unfamiliar intervals, as well as in single tones. According to the MMN amplitude data, the pitch change was larger in both subject groups when it was embedded in the familiar pattern (where the pitch shift also changed the pattern mode) than when it was embedded in the unfamiliar pattern. Moreover, the MMN amplitude was least obvious when the pitch change was presented in single tones as compared to both pattern conditions. In terms of the MMN latency, musicians reacted faster than non-musicians to a pitch change when it was presented among temporally complex patterns (with or without a modal context). Taken together, there seems to be a general neural facilitation to discriminate pitch changes in a musically familiar context in terms of tuning, with musicians faster than non-musicians in discriminating a pitch change within a temporally complex pattern.

According to the most recent views, the learning process commencing during infanthood plastically modifying our cortical organization for sound processing is mainly based on the statistical frequency of the sound events. This process finally leads to the parsing of those events into, for example, words or tone patterns (Seidenberg *et al.*, 2003; Saffran *et al.*, 1996). Such learning is implicit, in the sense that it occurs in an incidental manner without verbalization of what is learned and without conscious awareness by the subject (Seger, 1994; Tillmann

[1] The equal-tempered tuning largely used in Western music (e.g., in classical, rock, pop, and jazz) was introduced between the end of the Sixteenth and the beginning of the Seventeenth century (The Equal Tempered Harpsichord by Bach was first published in 1722). It reduced the amount of sounds to be included in an octave to only 12 (previously keyboards might have included up to 32 keys in order to produce mathematically perfect intervals; Finizio, 1950). The tuning serves to determine the sounds and intervals of a musical system (in the piano, tuning is fixed on the keys while in instruments such as the violin it can be chosen by performers). In the equal tempered tuning the smallest interval between sounds is the semitone (corresponding to a frequency difference of about 6%). A smaller interval would be 'wrong' in this tuning but, for example, correct in the tunings of other cultures (Arabic, Indian, Chinese, etc.).

et al., 2000). This was demonstrated by measuring brain evoked responses of subjects before and after they were shortly but intensely exposed to nonsense words: auditory brain potentials were facilitated at the beginning of each nonsense word only after subjects learned to segment them (Sanders *et al.*, 2002).

We hypothesize here that the segmentation and classification processes may become automatized thanks to the existence of hardwired neuronal models or templates in the brain (cf. Sokolov, 1963). These models correspond to what is called category and schema in cognitive psychology: while becoming familiar during long-term passive or active exposure to similar classes of stimuli, these sound classes get more permanently represented in the brain (e.g., those belonging to the music of a specific culture or to the native language). The incoming stimuli are encoded first into sensory representations and then integrated with the ones previously presented, i.e., with the acoustic context.

As we have previously seen, the auditory cortex is also capable of abstracting more general characteristics of these neuronal activations. These abstract models may or may not match with preexistent neuronal models stored most probably in specific cortical loci (Näätänen *et al.*, 2001)[2]. In other words, when we listen to music played by an amateur pianist we are better able to detect the mistakes in the performance especially when we know the piece. However, even if we have never listened to what the performer is playing we understand when a note is wrong on the basis of an internal musical representation, most likely corresponding to a neural template hardwired in the brain that matches or not with what we hear. Preliminary electrophysiological results seem to confirm this hypothesis (see Appendix).

However, it should be noticed that such neural templates probably do not exist when we listen occasionally to contemporary music, or it is merely limited to the extraction of acoustic or surface characteristics of the musical piece. Only expert listeners of that musical genre might be able to extract the underlying musical structures of a contemporary piece, due to the limited passive exposure naïve listeners usually have to that music genre. Moreover, in contrast with the more divulgated classical tonal music in which composers mainly followed the rules defined by two centuries of music theory reflections, musical structures in contemporary music are usually different for different pieces since they are independently chosen by each composer.

Thus, when the sound-evoked neuronal firing in the auditory cortex does not match the existing neural templates activated by the previous context (e.g., in case of a mistuned note), other neuronal populations fire probably in order to

[2] These models are based on the changes in the strength of connections between pre- and post-synaptic neurons. For example, transient modifications lasting seconds to minutes after repeated neuronal stimulation are based on the altered calcium levels at the active synapses. Long-lasting synaptic plasticity may involve also changes in gene expression that may eventually lead to more permanent changes in synaptic strength. This is what is possibly happening at the level of the auditory cortex for familiar intervals of a musical culture. Several mechanisms can cause the long-lasting plastic changes such as increase in the strength of synaptic connections, increasing or decreasing of transmitter release from presynaptic terminals, changes in the number or sensitivity of postsynaptic receptors, and addition or subtraction of synapses in the neural circuits (Purves *et al.*, 1997).

switch attentional resources towards the new sound while readjusting the neuronal model for the incoming acoustic signals. With Winkler *et al.* (1996, p. 241)'s words, 'when the incoming sound is incompatible with the inferences of the acoustic model, the mismatched elements of the model are adjusted to assimilate the new event'. Interestingly, such neural reaction occurs quite shortly after the onset of the deviating sound and may be triggered by a context consisting of chord cadences (Koelsch *et al.*, 2002) or even of very few notes without any accompaniment, such as in the case of unfamiliar melodies (Brattico *et al.*, in preparation; see Appendix).

Future lines of investigation should reveal whether an automatic neural facilitation for e.g., tonal hierarchies can be induced with simple musical stimulation in listeners possessing musical expertise and in what sense attentional focus is relevant for extracting cognitive musical categories. Moreover, studies in the future should also cover the neural bases of concrete memories for familiar songs or musical pieces, which probably exist in the brain in the form of plastic neural circuits specifically activated. These memory traces are most probably located in association areas of the auditory cortices and in the medial temporal lobe regions devoted to the storage of long-term episodic memories (Simons & Spiers, 2003).

VI: Conclusions

In light of the present evidence the views on (at least partial) modularity of auditory perception and cognition are justified. Speech and music sound processing seem to be based on functionally and also anatomically separate neural substrates. However, it remains to be elucidated how much this specialization results from acoustical and 'bottom-up' factors, that is, features intrinsic to music vs. speech sounds. In parallel, it should be investigated up to which extent this specialization is an outcome of more cognitive 'top-down' factors, possibly also modifiable by learning and enculturation. In the future, experimental investigations on e.g., tone languages, which uniquely combine both phonetic and musical information, might provide us with valuable evidence in this respect.

The literature reviewed above also indicates the amazing ability of the human brain to process highly variable and complex sound information without the necessity of conscious attention during encoding or retrieval. In fact, there is increasing evidence that at least in the case of pitch information, increased sound complexity facilitates rather than deteriorates pitch processing in several ways. In a similar vein, automatic sound encoding is not limited to acoustic sound properties but it also covers abstract, 'rule-based' sound features (e.g., direction of pitch change, contour of a short melody). The limits of automatic cognition, also called primitive intelligence (Näätänen *et al.*, 2001), are under increasingly intensive research efforts. As the most recent examples of this line of research are the findings indicating the ability of the human brain to represent and consolidate the representations of complex spectro-temporal sound patterns during sleep (Atienza *et al.*, 2001). It is possible that in the future, these findings change our views on auditory learning and memory by emphasizing the automatic, implicit forms of learning with regard to quite advanced sound features and regularities.

Investigations focused on musical pitch (i.e., pitch in a musical context) have provided tentative evidence for a new theory on the existence of preattentive musical cognition. For instance, in studying characteristics of interval perception we found that in intervals a perceptual quality such as dissonance vs. consonance overrules their acoustical quality (frequency distance between interval components) during automatic pitch-change processing. Correspondingly, also the familiar scale context advanced the discrimination of unpredictable, infrequent pitch shifts among short sound excerpts when compared with unfamiliar scale context.

Based on the reviewed evidence we might already conclude that musical attributes, based most probably on implicit and/or explicit learning, affect the way sound information is encoded by the human brain. It should be kept in mind, however, that in those studies the sound stimulation was somewhat repetitive in its nature. So far, only one study (Brattico et al., in preparation, see Appendix) used unfamiliar melodies to study the ongoing automatic discrimination by the auditory cortex of rare randomly placed tonal 'errors'. In particular, while in attentive condition both mistuned and out-of-key tones were neurally detected, in ignore condition this was the case only for the mistuned sounds. These data thus underline the existence of differential modes of music cognition, part of that depending on attentional listening strategies, but significant part being independent of the allocation of attentional resources even in untrained subjects.

Taken together, these results support the emerging view that musical sound perception is based on early largely automatic functions of the auditory system that dynamically store, in a way that is at least partially affected by past experience, separated sounds as organized regularities of the auditory scene.

Acknowledgments

We thank the Academy of Finland and the Pythagoras Graduate School (Ministry of Education, Finland) for financial support. We also appreciate the help of Ms I. Anourova and Mr M. Bregman in figure preparation and stylistic editing.

References

Alho, K. (1995), 'Cerebral generators of mismatch negativity (MMN) and its magnetic counterpart (MMNm) elicited by sound changes', *Ear and Hearing*, **16**, pp. 38–51.

Atienza, M., Cantero, J.L. & Escera, C. (2001), 'Auditory information processing during human sleep as revealed by event-related brain potentials', *Clinical Neurophysiology*, **112**, pp. 2031–45.

Besson, M. & Faita, F. (1995), 'An event-related potential (ERP) study of musical expectancy: Comparison of musicians with nonmusicians', *Journal of Experimental Psychology: Human Perception and Performance*, **21**, pp. 1278–96.

Besson, M., Faita, F. & Requin, J. (1994), 'Brain waves associated with musical incongruities differ for musicians and non-musicians', *Neuroscience Letters*, **168**, pp. 101–5.

Besson, M. & Macar, F. (1987), 'An event-related potential analysis of incongruity in music and other non-linguistic contexts', *Psychophysiology*, **24**, pp. 14–25.

Bharucha, J.J. (1987), 'Music cognition and perceptual facilitation: A connectionism framework', *Music Perception*, **5**, pp. 1–30.

Bharucha, J.J. & Stoeckig, K. (1986), 'Reaction time and musical expectancy: Priming of chords', *Journal of Experimental Psychology: Human Perception and Performance,* **12**, pp. 403–10.

Bharucha, J.J. & Stoeckig, K. (1987), 'Priming of chords: Spreading activation or overlapping frequency spectra?', *Perception and Psychophysics,* **41**, pp. 519–24.

Bigand, E., Madurell, F., Tillmann, B. & Pineau, M. (1999), 'Effect of global structure and temporal organization on chord processing', *Journal of Experimental Psychology: Human Perception and Performance*, **25**, pp. 184–97.

Bigand, E. & Pineau, M. (1997), 'Global context effects on musical expectancy', *Perception and Psychophysics*, **59**, pp. 1098–107.

Brattico, E., Näätänen, R. & Tervaniemi, M. (2001), 'Context effects on pitch perception in musicians and non-musicians: Evidence from ERP recordings', *Music Perception*, **19**, pp. 1–24.

Brattico, E., Näätänen, R., Verma, T., Välimäki, V. & Tervaniemi, M. (2000), 'Processing of musical intervals in the central auditory system: An event-related potential (ERP) study on sensory consonance', Paper presented at the Sixth International Conference on Music Perception and Cognition, Keele (UK).

Brattico, E., Tervaniemi, M. & Peretz, I. (in preparation), 'Automatic vs. attentive discrimination of "wrong" notes inside melodies'.

Brattico, E., Tervaniemi, M., Välimäki, V., van Zuijen, T. & Peretz, I. (2003), 'Cortical correlates of acquired deafness to dissonance', *Annals of the New York Academy of Sciences*, **999**.

Brattico, E., Winkler, I., Näätänen, R., Paavilainen, P. & Tervaniemi, M. (2002), 'Simultaneous storage of two complex temporal sound patterns in the human auditory sensory memory', *NeuroReport*, **13**, pp. 1747–51.

Bregman, A.S. (1990), *Auditory Scene Analysis: The Perceptual Organization of Sound* (Cambridge, MA: MIT Press).

Cheour, M., Leppänen, P.H.T. & Kraus, N. (2000), 'Mismatch negativity as a tool for investigating auditory discrimination and sensory memory in infants and children', *Clinical Neurophysiology*, **111**, pp. 4–16.

Dewar, K., Cuddy, L.L. & Mewhort, D.J.K. (1977), 'Recognition memory for single tones with and without context', *Journal of Experimental Psychology: Human Learning and Memory*, **3**, pp. 60–7.

Finizio, L. (1950), *Quello che ogni pianista deve sapere* (Milano: Edizioni Curci).

Fodor, J. (1983), *The Modularity of Mind* (Cambridge, MA: MIT Press).

Giard, M.H., Perrin, F., Bertrand, O., Pernier, J. & Bouchet, P. (1990), 'Brain generators implicated in the processing of auditory stimulus deviance: A topographic event-related potential study', *Psychophysiology*, **27**, pp. 627–40.

Heilman, K., & Van Den Abell, T. (1980), 'Right hemisphere dominance for attention: The mechanisms underlying hemispheric asymmetries of inattention (neglect)', Neurology, 30, pp. 327-330.

Jaramillo, M., Paavilainen, P. & Näätänen, R. (2000), 'Mismatch negativity and behavioural discrimination in humans as a function of the magnitude of change in sound duration', *Neuroscience Letters*, **290**, pp. 101–4.

Kameoka, A. & Kuriyagawa, M. (1969), 'Consonance theory Part I: Consonance of dyads', *Journal of the Acoustical Society of America*, **45**, pp. 1451–9.

Koelsch, S., Schröger, E. & Gunter, T.C. (2002), 'Music matters: Preattentive musicality of the human brain', *Psychophysiology*, **39**, pp. 38–48.

Koffka, K. (1935), *Principles of Gestalt Psychology* (London: Lund Humphries).

Kropotov, J.D., Näätänen, R., Sevostianov, A.V., Alho, K., Reinikainen, K., & Kropotova, O.V. (1995), 'Mismatch negativity to auditory stimulus change recorded directly from the human temporal cortex', *Psychophysiology*, **32**, pp. 418–22.

Krumhansl, C.L. (2000), 'Rhythm and pitch in music cognition', *Psychological Bulletin*, **126**, pp. 159–79.

Näätänen, R., Brattico, E. & Tervaniemi, M. (2003), 'Mismatch negativity (MMN): A probe to auditory cognition and perception in basic and clinical research', in *The Cognitive*

Electrophysiology of Mind and Brain, ed. A. Zani & A. Mado Proverbio (San Diego, CA: Academic Press).

Näätänen, R., Gaillard, A.W. & Mäntysalo, S. (1978), 'Early selective-attention effect on evoked potential reinterpreted', *Acta Psychologica*, **42**, pp. 313–29.

Näätänen, R., Tervaniemi, M., Sussman, E., Paavilainen, P. & Winkler, I. (2001), 'Pre-attentive cognitive processing ("primitive intelligence") in the auditory cortex as revealed by the mismatch negativity (MMN)', *Trends in Neurosciences*, **24**, pp. 283–8.

Näätänen, R., & Winkler, I. (1999), 'The concept of auditory stimulus representation in cognitive neuroscience', *Psychological Bulletin*, **125**, pp. 826–59.

Novitski, N., Tervaniemi, M., Huotilainen, M., & Näätänen, R. (in press), 'Frequency discrimination at different frequency levels as reflected by electrophysiological and behavioral indices', *Cognitive Brain Research.*

Opitz, B., Rinne, T., Mecklinger, A., von Cramon, D.Y. Schröger, E. (2002), 'Differential contribution of frontal and temporal cortices to auditory change detection: fMRI and ERP results', *NeuroImage*, **15**, pp. 167–74.

Paavilainen, P., Alho, K., Reinikainen, K., Sams, M. & Näätänen, R. (1991), 'Right hemisphere dominance of different mismatch negativities', *Electroencephalography and Clinical Neurophysiology*, **78**, pp. 466–79.

Peretz, I., & Coltheart, M. (2003), 'Modularity of music processing', *Nature Neuroscience*, **6**, pp. 688–91.

Plomp, R. & Levelt, J.M. (1965), 'Tonal consonance and critical bandwidth', *Journal of the Acoustical Society of America*, **38**, pp. 549–60.

Purves, D., Augustine, G. J., Fitzpatrick, D., Katz, L.C., LaMantia, A.-S., McNamara, J.O. (1997), *Neuroscience* (Sunderland, MA: Sinauer Associates).

Rauschecker, J.P. (1998), 'Cortical processing of complex sounds', *Current Opinions in Neurobiology*, **8**, pp. 516–21.

Rinne, T., Alho, K., Alku, P., Holi, M., Sinkkonen, J., Virtanen, J., Bertrand, O. & Näätänen, R. (1999), 'Analysis of speech sounds is left-hemisphere predominant at 100-150 ms after sound onset', *NeuroReport*, **10**, pp. 1113–17.

Saarinen, J., Paavilainen, P., Schröger, E., Tervaniemi, M. & Näätänen, R. (1992), 'Representation of abstract attributes of auditory stimuli in human brain', *NeuroReport*, **3**, pp. 1149–51.

Saffran, J.R., Aslin, R.N., & Newport, E.L. (1996), 'Statistical learning by 8-month-old infants', *Science*, **274**, pp. 1926–8.

Sams, M., Hari, R., Rif, J. & Knuutila, J. (1993), 'The human auditory sensory memory trace persists about 10 sec: Neuromagnetic evidence', *Journal of Cognitive Neuroscience*, **5**, pp. 363–70.

Sanders, L.D., Newport, E.L. & Neville, H.J. (2002), 'Segmenting nonsense: An event-related potential index of perceived onsets in continuous speech', *Nature Neuroscience*, **5**, pp. 700–3.

Schönberg, A. (1967), *Fundamentals of Musical Composition* (London: Faber and Faber Limited).

Seger, C.A. (1994), 'Implicit learning', *Psychological Bulletin*, **115**, pp. 163–9.

Seidenberg, M.S., MacDonald, M.C. & Saffran, J.R. (2003), 'Does grammar starts when statistics stop?', *Science*, **298**, pp. 553–4.

Simons, J.S. & Spiers, H.J. (2003), 'Prefrontal and medial temporal lobe interactions in long-term memory', *Nature Reviews Neuroscience*, **4**, pp. 637–48.

Sokolov, E.N. (1963), 'Higher nervous system functions: The orienting reflex', *Annual Review of Physiology*, **25**, pp. 545–80.

Tervaniemi, M. & Hugdahl, K. (2003), 'Lateralization of auditory-cortex functions', *Brain Research Reviews*, **43**, pp. 231–46.

Tervaniemi, M., Ilvonen, T., Karma, K., Alho, K., & Näätänen, R. (1997), 'The musical brain: Brain waves reveal the neurophysiological basis of musicality in human subjects', *Neuroscience Letters*, **226**, pp. 1–4.

Tervaniemi, M., Ilvonen, T., Sinkkonen, J., Kujala, A., Alho, K., Huotilainen, M. & Näätänen, R. (2000a), 'Harmonic partials facilitate pitch discrimination in humans: electrophysiological and behavioral evidence', *Neuroscience Letters*, **279**, pp. 29–32.

Tervaniemi, M., Kujala, A., Alho, K., Virtanen, J., Ilmoniemi, R.J., & Näätänen, R. (1999), 'Functional specialization of the human auditory cortex in processing phonetic and musical sounds: A magnetoencephalographic (MEG) study', *NeuroImage*, 9, pp. 330–6.
Tervaniemi, M., Maury, S. & Näätänen, R. (1994), 'Neural representations of abstract features in the human brain as reflected by the mismatch negativity', *NeuroReport*, **5**, pp. 844–6.
Tervaniemi, M., Medvedev, S.V., Alho, K., Pakhomov, S.V., Roudas, M.S., van Zuijen, T. & Näätänen, R. (2000b), 'Lateralized automatic auditory processing of phonetic versus musical information: A PET study', *Human Brain Mapping*, **10**, pp. 74–79.
Tervaniemi, M., Rytkönen, M., Schröger, E., Ilmoniemi, R.J. & Näätänen, R. (2001), 'Superior formation of cortical memory traces of melodic patterns in musicians', *Learning and Memory*, **8**, pp. 295–300.
Tiitinen, H., May, P., Reinikainen, K. & Näätänen, R. (1994), 'Attentive novelty detection in humans is governed by pre-attentive sensory memory', *Nature*, **372**, pp. 90–2.
Tillmann, B., Bharucha, J.J. & Bigand, E. (2000), 'Implicit learning of tonality: A self-organizing approach', *Psychological Review*, **107**, pp. 885–913.
Toiviainen, P., Tervaniemi, M., Louhivuori, J., Huotilainen, M., Saher, M. & Näätänen, R. (1998), 'Musical timbre: Convergence of neural, behavioral, and computational approaches', *Music Perception*, **16**, pp. 223–41.
Winkler, I., Karmos, G. & Näätänen, R. (1996), 'Adaptive modeling of the unattended acoustic environment in the mismatch-negativity event-related potential', *Brain Research*, **742**, pp. 239–52.
Zatorre, R.J., Belin, P. & Penhune, V.B. (2002), 'Structure and function of auditory cortex: Music and speech', *Trends in Cognitive Sciences*, **6**, pp. 37–46.

APPENDIX[3]

Prior knowledge influences the neural processing of incoming stimuli in the brain. Since this facilitation is so fast as to determine our almost immediate response to a mistuned ('wrong') note while we listen or play, we hypothesized the presence of neural long-term templates in the auditory cortex for the most basic musical structures, such as the equal-tempered tuning immediately activated even when the focus of attention is otherwise oriented. Additionally, we were interested in finding out whether musical structures, more cognitive than tuning, are automatically represented in the brain or whether neural detection of a deviation in the structure rules needs conscious processing to be produced. The musical structure we tested was tonality. Traditionally, the tonic represents the centre of any tonal succession. Psychologically, tonality is represented as a perceptual hierarchy: the notes of the tonic chord (in C major: *c-e-g*) are perceived as the most closely related to each other while the other notes of the diatonic scale (*d*, *f*, *a*, *b*) were perceived to be further apart in the tonal hierarchy (Krumhansl, 2000).

In order to determine the presence of neural templates for musical structures such as tonality and tuning in melodies without any accompaniment, we measured brain responses to pitch incongruities within unfamiliar melodies in subjects without any formal training in music (Brattico *et al.*, in preparation). Subjects were either ignoring the melodies (Ignore condition), or judging them

[3] The material in this appendix was inserted subsequent to refereeing, for the convenience of readers and to assist in following the argument in the main text. Hence its inclusion does not constitute peer-reviewed publication. — *Editor*

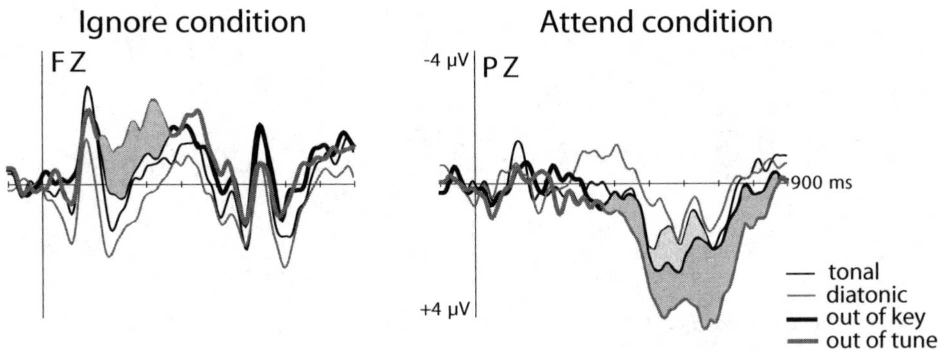

Figure in Appendix. Event-related potentials (ERPs) averaged across 9 subjects in response to pitch incongruities within unfamiliar melodies. In the Ignore condition (left) a long-lasting negative deflection (frontal electrode Fz) was elicited by the out-of-tune pitch only. In contrast, in the Attend condition (right; Pz) both the out-of-tune and out-of-key tones elicited larger positivities as compared to the other pitch stimulus categories.

according to their congruousness and incongruousness (Attend condition). In the melodies a pitch manipulation of four types occurred in the middle of the melodies: tonal (a large pitch shift from the previous sound) congruous with the melody context, diatonic (a whole tone pitch shift) also congruous with the context, out-of-key (a semitone shift) introducing a sound deviating from the key context of the melody, and out-of-tune (a quartertone shift) introducing a sound incongruous with the scale and tuning context of the melody. The behavioral results matched the expectations based on music theory rules: the most congruous melodies were the ones containing the diatonic sound manipulations while the most incongruous were the ones containing the out-of-tune manipulation. Similarly, the brain responses of the Attend condition showed a larger P3 to the out-of-tune and out-of-key manipulations than to the diatonic and tonal manipulations. Interestingly, an MMN was elicited in the Ignore condition by the mistuned pitch, but, in contrast with the Attend condition, we did not observe any MMN to the out-of-key note. These results suggest that automatic expectations for the familiar intervals and sounds on the incoming events may be formed even outside the focus of attention, allowing a fast processing of melodic sounds. At the same time, attention is needed for grasping the nuances of the cognitive musical structures of key and tonality.

Bruce F. Katz

A Measure of Musical Preference

Music exists not to be parsed, categorized, or otherwise processed, but because it provides enjoyment. Thus methodologies that concentrate on the cognitive aspects of music alone omit what is essential about this aesthetic form. This paper provides an alternative approach by proposing a measure of musical preference. Specifically, it is argued that a musical passage will be preferred to the extent that it induces synchrony in those brain structures that are responsible for processing the passage. It is first shown that this conception is consistent with time-honored principle of unity in diversity. It is then argued that the synchrony measure follows from more recent results regarding a possible solution to the binding problem. The bulk of the paper, however, is concerned with verifying the measure via simulation. It is shown, in particular, that the measure applied to a network of interacting integrate and fire neurons responsible for the processing of musical stimuli produces results consistent with human musical preference. This was carried out in three areas in the context of Western classical and popular musical forms. First, the model was applied to the laws of voice leading and other principles developed in the period of common harmonic practice. Next, it was shown that the three most salient aspects of melody, the preponderance of stepwise transitions, the theme and variation nature of phrase development, and increased positive affect with exposure all follow directly from the model. Finally, it was demonstrated how a steady rhythm can increase neural synchrony and presumably positive affect. Additional simulations run on Turkish art songs show that the synchrony measure may have some applicability to non-Western musical forms. The paper concludes by arguing that the synchrony measure may, in certain cases, apply to non-musical aesthetic stimuli.

Introduction

Consider a relatively simple aesthetic stimulus, a melody 32 notes long in a major or minor key, where each note is chosen over an octave range, and has four possible durations. There are $(8*4)^{32} \approx 10^{48}$ such melodies. Yet only a small

Correspondence:
Bruce F. Katz, Department of Computer and Electrical Engineering, Drexel University, 3141 Chestnut Street, Philadelphia, PA 19104, USA. *Email: katz@cbis.drexel.edu*

Journal of Consciousness Studies, **11**, No. 3–4, 2004, pp. 28–57

fraction of these would be deemed musically acceptable, and of this set, perhaps only a tiny proportion thereof would be found enjoyable by most listeners. To the extent that this reduced set is culturally and individually invariant, musical preference presents us with a problem that is well-defined, and to the extent that this problem is soluble, musical preference has the potential to provide insight into the nature of human consciousness.

That the study of musical preference is a tractable scientific endeavour hinges on the existence of a core set of what may be termed musical tendencies, i.e., trends that appear in most or the majority of musical examples, and ideally in differing genres. If this were not the case, if as the dictum goes, *de gustibus non est disputandum,* then models of preference would either be impossible or at the very least have to refer to individual histories or individual neural dynamics. To be sure, there are large individual differences in taste. The overlap between those who wish to attend a chamber music concert and a rap concert is probably minimal. And within a given genre, there are strong preferences if not passions for individual artists. Furthermore, the range of musical forms varies tremendously from culture to culture. It is not the intent of this paper, nor would it be possible with the theory to be proposed to explain these variations in full.

Rather, this paper will take a more proscribed approached by concentrating on the some of the simpler elements of music in a few selected musical forms. These elements, as will be argued, constitute the basis for the advancement of a hypothesis regarding musical preference based on the underlying neural dynamics of the listener, one that will be shown to be consistent with the musical forms studied, and may in the future may be more fully verified as the number of such forms increases. In particular, three fundamental aspects of harmony, melody, and rhythm will be investigated. In the case of harmony, the focus will be on the smooth transitions between successive chords. In the case of melody, the focus will be on the fact that phrases consist of motives and variations on those motives. Finally, in the case of rhythm, both the fact that rhythm works on a theme and variation basis, but additionally usually consists of a regular and steady beat accompanying these variations, will be investigated.

In all cases, musical affect in general will not be approached but rather a single dimension of affective experience, namely the preference or lack thereof for a musical passage will be studied. Other affective dimensions are certainly triggered by music, especially by longer movements or the piece as a whole. For example, it is well-known that pieces in a major key feel more lively and that minor keys evoke more somber feelings. There is also the interesting and under-explored possibility that a musical passage evokes emotions which do not correspond to anything that one might experience in everyday life and therefore there is no convenient linguistic label for the emotion engendered. Finally, to the extent that music evolved to meet bonding and/or communicative goals within the social structure, it may produce emotions that bear on the significance of the piece not just for the individual listener but also as it pertains to the place of the listener in the group (Benzon, 2001). Nevertheless, it will be argued that the single dimension of preference, for at least some of the more elemental aspects of music, can be approached within a relatively compact theoretical framework that looks at neural dynamics of an individual listener alone.

The structure of the argument leading up to this conclusion is as follows. First, a measure of preference based on neural synchrony is introduced. This measure is then justified in two ways, first by reference to the traditional principle of unity in variety, and then by a related argument that draws on recent research into synchrony and the binding problem. It is then shown that applying this measure to models of musical processing comprising networks of integrate and fire neurons yield results that are consistent with human preference. Simulations to this effect were carried out in three areas. First, harmonic progressions as dictated by the rules of common harmonic practice are described. Next, categorical and exposure effects in melodies are given. Finally, the measure is applied to a model of rhythmic processing. The paper then studies whether these results can be extended to a non-Western musical form. The paper concludes by arguing that the synchrony measure may have some applicability to other artistic forms.

The Measure

The measure of preference to be advanced in this paper is as follows:

> *A musical passage will be preferred to the extent that it creates synchrony in the neurons that are responsible for processing the passage.*

In other words, one can conceive of auditory processing as taking place within a neural network. This network will contain a certain number of neurons (or units, if one is talking about simulating those networks) which, at any given time, will be either firing or not firing. Synchrony refers to the degree of coincidence between the firing patterns of a given set of two units within one of these networks. The measure states that preference will be proportional to the sum of these individual synchrony measures over the entire network, i.e., the sum of the synchronies of the units taken two at a time.

There are two related arguments that would lead one to believe that this is the case. The first is based on the time-honored notion that the aesthetic quality of a stimulus is proportional to the extent that the stimulus exhibits unity in variety. As with many pivotal ideas in Western thought, this has its origins in Plato, who stated that if an object is found beautiful, then it must be allied with the One, rather than with the Many (Beardsley, 1966). The neo-Platonic philosopher Plotinus echoes this theme: ‘But where the Ideal-Form has entered, it has grouped and coordinated what from a diversity of parts was to become a unity: it has rallied confusion into cooperation: it has made the sum one harmonious coherence’ (Beardsley, 1966). Augustine (1942) continues this tradition in the same vein, but substitutes the supreme unity of the Christian God for the unity of the Ideal. The Romantic poet and literary theorist Coleridge offers a similar account (Beardsley, 1966). Beauty occurs when ‘that which in the many, still seen as the many, becomes one’. Note the change from a metaphysical notion of unity to a psychological one, in which the act of perception is the unifying force.

The move away from beauty, intrinsic to an object, and towards a psychological account can also be found in the writings of the twentieth-century American pragmatist, John Dewey (1934).

Unfortunately, this necessary move was not echoed in the work of those who attempted a more empirical approach to aesthetics in the prior century. For example, the mathematician Birkhoff attempted to provide a measure of the beauty of polygons based on two 'objective' factors that mirror unity and variety, order and complexity (he largely failed, viz. Katz, 2002). The same error was committed by Berlyne, who is widely regarded as the forefather of modern experimental aesthetics. Berlyne (1979) attempted to show, in a move that paralleled that of Wundt (1874) a century prior, that aesthetic worth was an inverted U-shaped function of what he termed arousal potential, which corresponds roughly to the notion of variety. Martindale (1984) argues that Berlyne's claim has only a loose correspondence to the experimental data.

More fatally, Berlyne never embedded his claim within a psychological model of the processing of the stimulus. Order, complexity, arousal — all of these notions depend on how the stimulus is processed. For example, no model-independent argument can be made as to why the dominant to tonic transition, considered in detail below, is the most forceful transition in both popular and art musics. Aliens may very well prefer other chord transitions, or even the sound of scratching on a blackboard, depending on how well they able to unify the stimulus. Or to take an example that depends more on individual differences, the arguments and equations involved in Einstein's development of general relativity are beautiful, but only to those who understand tensor calculus; otherwise, it appears to be an extremely complex description of nature, and therefore lacking in beauty.

In summary, if unity in variety is to be a useful notion, it will be so only in the context of some means of accessing the *psychological* value of these quantities. One method, to be defended shortly, of assessing perceived unity is to measure the synchrony of the neural cells processing the stimulus. If this is the case, then it can easily be shown that unity in variety can be gauged by observing the total synchrony of the cells responsible for responding to the elements (either

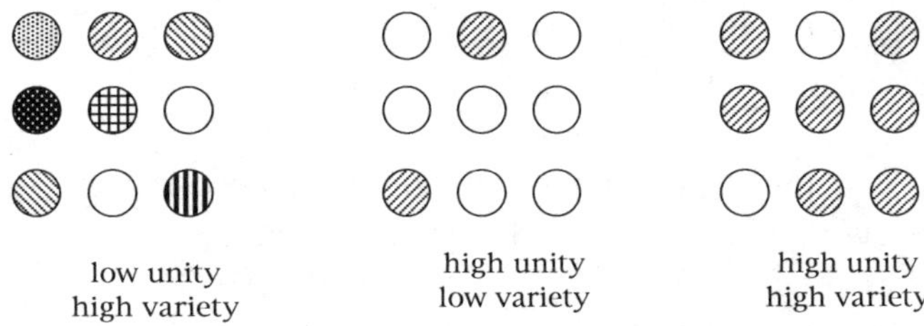

Figure 1. Nine cells assumed to be all causally related. Cells that fire are shaded, with phase relationships represented by the fill patterns. The leftmost and center panels have the same low overall synchrony. Large overall synchrony is only found in the third panel, which represents a stimulus that has variety but is perceived as unified whole (see text for further explanation).

low-level or constructed) of the stimulus. The leftmost diagram in Figure 1 shows a simplified diagram of the processing of a stimulus with a variety of elements but low perceived unity. Then, by hypothesis, the cells registering these elements will fire out of synchrony (firing cells have some enclosed pattern; cells firing in synchrony have the identical fill pattern). In contrast, if the stimulus exhibits a large degree of unity, but involves few elements, then the situation in the center panel results. The overall synchrony is the same as that of the first panel because relatively few cells are triggered. However, when there is both variety and perceived unity, the rightmost diagram results. Here the overall synchrony is greater than the two previous cases.

In summary, unity in variety may be assessed by a measure of overall synchrony between firing elements, if one assumes that synchronized firing correlates with perceived unity, and the number of elements that fire with the degree of variety. It may be comforting to know that the time-tested notion of unity in variety can be operationalized in this form; however, if the argument is to stand scrutiny, it must be recast in a form that accords with more contemporary notions. Accordingly, the following argument is offered to further clarify the relation between the measure and neural dynamics:

(i) The binding of the elements of a stimulus is proportional to the synchrony associated with the cells encoding these elements.
(ii) A stimulus will be rewarding to the extent that its elements can be bound into a unified whole.

Therefore the intrinsic reward of the stimulus can be measured by the synchrony associated with it.

It is clear that the conclusion follows directly from the premises, so it remains to justify the premises. One small word of caution is in order. The conclusion of the argument introduces a key word, "intrinsic". This is to distinguish aesthetic stimuli from non-aesthetic stimuli, which have rewarding properties extrinsic to their perceptual effects. It is unlikely that anyone finds a 100 dollar bill intrinsically much more beautiful than a one dollar bill, but the former will always have a greater rewarding effect. Aesthetics, whether it is neurally grounded or not, always must attempt to divorce the test stimuli from any extrinsic rewards they may be associated with.

Premise (i) is currently the subject of intense debate within the scientific community. It may be stated in various forms, but the form most applicable to the current topic is that phenomenological unity is achieved when there is short-term synchronization (< 10 ms) between the cells subserving the features in question (cf. Engel and Singer, 2001). This may be the result of phase-locking in the gamma range or simply due to short-term overlap between firing spikes. The evidence for this hypothesis is both theoretical and empirical. The primary theoretical motivation is the putative inability of a parallel model which encodes by firing rate and place to represent the enormous numbers of combination of features that could be combined (von der Malsburg, 1999; Gray, 1999). The alternative suggested by the premise is that those features that have firing trains running approximately in unison are those which are bound together. Numerous empirical studies can be mustered to support this notion; Engle and Singer discuss 25 such studies in the visual domain and other modalities. Perhaps the most telling set of studies are those that show greater synchrony between units in the visual cortex that are associated with the currently attended eye in a binocular rivalry paradigm (Fries *et. al.*, 1997). Critics of the binding hypothesis point out that the current evidence while extensive and growing, fails to fully account for how binding is achieved. For example, there is a currently no commonly agreed means by which higher order circuits respond to the temporal binding occurring at a lower level. 'Conventional' models which use rate encoding avoid this difficulty because convergence provides a natural means by which higher-order features are constructed from sets of lower-order ones. Furthermore, some argue that convergence may be able to solve the binding problem without help from temporal binding (Shadlen and Movshon, 1999).

A full discussion of this debate would take many pages. Nevertheless, it is worth mentioning that the phenomenological aspect of premise i) (as opposed to the computational aspect), which is the one of critical concern here, may receive support from an independent argument. Consider the situation in which phenomenology does not depend on precise temporal dynamics. This would imply that phenomenology, unlike any other natural phenomenon (with the possible exception of some non-local quantum mechanical effects), is not a function of local temporality. In other words, the route from neural states to brain states would necessarily involve non-locally temporal calculations. Many are no doubt willing to entertain this, given that consciousness, though a phenomenon of the natural world, is one that appears to be like no other. But it should be stressed that it is more economical to assume that what a brain is 'feeling' is a function of what the brain is doing right now. In other words, phenomenological binding through temporal correlation may simply be the consequence of the default (and parsimonious) assumption which states that all items concurrently represented are perceived as unified, where concurrency is defined as a suitably small window of time.

Premise (ii) has its roots in Ramachandran and Hirstein's (1999) observation that perceptual binding is directly reinforcing. Ramachandran argues that the binding together of the elements of a stimulus results in an 'aha' phenomenon due to internal reinforcement. This will be true, for example, when the previously disjointed elements of a visual scene come together, or, in perhaps a stronger case, when a number of previously unexplained phenomena are suddenly seen to follow from the same theory. The reason for the reinforcement is that the organism will experience clear benefits from the unification process. One way of stating this that is consistent with premise ii) is as follows. An organism will benefit to the extent that it can maximize the amount of information about its environment it can maintain in parallel. As an incentive to achieving this, an internal reward will be generated in proportion to the extent this occurs. This internal reward is then coupled with a possible external reward or punishment to yield a net reward. For example, a brain totally lacking in inhibition will always be able to unify its entire perceptual field, but it would very soon receive an external punishment that would more than outweigh any internal reward. Under non-pathological conditions, however, the ability to rapidly create a coherent and unified view of one's environment is something that evolution has appropriately chosen to reward.

In summary, there are at least two routes to the synchrony measure of preference proposed here. Ultimately, however, its worth is dependent on how well it explains that data at hand. This is treated in the following sections in the case of musical preference.

Testing the Measure

Ideally, one would like to muster direct empirical evidence for the synchrony hypothesis; unfortunately, the neurophysiological basis of musical enjoyment is imperfectly understood at the present, although a select number of intriguing studies have been carried out. Increase in theta power has been shown to correlate with the pleasantness of a piece of music (Ramos and Corsi-Cabrera, 1989); the origin of this increase in unknown. Recently, a PET study has shown that music that elicits chills or is well-liked is correlated with increases and decreases in blood flow in a number of areas implicated in reward including the left ventral striatum and dorsomedial midbrain (increases) and right amygdala, left hippocampus, and the ventral medial prefrontal cortex (decreases) (Blood, and Zatorre, 2001). This is consistent with Ramachandran and Hirstein's (1999) claim that the limbic system mediates the reinforcement associated with the binding process. Perhaps the most relevant physiological study to the current proposal is Bhattacharya and Petsche's (2001) finding that gamma band synchrony was significantly higher in musicians than non-musicians. While not a finding on musical affect per se, it is consistent with the results described below showing increased synchrony as a function of exposure (up to a certain point). Presumably, musicians have listened to and have attended to more music than non-musicians, resulting in both a larger affective response and higher synchrony by the mechanism to be proposed. One cannot rule out on the basis of current findings, however, that the physiological findings are due to either a different kind of processing in musicians versus non-musicians or possibly innate factors.

This paper takes an alternative route to testing the proposed measure, as a means of providing some degree of verification, and also in order to elucidate the mechanisms underlying musical affect. Specifically, the processing of various musical aspects is simulated with a neural network, and it is shown that the network exhibits increased synchrony on those musical stimuli that are known to be preferred. In order to carry this project out, two items are essential. First, there must exist a means of simulating neural activity, and then must be a way of operationalizing the preference measure as a function of this activity.

The current work uses an integrate and fire neuron, which stands at an intermediate level of complexity between rate encoding models and those that model the fine details of ion transport. The former is clearly insufficient to capture short-term synchrony, while the latter contains more details than are necessary. An integrate-and-fire neuron, as its name implies, integrates input activity over time and fires when this activity exceeds a threshold. At any given time, input activity is the sum of the synaptic efficacy (positive in the case of excitation, negative in the case of inhibition) of the cells which are both firing and connected to the cell in question. It is also characterized by a parameter representing leakage, or a reduction of the integrated activity with time, and in addition may fire in a noisy manner, i.e., roughly in proportion to the integrated activity, but not necessarily when this activity precisely reaches threshold. Appendix 1 describes the operation and parameters for the model neuron used in this paper in more detail.

Panel A in Figure 2 shows the hypothetical firing pattern of two cells. The top cell is receiving greater net activity and is therefore firing at a faster rate. Note that any given time, a unit is either firing or not; hence, the spikes in firing patterns. Synchrony can be measured by noting the temporal proximity of the spikes from the two model neurons.

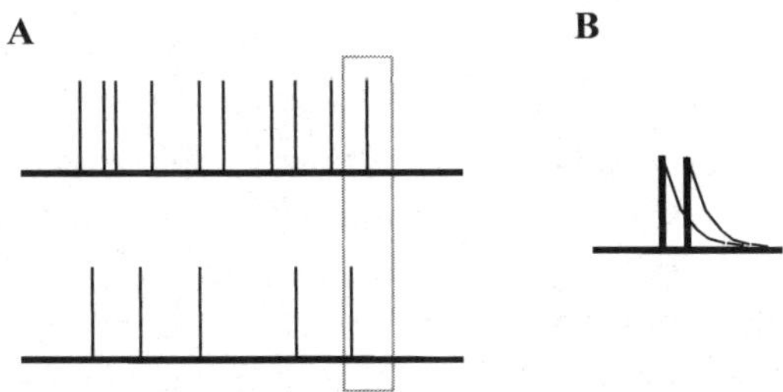

Figure 2. Synchrony between two integrate-and-fire neurons. **A**, typical firing patterns of two cells. **B**, measuring synchrony between the last spikes of these cells. The spike is convolved with an exponentially decreasing function, and these functions are then multiplied to yield a synchrony score (see text for details).

In this study, synchrony was measured by convolving all the spike delta functions of the two neurons in question with an asymmetric exponentially decreasing function, and then taking the product of the resulting convolutions, a measure first proposed by van Rossum (2001). This method has many desirable features over traditional binning measures including yielding a smooth value as a function of inter-spike distance, although none of the results reported here depend crucially on the measure used. Panel B in Figure 2 shows how the measure is applied to the two final spikes in panel A (enclosed by the rectangle). The result of the convolution is shown in both cases. Synchrony is measured simply by taking the normalized overlap between these two functions. If the synchrony of the spikes is exact, this value will be 1.0, if there is no overlap between the functions, then the product will be 0.0, with the value achieving some intermediate value if there is partial overlap, as in this case. Synchrony between the firing patterns is measured by taking the sum of all the individual synchronies between every spike in the first and every spike in the second (most of contributions will be zero because the distance between the spikes will be too great). When the synchrony between more than two units is assessed, the measured value is simply the sum of the individual synchronies computed two units at a time.

In general, synchrony or the lack thereof is a complex non-linear function of the underlying neural dynamics. However, in certain special cases, one can specify the origins of synchronous behavior. For example, one source of synchrony is a simple excitatory connection between two cells. Firing in one will immediately excite the other, and if the connection between the cells is sufficiently large, then near synchrony will result, regardless of the other inputs to the cells. A second, related source of synchrony occurs when two cells are both being fed by a third cell, which maintains an excitatory connection to both. This will be the primary origin of synchrony in the models to be considered here. For example, in the harmony model to be discussed, synchrony arises between ordinarily mutually inhibitory (and therefore, on average, desynchronized) chord units when they are fed by either the same note unit, or two different note units that are themselves synchronized.

The note recognition model

All of the simulations in this paper are based on a note recognition model first proposed in Katz (1994). The essential feature of this model, shown in Figure 3, is that a given input will trigger not only its counterpart in note recognition layer, but also to a lesser extent its neighbors a half step and whole step distant. The justification for this, given more fully in Katz (1994), is that inner hair cells respond in a Gaussian fashion to a range of frequencies centering on a central frequency. It was also hypothesized that cells responsible for recognition of a given note are fed by a number of hair cells that may respond to a given frequency in order to be maximally responsive in the presence of noise and/or hair cell deterioration. The net effect of these two facts is that a given note recognition cell will be responsive first to the characteristic frequency of this note, to a smaller extent notes a half step apart, and to a lesser extent still notes a full step apart. This is indicated in Figure 3 by the thickness of the connections. Not shown in the diagram are lateral inhibitory connections between all units in the note layer which serve to enhance contrast (all parameters for this and the other models in this paper are described in the Appendix).

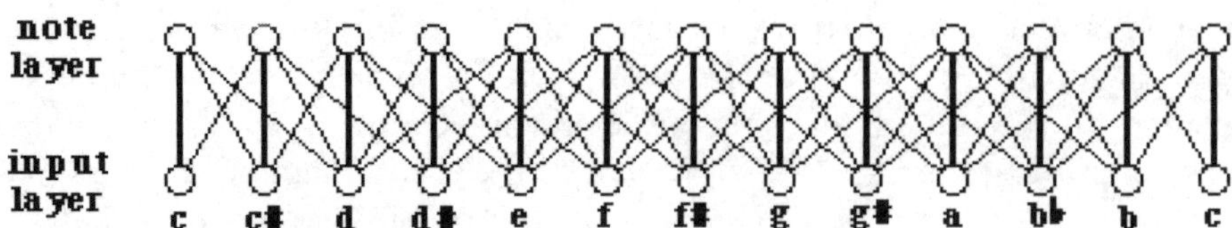

Figure 3. The note recognition model. Units in the input layer connect most strongly to their direct counterparts in the note layer, but also to neighboring units in that layer.

There are two related consequences of this model. First, perceptual blending between two notes should be a function of both their tonal distance and the transition time between notes. Second, ornamentation (presumably used to increase the aesthetic worth of a piece) should consist of rapid alternation between proximal notes. The former is readily verified by direct experience, and the latter by an examination of the musical corpus. It is rare to ornament a note with leaps or jump intervals (greater than a whole note).[1]

Both effects are immediately explicable given the central claim of this paper. Figure 4 shows typical firing patterns for the notes involved in a trill as a function of the distance between notes and note duration. Note onsets are given at the bottom of the diagram; units continue to receive exponentially decaying activation for a short time after triggering corresponding to the fading of the intensity of the sound. As can be seen, overlap between firing clumps and therefore synchrony is inversely proportional to both note duration and note distance (results for the whole step transition are intermediate between the illustrated cases). The former effect follows directly from the temporal dynamics of the situation; when the alternation is rapid, the unit previously triggered continues firing when the new unit becomes active. The latter effect is more complex and follows from the architecture illustrated in Figure 3. Let us say the transition is from an e to an f. When the unit corresponding to the f in the note layer is active, it provides excitatory support for both its counterpart directly above in the note layer, but also to the e. This activity under normal circumstance would be sub-threshold, and would not cause the e to fire. However, in conjunction with latent activity received by the exponential fading input to the e, it may be sufficient to sustain

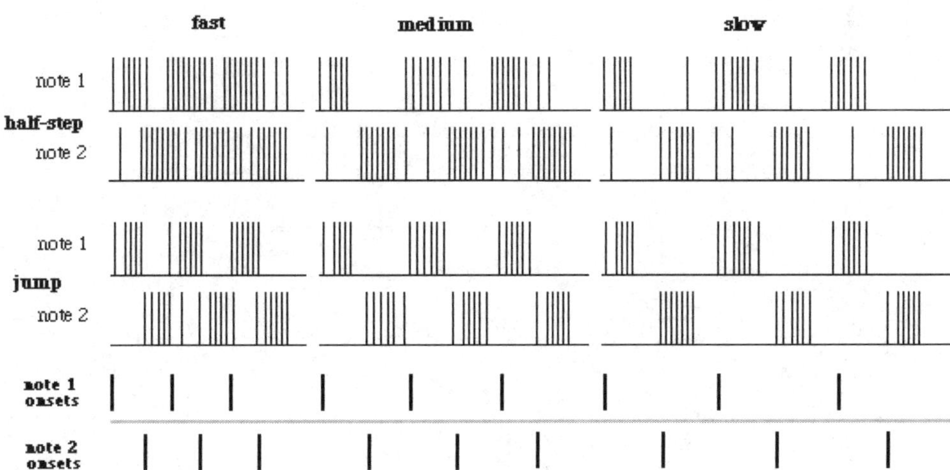

Figure 4. Sample firing patterns for the half-step and jump trills as a function of note length.

[1] These effects are horizontal, not vertical; i.e., they are concerned with the successive sounding of non-overlapping notes, not the formation of chords. The rules for chord-formation are completely different. In that case, factors such as the coincidence of overtones (e.g., between a note and a note a fifth above), contributing to the consonance of the chord, and inducing beating (e.g., between a note and a half note above) contributing to the dissonance of the chord, come into play.

some degree of activity in this unit. Synchrony between adjacent notes, and by hypothesis, increased preference for transitions between them, will prove crucial to the models of harmony and melody discussed below.

Harmony

The rules of harmony evolved during the period of common harmonic practice (approx. 1700-1850). Within the classical domain, the rules become somewhat looser in the late 19th century and 20th centuries, although many principles such as voice leading remained largely invariant. It is also noteworthy that popular music, in addition to also following these principles, relies heavily on dominant to tonic and subdominant to tonic progressions, as does classical. The goal of this section is to show that a model of chord recognition acting in concert with the synchrony measure makes predictions consistent with the rules of harmonic practice.

The chord recognition model is illustrated in Figure 5. The model, identical to that presented in Katz (1995), which, in turn was based on earlier model of Bharucha (1987), comprises the previously presented note recognition model and additionally a chord recognition layer. Bi-directional connections between chords and their respective notes form a resonance loop that allows both proper recognition and in addition accounts for top-down priming effects. The connection between the tonic of the chord and the chord unit is stronger than the other connections signaling that the presence of this note is a stronger indication of the presence of the chord than the other notes. The chord units (in this case those for the dominant and tonic chords) are engaged in a winner-take-all subnetwork consisting of excitatory self-connections and lateral inhibitory connections between the units.

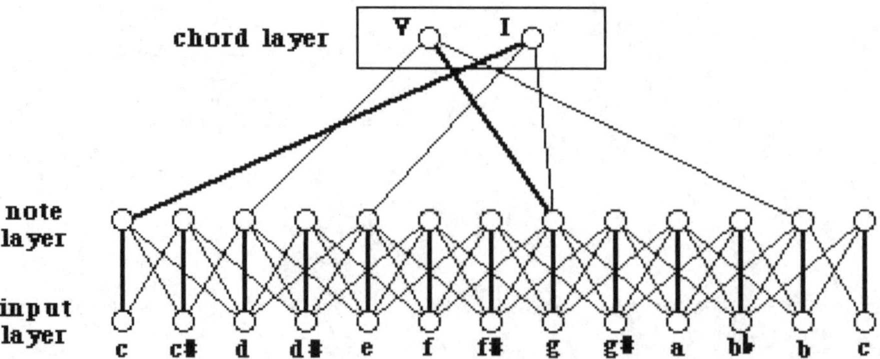

Figure 5. The chord recognition model. Notes are connected to their respective chord units, which are members of a winner-take-all recognition layer.

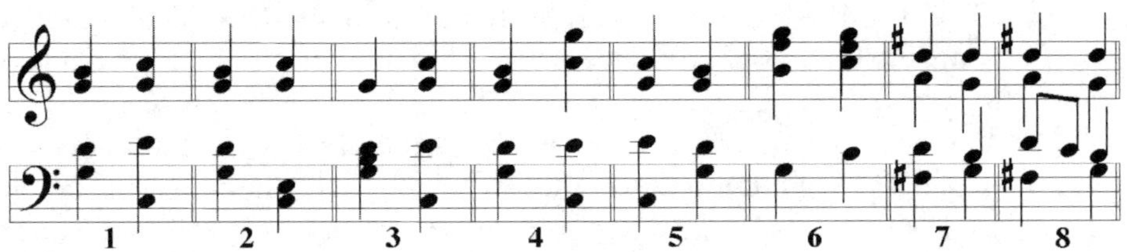

Figure 6. The chord sequences tested in this section

The model was tested on 8 chord progressions, shown in Figure 6. The progression in bar 1 is the dominant to tonic progression or perfect cadence, is considered the most powerful sequence (Pratt, 1984), and frequently ends classical pieces. There are three instances of voice leading in this sequence: the whole step resolution of the d to e, the half step resolution of b to c, and the fifth note (g) which remains constant. Progressions 2, 3, and 4 break several of these voice-leading rules, and therefore are less preferred. In 2, the whole step resolution is left out, in 3 the half step resolution is not present, and 4 omits the constant g. If the model is correct, these should all exhibit less synchrony than 1. Progression 5 is progression 1 in inverse order, or effectively a subdominant to tonic or imperfect cadence. It is also predicted that this should produce less synchrony that 1, consonant with the fact that it is considered less powerful than 1. Progression 6 is a dominant seventh to tonic cadence. The new seventh note (f) introduces a new half-step resolution with respect to the original cadence. As the period of common harmonic practice progressed, this cadence become more common, presumably because the ear became more accustomed to hearing the seventh as a proper member of the dominant chord (Pratt, 1984). To the extent that this is the case, this progression should be preferred, because it contains two half-step resolutions in contrast to the original cadence's solitary half-step resolution. Progression 7 is another perfect cadence, and progression 8 is a version of it with a passing note introduced. The passing note serves to bind together the d and b notes of the chords, thereby increasing the overall unity of the transition. Thus 8 should be slightly preferred to 7.

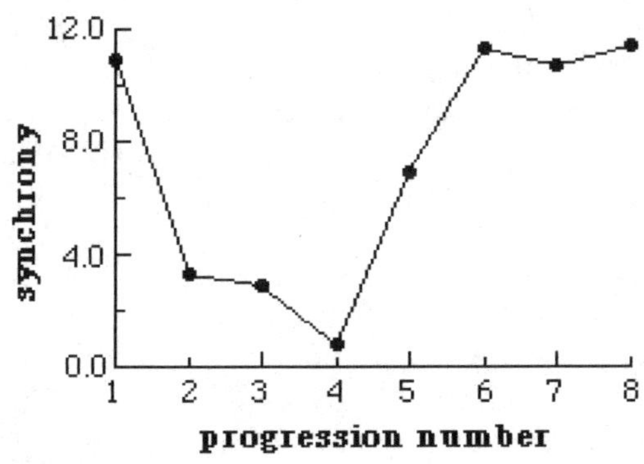

Figure 7.

Synchrony in the chord layer of the network as a function of the progression number in Figure 6.

Figure 7 shows the simulation results for these 8 sequences. The degree of synchrony during the entire chord transition is displayed for the two units representing the successive chords, using the previously described measure. That is, the spike patterns for the two units were first convolved with an exponentially decreasing function and the resulting total overlap over the resulting functions was assessed. All results are in accord with predictions. The perfect cadence outperforms its altered counterparts, progressions 2, 3 and 4. The lack of resolutions in 2 and 3 caused the leading note of the resolution pair not to be sustained as long as it was in the unaltered cadence. An even stronger effect was found for progression 4, in which the shared dominant note was removed. In the perfect cadence, the presence of this note in the second chord allows the first chord to continue to receive activity after the first chord stops sounding. This causes it to continue to fire for a brief period after the second chord is introduced, increasing the chance of overlap in the spiking patterns. Progression 5 exhibits a less obvious result but one in keeping with the rules of harmony. Reversing the progression does not result in a symmetrical effect in the model because of the greater magnitude of weight from the tonic note of a chord to its chord unit. In the forward direction (progression 1), the shared g note strongly supports the first chord for this reason. In the reverse direction (progression 5), this note only weakly supports the first chord, and thus the activity associated with this unit dies more quickly. The extra half-step resolution in progression 6 results in greater synchrony between the successive chords, in keeping with the ubiquity of the dominant seventh to tonic transition in the later classical period as well as in popular music. The results for progression 7 are identical to those of progression 1. Progression 8 shows an additional way of creating greater unity between the two chords, as evidenced by the slightly increased synchrony. The passing note supports both the prior and succeeding notes surrounding it, forcing slightly higher mutual support for the chords in the sequence.

In summary, the model makes predictions entirely consistent with the laws of harmony. A natural question is the following: if note resolutions increase the unity during chord sequences, why not include a surfeit of such. In fact, in certain genres such as barbershop harmonies this is precisely what happens. However, two factors mediate against this. First, the mind must be receptive to the dissonance in the chord that results from the addition of these notes. For example, addition of the seventh in progression 5 became prominent only when it was no longer heard as a dissonant note and was able to be incorporated into the chord. Second, shared notes, and especially the shared dominant note (as in the perfect cadence) are also important, and chord sequences in which these can be included in a natural fashion will be found to have greater unity.

Melody

Creating a good melody is most definitely an art rather than a science, and a working set of preference rules that would generate pleasing melodies (as opposed to merely passable ones) has yet to be proposed. Nevertheless, there are three fundamental facts about melodies that are not in doubt. First, melodies tend to include an inordinate number of steps rather than leaps. For example, Jeffries (1974) analysis of Western popular songs showed that major and minor second intervals were by far the most common. This is not to say that there are not some melodies which are not characterized by a more even distribution of steps and leaps, rather, that the norm is for a disproportionate number of steps. For example, an examination of melodies from a non-Western source, later in this paper, will show that a full 70% of transitions in this genre are steps. This effect is predicted by the results given above, in which it was shown that step transitions result in greater synchrony between the notes in question due to the mutual support from the input layer.

This section will concentrate on the other two facts regarding melodies. The first is that melodies improve with hearing; this will be considered later in this section. The other, and perhaps the most salient fact about melodies, is that successive phrases stand in a similarity relation to each other. A narrower hypothesis is that melodies are designed to elicit emotions by violating expectation (cf. Meyer, 1956). An example of such a transformation is the common jazz trope of repeating a phrase two or three times and then providing a new ending the last time it is played. However, this is just one of many similarity transformations. For example, one phrase is often simply the transpose of a previous phrase. Far from violating expectations, this permits the listener to complete the second phrase after hearing the first few notes. Other transformations include inversion of the contour, the keeping of the same notes but changing the contour, permutations of the rhythm, breaking a single note down into two or more, and changes in emphasis or timing. In short, the most concise summary of the relation between phrases is that the following phrase may be derived from the leading phrase by a similarity transformation that is easily computed by the listener.

Two additions to the model must be made in order to adequately reflect this fact. First, there must be some way of representing the phrases to capture rhythmic and contour similarities. This is accomplished in the current model with the single scheme shown in Figure 8. Panel A of the figure shows a phrase from the Chinese melody ‘Kangding Love Song’, and Panel B shows how this phrase is represented in the network model. The contour information is represented in five categories, representing leap up (greater than a whole note), step up (a whole note or less), repeat, step down (a whole note or less), and leap down (greater than a whole note), consistent with the fact that people can remember general

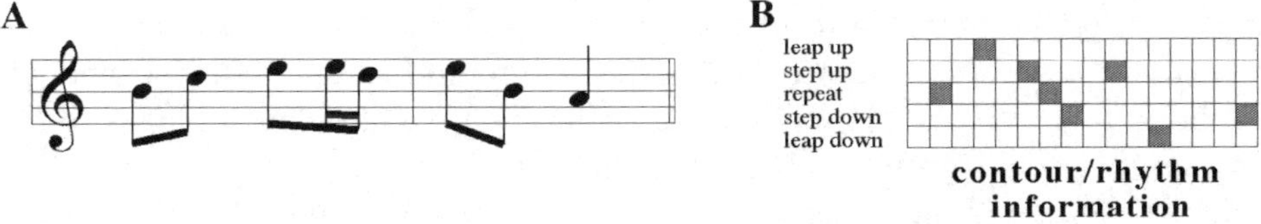

Figure 8. Contour and rhythm information in the model. **A** shows a typical melodic phrase, and **B** shows the representational scheme (see the text for details).

contours but have poor memories for exact interval information in a phrase (Davies and Jenning, 1977). Rhythmic information is represented by shading the appropriate box corresponding to the length of the given note. For example, in this example, each vertical column represents a sixteenth note. Thus, the first note, an eighth note, is indicated in the second column, and it is the first note, so it is placed in the repeat position by default. The next note, also an eighth note, is placed in the fourth column, and the relation between it and the previous note is a leap, so it is placed in the top row. This representation captures the vast majority of similarity transformations found in melodic development, although it does have some weaknesses. For example, occasionally extra notes are added at the start rather than the end of the phrase; this representation would not capture the resemblance between phrases altered in this way. It is unlikely that the qualitative nature of the reported results would be altered by including a shift mechanism to capture this relation, however.

In addition to representing the phrases, there must be some means of capturing the similarity between successive phrases. In the current model, this is done with an ART-like (Grossberg, 1980) unsupervised learning model. The justification for using an unsupervised model is that music is not normally accompanied by instructions as to what is occurring. It is up to the listener to place items such as phrases in created categories. The justification for using an ART inspired model is that this type of network allows one to explicitly control how close two input examples must be in order be placed in the same category via what is known as a vigilance parameter. For example, when this parameter is set to a relatively high value, examples must be almost identical to be classified together. By constructing a network with a variety of clusters, each one controlled by a unique vigilance parameter, one can effectively form an unsupervised distributed representation of the input pattern, and do so in time-efficient manner (see Katz, 1994 for details). The net effect of this scheme is that a distributed representation of the phrase is formed in the category layer, i.e., the overlap of the units representing the two phrases will be proportional to the similarity between the phrases.

This scheme is realized as shown in Figure 9, in which multiple winner-take-all networks, or clusters (10 of which are present in the full model), independently receive information about the notes that were sounded in the phrase, from the note layer, and the rhythm and contour information. Learning takes place only at the phrase junctures, and one phrase is learned at a time. The reason for learning only at the phrase junctions is that these are, from the point of view of melody, the most psychologically significant boundaries within a melody (Lehrdal and Jackendoff, 1983), apart from fundamental boundary between the notes themselves. There is also occasionally thematic development within a phrase itself, and groups of phrases often stand in thematic relation to one another. Neither of these is treated here, although Katz (1994) describes how the latter may be handled.

The model in conjunction with the synchrony measure favours phrase transitions that are neither too similar nor too different. Consider almost identical

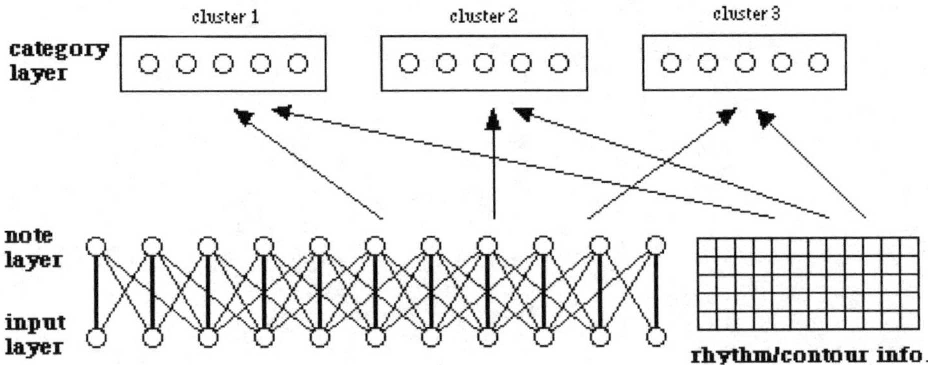

Figure 9.
The phrase processing scheme. Winner-take-all category clusters classify each phrase according to both the notes present in the phrase and also the rhythmic and contour information in the phrase.

phrases. Then a transition within a cluster will entail a relatively large overlap between the firing of the units categorizing the phrases, and potentially a large amount of synchrony, because the first unit will be supported during the transition by features in common between the phrases. However, there will be relatively few such transitions, because the distributed representations will be almost identical. Alternatively, consider two widely disparate phrases. Many transitions will take place in the category layer, but the lack of shared features implies relatively low synchrony between the units in question. Optimal synchrony results when there is a modicum of similarity between phrases, which is what is seen with actual melodies. In summary, maximal synchrony for phrases of moderate similarity is an emergent property of a system that forms an unsupervised distributed representation of phrases, and not one that must be explicitly designed into the system.

To test these ideas, eight popular and eight jazz melodies, chosen at random from songbooks were examined (the list of melodies is given in Appendix 2). The principle of melodic degradation (Katz, 1994), which states that it is unlikely that a well-liked melody will improve by a random alteration, was invoked. A model that predicts preference should therefore also exhibit a decreased response as a melody is altered. Alteration was accomplished in this study by replacing a given proportion at notes with randomly generated notes in the same pitch range and duration range as the original melody. Phrase boundaries were assessed in accord with the principles outlined in Lehrdal and Jackendoff (1983) by the experimenter, and the network learned only at such boundaries.

Figure 10 shows the averaged synchrony for each musical category as a function of percent alteration. Synchrony was assessed by summing over the synchrony for each category cluster, where this was computed by summing over the synchrony for all the units in the cluster, taken two at time, and applying the measure shown in Figure 2. The results are shown normalized to the total synchrony obtained in the no alteration condition. As desired, there is degradation in the

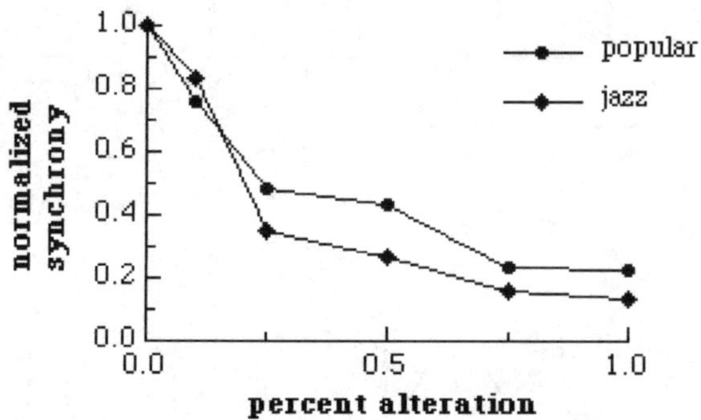

Figure 10. Synchrony in the clusters in the category layer as a function of melodic degradation for two sets of melodies.

models' assessments of the songs as a function of the percent of notes altered. In addition, the degradation is non-linear, with a disproportionate effect occurring with a small proportion of notes altered. This is arguably a plausible reflection of the human response, in that only few notes changed in a good melody will likely convert it into a mediocre one.

One aspect of melodic preference that was captured, also as an emergent property of the learning scheme, is the exposure effect. As with many other areas, preference in music is a function not just of the intrinsic merit of the piece but also how often one has been exposed to it (Zajonc, 1980). This is one reason radio time is so critical in developing the market for popular songs. Exposure not only publicizes the song but also increases preference for it.

It is easily seen that increased synchrony as a function of exposure is a direct effect of the proposed model. Categorical units respond in proportion to the amount of training time. If these are not responsive, there is no opportunity for synchrony to develop during the transition between categories. Figure 11 shows the normalized synchrony, measured as before within clusters, for all 16 songs (the performance of the popular and jazz melodies was nearly identical), as a function of training cycle. A smooth, monotonically increasing S-shaped curve

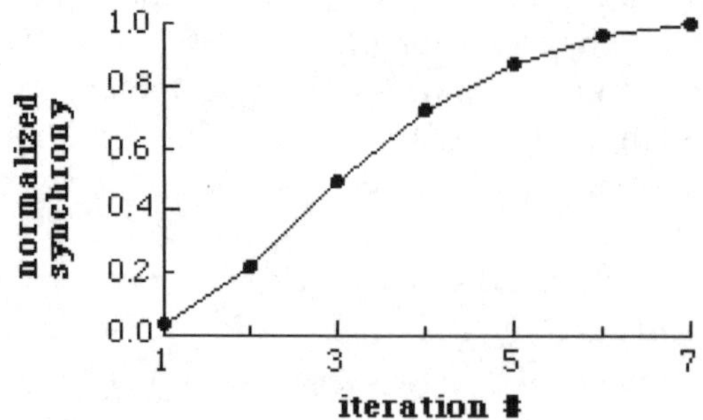

Figure 11. Synchrony rises monotonically as a function of the learning iteration.

was produced. This curve does not reflect a downturn in positive affect as a function of overexposure (Boornstein, 1989). Katz (1995) suggests an additional habituation mechanism based on increased lateral inhibition to explain this effect. This mechanism was not implemented in this case but would also be applicable to the current model because synchrony decreases with increasing inhibition between cells.

In summary, three primary preference effects relating to melody are explained by the current model. The first, the preponderance of stepwise movement, is explained by the basic note recognition model. The last two, phrase similarity and increasing preference as a function of exposure are explained by an unsupervised distributed learning scheme which classifies the phrases.

Rhythm

The previous section treated rhythm, but it treated it categorically. That is, rhythmic information was pertinent only to the extent that it influenced how a particular phrase was categorized. But rhythm also has a dynamic effect on the perception and preference for music. The most salient fact about the dynamic aspect of rhythm is that all music is either accompanied or contains a relatively steady beat. In popular musics, this beat is usually reinforced by a percussion instrument, and in art musics, it is implicitly present in the notes themselves and in emphasis cues. Typically, not every beat will be present in more complex musical forms. However, in a piece of art music in 4/4 time, for example, almost every measure will begin with a note (corresponding to the first beat), the vast majority of measures of measures will have a note onset on the third beat of the measure, and in at least a simple majority of cases there will be a note onset corresponding to the second or the fourth beats or both. This regularity, though not perfect, is something that calls for an explanation.

The simplest explanation consistent with both the current model and psychological fact is that a steady rhythm sets up an expectation that succeeding notes will fall in certain places. For example, most people can tap their feet in time with the underlying meter of a song, regardless of whether this meter is strongly or weakly indicated. This expectation may be thought of as top-down process, which anticipates and thereby serves to prime the notes to come. This priming sends simultaneous activity to units that may already be in some degree of synchrony, thereby increasing the net synchrony between the units and increasing the preference for the heard music by the central hypothesis of this paper. When timing is erratic, the priming signal will not match the onset of the coming note, and therefore its effect will be accordingly diminished.

Figure 12 shows how this is accomplished in the current model. An oscillator layer contains units that beat with a given period. Prior studies have shown how it is possible for integrate and fire units to induce this beat (Large and Kolen, 1994; Eck, 2002). For simplicity, in this study it is assumed that only two such units with fixed periods are present, corresponding to the fundamental beat length and the measure length, with phases set to the start of the song. For

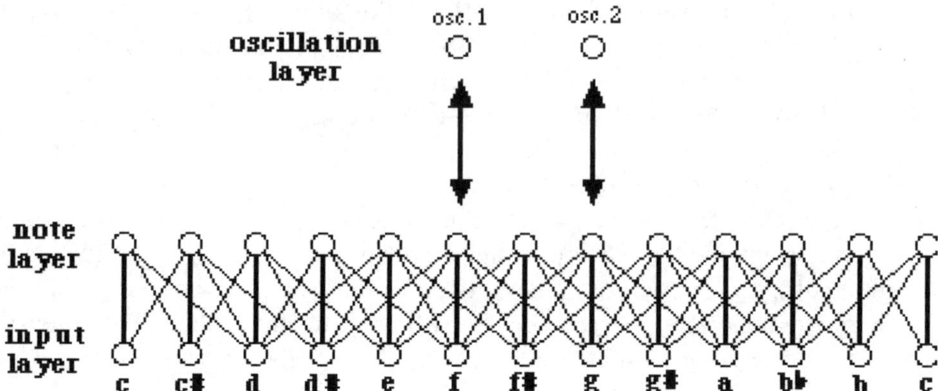

Figure 12. The model of dynamic rhythm processing. Two oscillators, with periods for the fundamental note duration and the measure duration provide top-down expectation and in turn are affected by the incoming beats.

example, if the melody was in 3/4 time, the period of the first oscillator would correspond to a quarter note and that of the second oscillator would be three quarter notes. As in the induction studies, however, the tendency to fire for these units is proportional to the degree that a note has recently fallen in phase with the oscillator. Thus, in an irregular rhythm, these units would have a tendency not to fire, and for a very steady beat, eventually they would fire every period. When they do fire and if they meet an incoming note being triggered at the same time, the descending priming increases the likelihood of firing of the corresponding note unit when it is first activated. This in turn increases the likelihood of overlap between this note and residual firing of other notes, and thereby the likelihood of synchrony.

To show that this mechanism can enhance synchrony, the effect of a steady beat on stepwise resolution (the trills first illustrated in Figure 4) was first assessed. For the purposes of these simulations, it was assumed that the trills appeared somewhere after the very start of the melody, and therefore the oscillators were already well primed and ready to fire on their respective beats. This additional source of excitation, providing top-down priming to the note units, did in fact increase the degree of synchrony between the note units during the resolution in almost all cases, as Figure 13 illustrates. This figure shows the *difference* in synchrony between the oscillator absent condition, and the current simulation where the oscillators were present. The graph also reveals, however, a number of interesting results besides this basic effect. Note that the priming has almost no effect on the whole step and jump resolutions as the note length is increased. In these conditions, there is no overlap in firing between the successive notes, and the sub-threshold top-down priming from the oscillators can do nothing to change this. Alternatively, there is a very large synergistic effect for the half-step resolution for medium and longer note lengths. The priming serves to sustain the firing of the prior note which would otherwise fade because of the relatively long interval before the next note. These results illustrate that the

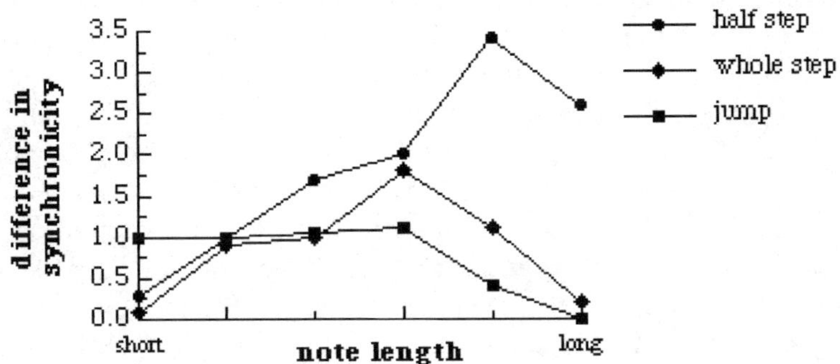

Figure 13.
Difference in synchrony between the oscillator present and the oscillator absent conditions.

model is capable of making non-trivial predictions about interaction between multiple factors, in this case, rhythmic and melodic. The human data on the confluence of multiple factors on preference is as yet too sparse to be compared to the current results, however.

As a further verification of the model, a similar experiment was carried out to the one in the previous section, in which the sixteen melodies were degraded by replacing randomly selected notes. In this case, however, only the note durations were changed, by displacing it by either a 1/32 note before or after its actual occurrence if the note was selected for degradation; the note values themselves were left unaltered. In addition, synchrony was measured in the note layer only; no category layer was present in this simulation. As expected, there was a decline in synchrony with increasing degradation for both the popular and jazz melodies, as can be seen in Figure 14 (the Turkish melodies are treated in the section below

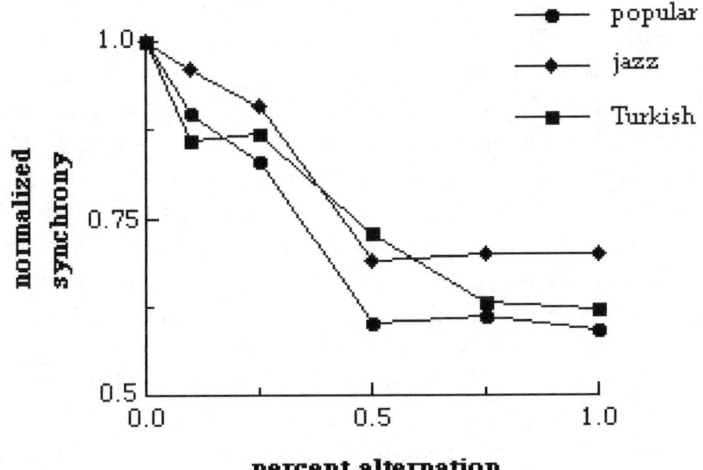

Figure 14. Synchrony in the note layer as a function of melody degradation.

on cross-cultural validation). This was due to two factors. First, the increasing irregularity of the rhythm caused a decline in firing of the oscillator units. Additionally, the irregularity of the beat with increasing degradation meant that there was decreased probability of the note being triggered in conjunction with a top-down prime.

Clearly, much more work need to be done in both gathering experimental data regarding human preferences to various rhythms and in the modeling thereof. Nevertheless, the current model does indicate why there is a trade-off between the dynamic and categorical aspects of rhythm. The former would like there to be as steady a beat as possible, while the latter needs variation in order to induce maximum synchrony. In fact, what would be ideal from the point of view of both would be for some instruments to keep a steady beat while others are able to weave in and out of the underlying rhythm. This, of course, is precisely what is seen in popular musics, and to a lesser extent, art musics.

Cross-cultural and further validation

The synchrony measure has been shown to be consistent with some of the simpler aspects of Western classical and popular forms. If the measure is to aspire to universality, then it must be shown to be valid both cross-culturally, and within more complex Western forms. Such an undertaking, even on a limited scale, is not possible within the scope of a single article, however, as it would entail the production of simulation results over an enormous range of musical forms. Nevertheless, it is hoped that a few extra points of confirmation will enhance the credibility of the proposed theory.

In particular, let us begin by examining some aspects of Turkish art music, a rich musical tradition extending back at least 800 years. Turkish art music, like many middle-eastern forms, revolve around maqams. Maqams, like the Western modes of major and minor, select a subset of possible notes from the set of all notes as the basis for the composition, and may revolve around a tonic note (the key in Western music). However, the core of a maqam is usually not a single note, but rather a characteristic sequence of ascending or descending notes. This sequence serves as both a theme and point of departure, and has no precise counterpart in the Western classical tradition. Furthermore, maqams may contain microtones not found in the Western scale. In addition, Turkish music is often written in what would be unusual time signatures for Western music (especially outside the realm of jazz), such as 9/4, 9/8, or even 28/4. Finally, Turkish art music, though sharing some instruments with Western classical music, most notably the violin and the clarinet, developed almost completely independently from this tradition. Thus, it is an ideal candidate for independent verification of a musical theory.

The first and most obvious question revolves around the interval incidence of Turkish art songs. Earlier it was argued that stepwise intervals between successive notes should be disproportionately favoured because of the increased synchrony between notes in this relation, and this relation should hold regardless of

	Leap down	Step down	Identical	Step up	Leap up
Popular	14%	32%	15%	24%	15%
Jazz	13	28	17	32	10
Turkish	3	46	21	24	6
Average	10%	35%	18%	27%	10%

Table 1. Percentage of types of intervals in three different musical forms.

the musical type. Table 1 shows that this is indeed the case for both the songs studied earlier and for Turkish art songs. For the purposes of this table, a step was anything less than or equal to a minor third interval. In the case of the Turkish songs, this included non-Western intervals (between microtones or between microtones and 'standard' notes) within this interval.

The table shows that in all forms, stepwise intervals predominate. This effect is even stronger in case of the Turkish songs, in which fully 70% of all intervals are steps. The table also reveals that identical note progressions (the same note repeated but with possibly a different duration) are also disproportionately represented. For example, in the Turkish songs, they far outnumber all leaps combined. Although the full results will not be presented here, this can be shown to be a type of priming, whereby the second identical note in the series of notes fires more fully by being anticipated by an identical note (recall that an integrate-and-fire neuron integrates prior input; thus, a prior sounding can serve to 'kick-start' a unit which is currently off). This, in turn, will cause an increase in synchrony with between this primed note and subsequent notes, and thus the relatively high incidence of repeated notes is consistent with the current claims.

Let us also examine in more detail how microtones resolve in Turkish music. In particular, the 'koma', or reduced flat plays an important role in many maqam families. Figure 15 shows the position of b koma on the scale. It is approximately 1/5 of the way between b and b flat (the frequency ratio between b and b flat is approximately 1/1.0679, between b and b koma is 1/1.0136).

A normal b flat would stand in closest relation to the a below it, and thus one would expect that resolutions to or from this note would predominate. Note, however, that the b koma is closer to c. Thus, the current theory would predict that this direction would be preferred. Table 2 shows that this is the case. All possible stepwise resolutions of the b koma are shown for 2 songs chosen at random from each of the maqam families containing this note. The koma preferentially resolves to or from the c 54% of the time, as opposed to the a 32% of the time.

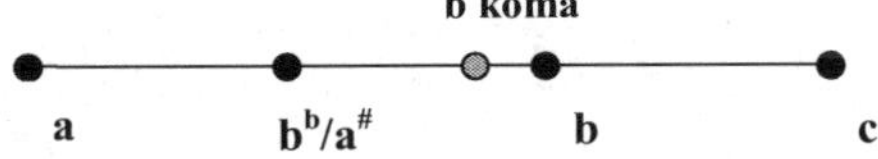

Figure 15. Position of the b koma relative to other notes in its vicinity.

Furthermore, 7% of the time that it does resolve to the a it is altered into a regular b flat to bring it closer to the a, and an additional 7% of the time the opposite transformation is effected, i.e., a is raised to an a# with the koma left untouched. In summary, a total of 68% of the time the koma resolves to or from the nearest note, or the sequence is modified so as to keep the interval small. This, in conjunction with the previous results, suggests that small intervals are strongly favoured in Turkish music, as in Western music.

Maqam family	'b koma' to 'c'	'b koma' to 'a'	'b flat' to 'a'	'b koma' to 'a sharp'
hicazkar	38%	24%	38%	0%
huseyni	57	43	0	0
huzzam	45	11	11	33
karcigar	70	30	10	0
evc	41	44	0	15
mukayyer	59	34	7	0
rast	53	42	0	5
saba	57	43	0	0
segah	68	6	0	26
ussak	52	32	7	7
Total	54%	32%	7%	7%

Table 2. Percent resolutions of the koma for different maqam families.

Another aspect of melody that was previously investigated was the theme and variation nature of melodic phrasing. As discussed, synchrony between units processing the phrases in a song is maximized when successive phrases are variations of each other, i.e., neither too similar nor too distinct. The question arises as to whether this is also the case for the Turkish art songs. Rather than run the previous simulation, which showed a degradation in synchrony with increasing noise added to the song (Figure 10), here a more direct comparison was made between the three song types by comparing vectors containing various aspects of the phrases. The similarity between the vectors for the successive phrases was measured by computing the cosine of the angle between the vectors. Three vectors were constructed. The first simply contained the notes present in the phrase, with element set to 1.0 if that note was present, and 0.0 otherwise (there was no representation of multiple appearances of the same note). The second vector represented the rhythm information, with each element representing successive 1/32 note duration intervals, and with the element set to 1.0 if the note was introduced at that time, and 0.0 otherwise. A third vector contained contour information, with 5 elements for each note, representing leap down, step down, identical, step up, and step down intervals, with steps and leaps as defined previously. Finally, a vector representing the entire phrase was constructed by appending the three vectors together.

	Note values	Rhythm	Contour	Entire vector
Popular	.52	.52	.31	.44
Jazz	.51	.57	.52	.54
Turkish	.44	.52	.32	.43
Average	.49	.54	.38	.47

Table 3. Similarity between successive phrases as measured by the note values, the rhythm, and the contour for the three song groups, as measured by the cosine of the angle between the vectors.

Table 3 shows the results of these comparisons for all three music types. Note that for all music types, and for all measures, phrase similarity is somewhere between perfect repetition and complete difference, and that the average for the entire phrase vector comparisons is very close to 1/2. In addition, there is no reason to believe from this data that the Turkish songs have a fundamentally different structure than the Western ones, although overall similarity for the Turkish songs is slightly less than the other two. One possible reason for this is that polyphony and therefore harmonic variation is absent from Turkish music, and therefore more variation is found in the purely melodic elements that are present. This conclusion would require further examination of the use of harmonic variation in the Western songs both as they are written, and especially in the case of jazz, how they are actually played, however.

Table 3 suggests that Turkish songs treat rhythm categorically in a similar fashion to the Western songs. Another question is whether the dynamic aspects of rhythm are also similar. Figure 14 indicates that there is no significant difference in synchrony as a function of rhythmic degradation between the musical forms; the Turkish curve lies approximately between the other two. This suggests that Turkish music, like Western forms, relies on a steady beat, the disruption of which reduces the quality of the song.

However, there are other key differences not indicated by this simulation, one of which is the use of non-Western time signatures. In particular, Turkish songs often contain time signatures (e.g., 9/8 and 9/4) in which measures end in an emphatic note, or downbeat, as opposed to the most common signatures in Western music (e.g., 2/4, 4/4, and 3/4) which all end on an upbeat. This imparts a different emotional quality to much of Turkish music, and for the reasons originally discussed in the introduction, this effect will not be treated here.

However, there is one aspect of Turkish songs in 9/8 and 9/4 that can be discussed in the current context. The increased emphasis on the final note of the measure implies that any other means that would increase synchrony between the final note and its predecessor would be accordingly enhanced (recall the synergistic effects of rhythm and resolution shown in Figure 13). In effect, it is posited that dynamic emphasis in conjunction with the stepwise resolution acts to both maintain the firing of the unit representing the note prior to the final note as well as helping to trigger firing of the unit representing the final note itself. Thus one would predict that the final eighth note in 9/8 time or the final quarter note in 9/4 time in each measure would be arrived at by step in a disproportionate number of instances relative to other notes. In fact, as Table 4 illustrates, this is exactly what is seen. The final note in each measure in 20 songs (10 in 9/4, 10 in 9/8) from a number of different maqam families is approached by step 79% of the time, compared with 70% of the time for all notes in the previously studied Turkish songs, and 58% of the time for the Western songs previously studied.

	Leap down	Step down	Identical	Step up	Leap up
final note in 9/8;9/4	2%	47%	14%	32%	5%
all notes Turkish	3	46	21	24	6
all notes Western	14	30	16	28	12

Table 4. Percent intervals between notes for the last note in 9/8 and 9/4 time in selected Turkish songs, and in all notes in the previously studied Turkish and Western melodies.

Ideally, one would like to extend the prior results regarding harmony to Turkish music also. Unfortunately, Turkish music derives its richness from melodic and rhythmic complexity; there is no polyphony to speak of in the typical composition. Thus, here we will reprise one of the earlier results in the context of jazz, a music that has done a great deal to expand the boundaries of harmonic possibilities since the time of common harmonic practice. As can be seen in the three chord cadence in Figure 16, jazz chords are typically built around the tonic, the third, and the seventh (ignore the shaded notes for now). This presents an immediate problem for the current theory, in that the shared fifth note in this type of cadence serves to maintain the activity of the prior chord when the new chord is sounded (for example, the ‘g’ in ‘I’ below keeps the ‘V’ chord active). If this is removed, then, as previously argued, the affective force of the cadence should be considerably reduced.

The resolution of this apparent contradiction with the proposed theory lies in two additional claims:

(i) Even when removed, the fifth in the resolving chord, and the tonic of the leading chord (the shaded notes), are virtually present. The reason for this is that these notes are overtones of the bass notes; i.e., they will be acoustically present (to a degree depending on the instrument) by virtual of being integer

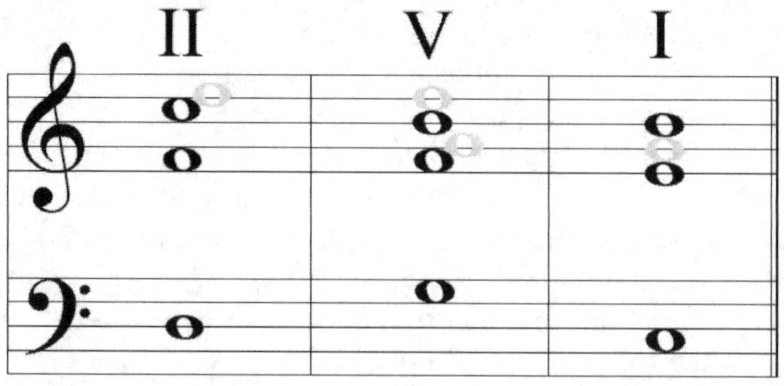

II V I

Figure 16. A sequence of jazz chords. The shaded notes are typically not present, but are virtually present in the form of overtones.

multiples of the underlying bass tone (Buser & Imbert, 1992). The net effect of this is that a chord with the fifth removed, other than sounding a little thinner to the ear, sounds almost the same as if these notes are present.

(ii) The explicit presence of these notes creates inertia if a chord sequence with a large number of chords is played relatively quickly (Alldis, 2000). That is, the presence of these notes, by doing such a good job of maintaining the chord prior to the current one, slows down the transition from one chord to the next, eventually creating a 'backlog' of chords in a longer chord sequence that will clash in the mind's ear. In the current model, this occurs because the chord units are connected via lateral inhibition. For example, in a fast sequence from chord 1 to chord 2 to chord 3, chords 1 and 2 may still be active when chord 3 is triggered, inhibiting the firing of the unit for this chord (chord 3), and thus, lowering the potential synchrony between chords 2 and 3.

The graph in Figure 17 shows normalized synchrony in the chord layer in the model in Figure 5 as a function of the strength of the overtones in Figure 16 (0.0 means the overtone is absent, 1.0 means that the note is triggered to the same degree as the non-virtual notes), for a five chord 'cycle of fifths' sequence, in which a relatively short time for each chord was allowed. Note that maximal synchrony is obtained when the virtual notes are somewhat reduced in trigger strength relative to their being actually present in the chords. An examination of the actual firing patterns shows that this occurs for the reason stated, namely, that the entry of the later chords is delayed, via lateral inhibition, by the continued firing of the earlier chords, effectively limiting the possibilities for synchrony between these chords. These results are consistent with the fact that in a musical form that is typically light on its feet like jazz, with relatively rapid alternations between chords, it may be better to suppress the fifth in the chord, and let acoustical properties of the instruments partially but not completely fill them in.

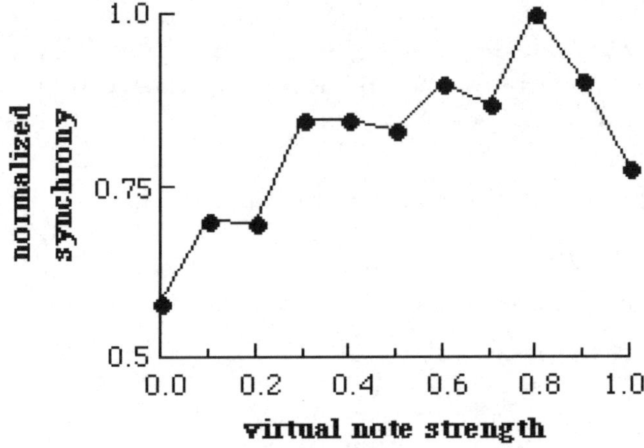

Figure 17. Synchrony in the chord layer as a function of the trigger activity supplied to the virtual notes for a five chord 'cycle of fifths' sequence.

Discussion

A method of musical preference dependent on the degree of neural synchrony has been proposed. It has been shown that this measure adequately predicts some of the simpler aspect of Western harmony, melody, and rhythm. In addition, it has been shown that many of these effects extend to Turkish music, either by direct simulation or by tabulation. It was also shown that some unique aspects of Turkish music, namely, the resolution of microtones, and the resolution of the final beat in 9/8 or 9/4 time, is consistent with the proposed model. Finally, it was demonstrated that the model makes an interesting non-monotonic prediction, namely, that there is an optimal level of the presence of the fifth of a chord where the prior chord is the dominant of the subsequent chord in a relatively fast sequence of multiple chords, consistent with chord phrasing in jazz harmony.

These results, of course, only begin to touch on the vast number of examples that could be drawn from the musical corpus, within Western harmony, melody, and rhythm, and within these elements from non-Western musical forms. In addition, relatively little has been said about the interaction between these elements. Finally, only the simpler aspects of elements have been treated. Full confirmation of the measure therefore awaits further simulation studies, ideally backed up direct brain imaging studies that assess synchrony.

Nevertheless, the correspondence between synchrony and putative degrees of preference on a number of different cases should inspire some degree of tentative confidence in the proposed measure. In addition, it may be possible to extend these results other art forms. For example, Bornstein's (1989) meta-analysis of the exposure effect (and downturn in affect with overexposure) shows that this is an almost universal effect, and thus likely to apply to types of aesthetic stimuli other than music. To the extent that the synchrony measure can be applied to these stimuli, then it may also be applicable to these other forms. Another aspect of music, theme and variation, may also have more general implications for aesthetic stimuli in other modalities. This method appears most notably in dance and in abstract visual art. In summary, the preference measure based on neural synchrony, while still in its infancy, has the potential for providing greater insight into why music is such a powerful artistic form, and also why other artistic forms share some of the characteristics of music.

APPENDIX 1: Simulation Details

The integrate and fire neuron

A spike is generated with probability P(H) with

$$H(t) = H_{som}(t) + H_{ref}(t)$$

where

$$H_{som}(t) = H_{som}(t-1)\exp[-\Delta t/\tau] + I(t)$$

is the integration of the signal at the soma, with I(t) the net input to the unit, and

$H_{ref}(t) = -\text{infinity}$ when $t - t_f <= t_{abs}$, and $-1/[t-t_f-t_{abs}]$ otherwise,

is the refractory potential where t_f is the last time the spike was generated, and

$P(H) = 1 - \exp[-\Delta t/[\tau_o \exp[-\beta(H-\theta)]]$.

For all simulations, parameters values were as follows:

$q = 1.0$; $b = 8.0$; $\tau = 5.0$; $\Delta t = 1$; $t_{abs} = 2$; $\tau_o = 1$;

Note recognition

All units in the input layer are connected to their counterparts in the note layer with a weight of 1.25, to units in the note layer a half step distant with a weight of 0.62, and to units a whole step distant with a weight of 0.25. All units in the note layer are connected to every other unit in this layer with an inhibitory connection of -.2. With the exception of the harmony simulation, in which case all relevant notes continuously receive constant I(t) = 1.0, input layer units receive an initial I(t) = 2.0 on note onset and an exponentially decreasing value of I(t) = 0.95 I(t–1) thereafter. Note durations for the trill simulation were 48, 96, and 128 time cycles for the fast, medium and slow cases respectively.

Harmony

Non-tonic notes are connected to chord layer units with a weight of 0.5, and tonic units with a weight of 0.75. The descending connection from the chord units to all elements of the chord was 0.1. Chord layer units are connected to themselves with a weight 0.5 and to the other chord units with a weight of –0.25. Each chord was triggered for 64 time cycles.

Melody

Ten clusters consisting of 12 units each with excitory self-connections of 0.5 and inhibitory lateral connections of –0.25 were used; vigilance ranged from 0.5 to 0.95 for the clusters. Learning followed the rule

$\Delta w_{ij} = \lambda (a_i - w_{ij})$,

where w_{ij} is the weight between a unit in the note or contour/info. layers, a_i is 1 if the unit is active and 0 otherwise, and λ is the learning rate. For the first simulation, λ was 1.0, i.e., the network learned in a single pass, and for the exposure simulation, λ was 0.1.

Rhythm

Each oscillator was characterized by a net input which was applied to the oscillator once per period. If an incoming note onset matched the oscillator's potential firing time, then the oscillator input was increased by 0.25, otherwise it was decreased by 0.25. Thus, the periodic firing of an oscillator was proportional to the existence of note onsets when it was scheduled to fire. The descending connection from both oscillators to all units in the note layer was 0.4. In the first simulation, the note lengths ranged from 48 to 128 time cycles.

Jazz harmony

Parameters were identical to the prior harmony simulation except that chords were triggered for 24 time cycles only. In addition, the virtual notes received an input I(t) corresponding to the independent variable in Figure 17.

APPENDIX 2: List of Songs Used in Simulations

Popular

1. The joker
2. Good morning heartache
3. Thirteen women
4. Sons of the sea
5. Oh Julie
6. The frim fram sauce
7. Caterina
8. Sometimes

Jazz

1. God bless the child
2. Maybe this time
3. Come rain or come shine
4. Summertime
5. My funny valentine
6. The thrill is gone
7. Lazy afternoon
8. That's all

Turkish

1. Daglari hep kar aldi
2. Unutmadim seni ben
3. Umitsiz bir aska dustum algarim ben halime
4. Gitti gelmeyiverdi
5. Otomobil ucar gider
6. Askimin ilkbahari ilk heyecanim benim
7. Antalya bir yere
8. Dil seni

References

Alldis, D. (2000), *A Classical Approach to Jazz Piano* (Milwauke: Hal Leonard).
Augustine (1942), *De ordine*, trans. Robert P. Russell (New York: Cosmopolitan Science & Art).
Beardsley, M.C. (1966), *Aesthetics from Classical Greece to the Present* (New York: Macmillan).

Benzon, W.L. (2002), *Beethoven's Anvil: Music in Mind and Culture* (New York: Basic Books).

Berlyne, D.E. (1971), *Aesthetics and Psychobiology* (New York: Appleton-Crofts).

Barucha, J.J. and Stoeckig, K. (1987), 'Priming of chords: Spreading activation or overlapping frequency spectra?', *Perception & Psychophysics*, **41**, pp. 519–24.

Bhattacharya, J. & Petsche, H. (2001), 'Enhanced phase synchrony in the electroecephalograph gamma band for musicians while listening to music', *Physical Review E*, **64**, pp. 1–4.

Blood, A. & Zattore, R.J. (2001), 'Intensely pleasurable responses to music correlate with activity in brain regions implicated in reward and emotion', *Proceedings of the National Academy of Sciences*, **98**, *pp.* 11818–23.

Bornstein, R.F. (1989), 'Exposure and affect: Overview and meta-analysis of research, 1968–1987', *Psychological Bulletin*, **106**, pp. 265–89.

Buser, P. & Imbert, M. (1992), *Audition* (Cambridge, MA: MIT Press).

Davies, J.B. & Jennings, J. (1977), 'The reproduction of familiar melodies and the perception of tonal sequences', *Journal of the Acoustical Society of America*, **61**, pp. 534–41.

Dewey, J. (1934), *Art As Experience* (New York: Putnam).

Eck, D. (2002), 'A network of relaxation oscillators the finds downbeats in rhythms', DETAILS??

Engel, A.K & Singer, W. (2001), 'Temporal binding and the neural correlates of sensory awareness', *Trends in Cognitive Sciencs*, **5**, pp. 16–25.

Fries *et al.* (1997), 'Synchronization of oscillatory responses in visual cortex correlates with perception in interocular rivalry', *Proceedings of the National Academies of Science, U.S.A.*, **94**, pp. 12699–704.

Gray, C. (1999), 'The temporal correlation hypothesis of visual feature integration: Still alive and well', *Neuron*, **24**, pp. 31–47.

Grossberg, S. (1980), 'How does the brain build a cognitive code?', *Psychological Review*, **87**, pp. 1–51.

Jeffries, T.B. (1974), 'Relationship of interval frequency count ot ratings of melodic intervals', *Journal of Experimental Psychology*, 102, pp. 903–5.

Katz, B.F. (1994), 'An ear for melody', in *Musical Networks*, ed. N. Griffith and P.M Todd (Cambridge, MA: MIT Press).

Katz, B.F. (1995), 'Harmonic resolution, neural resonance, and positive affect', *Music Perception*, **13**, *pp.* –9-108.

Katz, B.F. (1995), 'Mere exposure effects: Merely total activation?', *Proceedings of the Conference of the Cognitive Science Society* (Pittsburgh).

Large, E.W. & Kolen, J.F. (1994), 'Resonance and the perception of musical meter', in *Musical Networks*, ed. N. Griffith and P.M Todd (Cambridge, MA: MIT Press).

Lerdahl, F. and Jackendoff, R. (1983), *A Generative Theory of Tonal Music* (Cambridge, MA: MIT Press).

Katz, B.F. (2002), 'What makes a polygon pleasing?', *Empirical Studies of the Arts*, **20**, pp. 1–19.

Martindale, C. (1984), 'The pleasures of thought: A theory of cognitive hedonics', *The Journal of Mind and Behavior*, **5**, pp. 49–80.

Martindale, C. (2001), 'How does the brain compute aesthetic preference?', *The General Pyschologist*, **36**, pp. 25–35.

Meyer, L.B. (1956), *Emotion and Meaning in Music* (Chicago, IL: University of Chicago Press).

Pratt, G.P. (1984), *The Dynamics of Harmony: Principles and Practice* (Buckingham: Open University Press).

Ramachandran, V.S. & Hirstein, W. (1999), 'The science of art: A neurological theory of aesthetic experience', *Journal of Consciousness Studies*, **6** (6–7), pp. 15–51.

Ramosm J. & Corsi-Cabrera, M. (1989), 'Does brain electrical activity react to music?', *International Journal of Neuroscience*, **47**, pp. 351–7.

Shadlen, M.N. & Movshon, J.A. (1999), 'Synchrony unbound: A critical evaluation of the temporal binding hypothesis', *Neuron*, **24**, pp. 67–77.

van Rossum, M.C.W. (2001), 'A novel spike distance. *Neural Compuation, 13,* 751-763.

von der Malsburg, C. (1999) The what and why of binding: The modeler's perspective', *Neuron*, **24**, pp. 95–104.

Wundt, W.M. (1874), *Grunduzgeder physiologischen Psychologie* (Leipzig: Engelmann).

Zajonc, R.B. (1980), 'Feeling and thinking: Preferences need no inferences', *American Psychologist*, **39**, pp. 117–23.

Neus Barrantes-Vidal

Creativity & Madness Revisited from Current Psychological Perspectives

Abstract: *Both scientific evidence and folklore have suggested that madness is associated with creativity, especially in the arts. Recently, more rigorous studies have confirmed to some extent these previous observations. The current view is that it is not severe and acute insanity that is related to heightened creativity, but the personality roots and soft manifestations of both schizophrenic and bipolar psychoses. The affective and cognitive peculiarities associated with schizotypic and hypomanic personalities may be preferentially related to different kinds of creative endeavours, such as the sciences and arts, respectively. The connection between personality traits and creativity is produced because they share some biological–cognitive–personality features, such as cognitive disinhibition. Additionally, it has been shown that the genetic liability for both bipolar and schizophrenic psychoses is related to creativity. A prevailing hypothesis is that creativity may be one type of 'compensatory advantage' for those carrying the genes for psychosis.*

Nullum magnum ingenium sine mixtura dementiae
(No great imaginative power without a dash of madness)
Seneca

I: Introduction

Many philosophers, artists and old folklore beliefs have maintained for centuries that there is a hint of genius in the madman and, conversely, that creativity demands some degree of lunacy. Shakespeare put it nicely in Theseus' speech from *A Midsummer Night's Dream*: 'The lunatic, the poet, and the lover are of imagination all compact'. As Nettle (2001) points out, Shakespeare identified a common psychological trait in all three, that is, strong imagination: 'Lovers and madmen have such seething brains, such shaping fantasies, that apprehend more than cool reason ever comprehends'.

Correspondence:
Neus Barrantes-Vidal, Departament de Psicologia de la Salut, Facultat de Psicologia, Universitat Autònome de Barceleona, 08193-Bellaterra (Barcelona), Spain. *Email:* *neus.barrantes@uab.es*

Journal of Consciousness Studies, **11**, No. 3–4, 2004, pp. 58–78

On the one hand, many geniuses have suffered from some sort of mental disorder, a fact that has insinuated that madness may be the price for possessing one of the most sublime human gifts; on the other hand, there is some intuitive similarity between the unconventional ideas produced by the mentally ill and the truly innovative and creative insights of eminent creative individuals. The present paper will review the theoretical and empirical literature examining this question, beginning with a brief review of how psychology defines and understands creativity and madness.

II: Defining the Indefinable: What is Creativity?

There are many definitions of creativity, but none of them is a consensual definition in psychology. A starting point could be that 'creativity is the ability to produce work that is both novel (i.e., original, unexpected) and appropriate (i.e., useful, adaptive concerning task constraints)' (Sternberg, 1999, p. 3). A key point in differentiating true creativity from odd or capricious products is that creative output must not be idiosyncratic and only understandable by the creative individual, but meaningful for those belonging to the particular field of the creative endeavour.

Creativity is a multidimensional construct that can be studied from different *approaches*: what features define a *product* as creative; the biological, personality and cognitive characteristics of the creative *person*; the environmental and sociocultural *conditions* that favour creativity; and, lastly, the elements that compose the creative *process*. This diversity is also reflected in the wide range of tests designed to *measure* creativity: creative cognition, personality, attitudes, interests, biographic inventories, etc. Most research has been done with tests of creative cognition, mainly with *divergent thinking* tests, in which individuals are asked to produce a range of solutions to an open-ended problem for which there is neither a single correct response, nor an apparent solution. Examples include tests that ask for different uses of an item, unusual uses of a common object, listing remote consequences of a hypothesis, etc. The responses to these tests are scored attending to: *fluency* (number of meaningful responses), *cognitive flexibility* (the ability to produce varied responses belonging to different domains or conceptual categories), *originality* (the ability to produce ideas far from obvious, measured by the capacity to give infrequent answers), and *elaboration* (the capacity to provide additional details to embellish the basic response).

A challenging aspect linked to the definition of creativity is its differentiation from intelligence. For some authors creativity necessarily implies the *discovery* of a problem and finding a solution. This differs from the sole *recognition* of a problem, that is, the capacity to understand what the problem is and finding the correct solution (i.e., convergent thinking), the process that is usually assessed by conventional intelligence tests. Several longitudinal studies of children with remarkably high intelligence quotients (IQ) have shown that intelligence is a necessary but not sufficient condition for creativity (Cox, 1926; Terman, 1925), and it is presently accepted that intelligence and creativity have a high correlation and interdependence up to a superior intelligence (IQ 120) level at which these two cognitive abilities seem to become independent (Eysenck, 1995).

The traditional *associative models* of creativity defined the creative *process* as the formation of new combinations through the association of remote elements (Spearman, 1931; Mednick, 1962). The more remote the elements were, the more creative would be the process. A current view of creativity is that it is a *'cognitive disinhibition syndrome'* characterised by a broad associative horizon and a state of defocused attention. Martindale (1999) argues that creativity derives from the tendency to oscillate back and forth along a cognitive continuum. One end of this continuum is characterised by analogical, free-associative, irrational thinking, accompanied by defocused attention and low cortical arousal. These would be the cognitive conditions that favour the creative insight or 'illumination' stage of the creative process. The other end of the continuum is characterised by logical, abstract, reality-oriented thinking, accompanied by focused attention and higher levels of cortical arousal, a state necessary for discovering a problem and verifying the viability of the new creative insight. According to this model, individual differences in the variability of the general level of cortical activation, focus of attention, and type of thought account for individual differences in creativity.

III: One Key to the Problem: Views of Madness

The association between madness and genius raises a considerable paradox: how can the morbid traits of chaotic thinking, disconnection from reality, bizarre affect, perceptual anomalies, and erratic behaviour be related to the superior mental processes and effective production necessary for creativity? Even more puzzling is the fact that biographical evidence on which the madness–genius connection has been founded suggests that the mental disorders linked to creativity are the *psychoses*, a group of illnesses considered to be the severest form of psychopathology.[1] Obviously, it would be absurd to relate any severe mental state of insanity with creativity. So what then is the solution?

A reasonable answer to this paradox has emerged quite recently from the view that mental disorders are dimensional phenomena (e.g., Claridge, 1998; McGorry *et al.*, 1998; Poulton *et al.*, 2000; Johns & van Os, 2001); that is, that they are continuously connected with 'normality', as suggested by the wide margins of intermediate shades that surround the dichotomous and often artifactual border between illness and health (Claridge, 1995). Indeed, the *dimensional view of psychoses* argues that these disorders are extreme or pathological variants of otherwise normal personality dispositions (Eysenck & Eysenck, 1976). This notion suggests that the difference between clinical psychosis and its

[1] The traditional classification in psychopathology has distinguished between two broad groups of mental disorders: psychoses and neuroses. The *psychoses* are the most severe forms of pathology, the true madness where a break with reality is almost inevitable. Paranoia, manic-depressive illness and the different types of schizophrenia are included in the psychoses (a description of these disorders will follow later). The *neuroses* encompass milder forms of suffering that usually do not extend to the whole sphere of mental functions (e.g., depression, obsessions, anxiety and phobias).

temperamental basis, 'psychoticism', is quantitative and not qualitative. The personality dimension 'psychoticism' is composed of traits that are phenomenologically similar to the symptoms present in the psychotic disorders but are stable and have a mild, possibly adaptive, manifestation.

This dimensional view is readily applied to other psychopathologies, for instance, anxiety. Anxiety disorders are the extreme manifestation of a personality dimension, anxiety, that is present in all people to differing degrees. Furthermore, within normal limits, anxiety has a *necessary* and *adaptive* function, that is, to be a vigilance mechanism that signals potential dangers. However, it has been conceptually much harder for many researchers to accept that there is a personality dimension, psychoticism or schizotypy, that (analogous to anxiety) may have advantageous features (Claridge, 1995).

There is a second issue of dimensionality that is crucial for understanding the creativity–madness dilemma, that is, whether mental disorders should be considered distinct *categories* or a cluster of symptoms from different psychopathological *dimensions*. For psychiatry, which adopts a categorical view, the main question in this field is to establish *what* psychosis relates to creativity. Kraepelin (1919) distinguished two major forms of psychoses: an *affective psychosis* or manic-depressive illness, and a heterogeneous set of non-affective psychoses named '*dementia praecox*' that was later relabelled as 'the schizophrenias' by Bleuler (1911/1950). Manic-depressive patients tend to experience alternating episodes of depression and mania (the reversal of depression, with elated mood, racing thoughts, hyperactivity, increased self-esteem) interspersed with symptom-free periods, with some patients experiencing psychotic symptoms (e.g., hallucinations and delusions) during the periods of affective symptoms. In contrast, *schizophrenia* is usually a more pervasive disorder causing the impairment of a wide spectrum of mental functions: perception (e.g., hallucinations), thought (e.g., delusions, distorted thought processes), language (e.g., distorted speech patterns), emotion (attenuated or inappropriate affect), and motivation. While the outcome can be variable, schizophrenia tends to have a chronic course punctuated by recurring episodes of psychosis, with some recovery of functioning between episodes.

Recent evidence has cast doubt on the sharp distinction between these disorders: they are not so easily distinguishable at the clinical level, something that prompted the creation of an intermediate diagnosis, 'schizoaffective' disorder. Furthermore, patients can alternate diagnoses; genetic liability seems to be common for both; many severe features of schizophrenia seem to be present in affective disorders than was once thought (e.g., deteriorating course and impaired cognition); and there is a conspicuous interchangeability of treatments between the two forms of psychosis (Taylor, 1992). One attempt to refine the classification of these disorders has involved defining subtypes of each psychosis that differ in the degree of severity and some clinical features. We currently talk about the *schizophrenia and bipolar spectrums* that encompass a variety of disorders that range from severe illness to the subtle personality traits referred to as 'schizotypy' and 'affective temperaments', respectively (with Eysenck's term 'psychoticism' referring to the personality roots of psychosis in general).

Indeed, categorical distinctions do not satisfactorily apply to many forms of psychopathology. Instead, there seems to be a continua of mental dysfunction rather than a collection of clear-cut morbid entities. This *continuum hypothesis* argues that there are different dimensions of pathology continuously distributed in nature (e.g., delusions, depression, mania, thought disorder, paranoia) and that these dimensions are not exclusive to any mental disease (van Os & Verdoux, 2003). Consequently, from this dimensional or continuum viewpoint the question of what particular illness relates to a creative advantage becomes superfluous to some extent (Claridge, 1995).

The acceptance of this continuum or dimensional view makes it possible to understand the connection between creativity and madness. Logically, it is not the extreme variants of psychoticism, the psychotic *states*, that mediate the connection with creativity, but it is possible that the personality *traits* that underlie psychosis share some biological, emotional, and cognitive features with creativity. The presence of these traits *per se* would not guarantee a creative advantage; most likely many other factors need to be favourable for a creative outcome to happen, both from an individual (e.g., high intelligence, persistence, etc.), and from a situational perspective (e.g., a stimulating environment, an adequate sociocultural milieu, etc.). Additionally, it allows us to understand that creativity will not be related to a single psychological profile since, as referred to above, dimensionality also operates *within* the pathological realm (Claridge, 1998).

The idea of a *common factor* that mediates the co-occurrence of creativity and madness has gained acceptance in the last decades. This hypothesis tends to view this common factor as causative, even if it is not a sufficient condition. Most researchers subscribe to this view even if there are different opinions about the nature of the third factor(s) (e.g., the relative importance of genetic liability, cognition, temperament, etc.). This perspective has overcome two alternative models of the relationship between creativity and psychopathology (Richards, 1981; 2000–2001). One model claims that *psychopathology causes creativity*, either directly or indirectly. A *direct* relation would be, for example, that strange thoughts and bizarre perceptual processes may be vital for the creative process. For example, so-called overinclusive thinking (Cameron, 1938), defined by the loss of the capacity to limit associative processes, is thought to contribute to creative insights when it does not reach severe forms that lead to complete incoherence. An *indirect* relation would be that pathology leads to cathartic writing, which, in turn, enhances the creative quality of a given work. The other model sustains that *creativity causes psychopathology*. A *direct* relation would be, especially in the arts, that creativity implies facing high levels of psychic tension, leading to psychological imbalance. An *indirect* relation would be that the conflicts created by creativity might result in maladaptive coping strategies such as drug abuse.

IV: Historical Roots of the Creativity–Madness Connection: Psychobiographical and Family Studies

An aspect that has usually been overlooked in this field is the importance of the historical and cultural influences on the concept of creativity and the extent to which these factors have influenced our understanding of the relationship between creativity and mental disorders. Psychology and psychiatry tend to assume a transhistorical and transcultural nature of creativity, but some authors have cast doubt on such assumptions.

The history of the creativity–madness hypothesis can be traced back to classic antiquity. Socrates conceived the 'demon' as a divine gift granted to a few individuals (the philosopher, the poet, the priest . . .) that enabled them to communicate with the gods. Aristotle stated in his *Problemata XXX* that the *homo melancholicus* was gifted with sublime capacities and inextricably prone to madness: 'Those who have become eminent in philosophy, politics, poetry, and the arts have all had tendencies toward melancholia'. It is important to note that they did not assume that insanity was the key for creativity, but rather that the liability to experience states of melancholia was linked with creativity. The trespass into the realm of true madness would depend for Aristotle on the balance of a subject's humours.

The Italian Renaissance notion of *pazzia* or melancholia revived this tradition and, later, the Enlightenment stressed the necessity for genius to combine an active imagination with judgement or reason. It was Romanticism that changed the concept and function of genius. During the late eighteenth and nineteenth centuries, men of genius, generally lacking in wealth or status, attempted to challenge the hierarchical order of social values by considering innate creative ability as the supreme criterion for the evaluation of men. According to Becker (1978), the aspiring artist and men of ideas did not have a clear status in this historical period, feeling engulfed in the anonymous masses. The recovery and magnification of the classic ideas of divine madness as the source of inspiration and creativity instantiated a sense of identity and endowed the creative individual with a mystical and superior quality. As a result, spontaneous and irrational imagination became the essence of genius, leading to a necessary connection between madness and creativity.[2]

---

[2] From a sociological viewpoint, Becker (2000–2001) hypothesises that this imposed on the creative individual the *role expectation* of experiencing and manifesting mental suffering as one constitutive element of creative inspiration. It may well be that this role expectation influenced the biographical studies of eminent creators. Specifically, this cultural expectation may bias how creative individuals describe their mental problems in psychological examinations and how history has viewed their mental functioning, due to the definitional value of this deviance in the cultural concept of creativity. As a result, the perceived relationship between insanity and creativity may have become a sociological self-fulfilling prophecy. However, the evidence produced by studies conducted with non-eminent populations has overcome such a problem. While the adherence to role expectations by those with a creative career or eminent genius may bias the results of their psychological assessment, it seems unlikely that this can have a significant effect in non-artist populations whose self-concept is not that of a creative genius.

This polemic question only started to be systematically analysed by scientists one century ago. The first psychobiographic[3] study, *'The Men of Genius'*, was published in 1895 by an Italian psychiatrist, Cesare Lombroso, who carefully studied biographies of creative individuals from diverse fields (e.g., Julius Caesar, Newton, Schopenhauer. . .). Lombroso reached several conclusions that later studies have supported with more refined methods: 'Between the physiology of the man of genius and the pathology of the insane, there are many points of coincidence; there is even actual continuity'. He also established that creativity is genetically intertwined with the predisposition to affective and schizophrenic psychosis, psychopathy, and alcoholism.

Later on the association between psychopathology and creativity shifted towards neurosis. It coincided with the rise of psychoanalysis starting at the beginning of the twentieth century and the preferential interest that Freud gave to these disorders. From his perspective, creativity was a means to dampen the neurotic states. Subsequently, many humanists (e.g., Fromm, Rogers) defended the opposite notion, that mental health was necessary for creativity to occur.

As Becker (1978) concluded from an analysis of the psychobiographic studies published until 1950, the vast majority validate the anecdotal observation of an excess of psychopathology in eminently creative people. There are two main exceptions. Havelock Ellis (1904) found that only 4% of 1,020 British geniuses he studied suffered from a clearly diagnosable mental disorder, while Bowerman (1947) found similar results in the analysis of American geniuses. However, as Claridge *et al.* (1998) point out, although both authors refuted *a priori* the connection between creativity and madness, they agreed upon the existence of characteristic temperamental traits such as hypersensitivity, irritability, a tendency towards melancholy and affective instability; traits that belong to the 'affective temperaments' or soft end of the spectrum of affective disorders. It is also important to note that they selected subjects who appear in the Dictionary of National Biography, that is, subjects with a noteworthy role in the public life of their country, which does not necessary mean that they were truly and eminently creative (Andreasen & Canter, 1974).

There were two influential psychobiographical studies in the first half of the twentieth century. Lange-Eichenbaum (1932) focused on the temporal relation between creativity and psychosis. It was one of the first studies to signal that creative work is not performed during the active psychotic periods but in periods of remission, and that often psychosis follows intensely creative phases. Logically, the acute and severe psychotic state did, if anything, diminish the possibility of any creative output. As Sylvia Plath wrote eloquently: 'When you are insane you are busy being insane — all the time. . . . When I was crazy that was *all* I was'. Juda (1949) studied for 26 years a sample of 19,000 subjects of whom 204 were highly gifted scientists and artists. It was concluded that 'geniuses show a much

[3] The *psychobiographical method* consists in the detailed analysis of creative subjects' biographies, self-biographies, and available clinical records in order to study the presence of psychopathology and its relation to his/her creative productions. Obviously, one of the main limitations of these studies lies in their retrospective nature and the impossibility of contrasting the author's diagnostic judgement.

higher incidence of psychosis and psychoneurosis than the average population (. . .) schizophrenia occurred only in the artists, and manic-depressive insanity only in the scientists, in a frequency 10 times the incidence of the average population'.

In the second half of the twentieth century, psychobiographical studies dramatically improved their reliability by using consensual diagnoses and standardised diagnostic interviews when dealing with live cases. Most of them have focused on artists and especially writers (Obiols & Barrantes-Vidal, 1997).

Claridge *et al.* (1998) applied several sets of diagnostic criteria to the biographies and medical records of ten psychotic writers (e.g., Margery Kempe, Virgina Woolf) and concluded that they all suffered from schizophrenia or schizoaffective disorder, with varying results according to the diagnostic criteria used.

Jamison (1993), a psychiatrist and sufferer of a bipolar disorder, studied the most important British and Irish poets of the eighteenth century. She found a strikingly high rate of affective disorders, suicides, and institutionalisation in both poets and their relatives (e.g., Blake, Scott, Coleridge).

Ludwig (1994) reported an increased rate of suicidal behaviour in poets (18% versus 1% in the general population). He studied 59 female writers and 59 female control subjects matched on education and socioeconomic level (although not on intelligence) and found higher rates of affective, anxiety, drug abuse, and eating disorders, as well as more psychopathology and creativity in the family trees of the female writers. Interestingly, both personal and maternal psychopathology were significant predictors of creative performance. Furthermore, the exposure to sexual or physical abuse during childhood was also a significant predictor of creativity, suggesting a complex interaction between hereditary and environmental factors. Ludwig conceived of the connection between creativity and psychopathology as resulting from verbally talented individuals using their writing skills to communicate their experiences within a narrative structure, thus putting order in their prone-to-chaos internal milieu.

Similarly, Schildkraut *et al.* (1996) found that affective disorders were ten times more prevalent and suicidal behaviour was three times greater in the New York abstract expressionist painters (e.g., Pollock, Rothko . . .) than in the general population.

A few studies have compared creative people from different fields of endeavour. Post (1994) selected 291 eminent and recognised creative men (only men were included due to the lack of accurate biographies of creative women) from many different fields (visual artists, philosophers, scientists, politicians, composers, novelists, and playwrites). He found that 54% of them presented with personality disorder traits and 69% had suffered some kind of mental disorder. A comparison between different fields showed that scientists were the least affected group. A significant proportion of novelists and playwrites had a florid history of familial psychopathology, problematic family environments during childhood, depressive episodes, drug abuse, and marital problems. Artists and intellectuals had significant psychosexual difficulties and a greater presence of alcoholism than scientists. In a later study, Post (1996) analysed a larger number of biographies and confirmed that schizophrenia was less prevalent in this sample than in the general population, whereas affective disorders and alcoholism were strikingly high among writers. Bipolarity was specifically higher in poets, whereas the other writers as a whole presented more alcoholism, psychosexual problems, and depression. Post (1996) hypothesised that the combination of a high level of emotional imagination, the intense neural activity involved in writing, and depressive personality traits, may account for writers' increased risk of affective disorders. At the same time, as Storr (2000) points out, the act of writing can be contemplated as a way of objectifying negative emotions and enabling the writer to control grief and despair. As Graham Greene expressed it: 'Writing is a form of therapy; sometimes I wonder how all those who do not write, compose or paint can manage to escape the madness, the melancholia, the panic fear which is inherent in the human condition' (Greene, 1981, p. 211; cf. Storr, 2000).

Ludwig (1995) also compared different fields of creative endeavour by analysing 1,005 biographies. He found a positive correlation between the presence of severe psychopathology and the magnitude of the creative achievements. Again, scientists presented with fewer problems, while poets had the highest rate of mental disorders (87%), including more suicide and psychosis.

Psychobiographical studies have been complemented with *family studies* since the end of the nineteenth century. At that time it was already believed that both creativity and psychopathology were *heritable phenomena* and that, as Lombroso (1895) defended, these traits were cosegragated (i.e., inherited together and therefore expressed in the same subject). Two questions are posed: to what extent is creativity heritable and to what extent is there an association between creativity and psychopathology in families?

Is creativity a genetic trait? Currently, creativity is widely viewed as an '*emergenetic*' trait (Lykken, 1998), that is, a second-order trait that results (or emerges) from the synergistic interaction among a cluster of more fundamental characters (e.g., novelty seeking, analogical thinking, capacity for extreme hard work, high self-confidence, love of mental activity, high ego strength, etc; Martindale, 2000). To the extent that these traits are at least partially under genetic control, they will have a better chance to be more present in certain families.

The possible *genetic link between creativity and psychopathology* has been explored systematically in a few family studies. Heston (1966) showed that half of the children of schizophrenic mothers who were separated early from their biological mother and reared in adoptive families achieved an excellent adaptation, an exceptional talent on different creative fields, and, as expected, a higher risk of developing schizophrenia. Karlsson (1970) carried out a retrospective family study in which the professional status of all first-degree relatives of psychiatric patients admitted into hospital (that is, most likely with severe disorders like psychosis) in Iceland from 1851 to 1940 were recorded. He found that these relatives had a creative profession more often than the standard level in the general population, with twice as many writers than expected. Jamison (1993) analysed the family trees of many geniuses (Schumman, Woolf, van Gogh,

Hemingway, James) and also showed an excess of affective pathology in the biological relatives of these individuals. Andreasen (1987) did a study for 15 years in which 30 eminent American writers attending the prestigious Iowa writing workshop were compared to 30 carefully matched control subjects. There was an overall higher rate of affective disorders in the writers, especially bipolar forms, and alcoholism. The writers' first-degree relatives also exceeded the relatives of the control group in the rate of affective disorders and also had more creative professions. These studies suggest that there is some commonality in the genes that convey the risk for psychosis and creativity.

Richards *et al.* (1988) found that first-degree relatives of manic-depressive patients obtained the highest creativity scores when compared to normal control subjects, manic-depressive patients, and cyclothymic patients (a milder form of bipolar disorder). The difference was not explained by the effects of education or intelligence. The creative advantage found in these relatives may be extended to a large number of people if we take into account that around 1% of the general population suffers from manic-depressive illness.

Kinney *et al.* (2000–2001) studied the adoptees of biological parents with schizophrenia and a group of demographically matched control adoptees with no family history of psychiatric hospitalisation. It was found that the adoptees with genetic liability for schizophrenia who did not manifest the disorder were rated as more creative by blind independent researchers. Furthermore, adoptees who showed signs of personality traits that mimic schizophrenia (schizotypy) were rated as even more creative. Interestingly, schizotypic signs share a genetic relationship with schizophrenia. This study avoids the *post hoc* nature of most previous work and adds further evidence to the notion that there may be an adaptive value to certain genes for psychopathology, like those for both affective and schizophrenic psychosis.

How is the relationship between liability for psychosis and creativity explained? The *evolutionary hypothesis*[4] linking madness to creativity suggests that the genes that carry the liability for the psychoses have been retained in human evolution because they also convey a *compensatory advantage*: enhanced creativity may be one type of compensatory advantage to the genes that convey the liability for psychosis. This would help to maintain these putative genes in the population despite the low mating and fertility rates of psychotic patients (Kinney & Mathysse, 1978; Richards *et al*., 1988; Kinney *et al*., 2000–2001).

V: What Form of Madness is Associated with Creativity?

As introduced earlier, one of the main debates in psychiatry has been to establish the link between creativity and some particular form of mental disorder. For much of the twentieth century the connection was established with schizophrenia, whereas in recent years the situation shifted towards almost a denial of any link between creativity and the schizophrenia spectrum and the assumption of a

[4] For a Darwinian theory of creativity see Simonton (1999).

strong link between milder forms of bipolarity with creativity. This dramatic change is mainly related to two factors.

First, the diagnosis of affective psychosis, in particular bipolar disorder, was revived in the latter half of the twentieth century, broadening the affective spectrum cases and narrowing the schizophrenia spectrum. This is reflected in the fact that the psychobiographical analyses of the same geniuses led to different diagnoses from author to author. Those who are schizophrenic in one analysis appear as bipolar in another and vice-versa.

Secondly, the psychopathology–creativity link was restricted to schizophrenia because it was assumed that the *cognitive* rather than the *affective* characteristics of personality and psychopathology would account for the connection and schizophrenia is more fundamentally defined by cognitive symptoms (e.g., thought disorder and language peculiarities) than affective psychosis (Claridge, 1998).

In the 1970s research focused on the similarity between creative thinking and schizophrenic formal thought disorder,[5] establishing that there was a cognitive continuum ranging from normality through creativity to disorder (Hasenfus & Magaro, 1976). McConaghy (1960) defined two cognitive styles that may reflect predispositions to psychosis and to creative cognition: *allusive thinking*, in which filtering mechanisms are impaired and permit the intrusion of irrelevant associations, with vague thought processes dominated by intuition; in the other style the capacity for making logical attributions is enhanced, and the adherence to the conclusion arrived at is greater than normal devotion. This cognitive style is more dominated by logic than common sense and has been hypothesised to predispose to both scientific thinking and paranoid ideation. Other thinking styles include pathological *overinclusive thinking* (Cameron, 1938), in which the person is not able to establish boundaries between ideas and images, and its healthier counterpart, *divergent thinking* (Guilford, 1970).

However, in the last decades, schizophrenia research returned to a focus on the deteriorating, dementia-like view of the disorder and the *negative or deficit symptoms,* considered by Bleuler (1911/1950) to be the core feature of schizophrenia. 'Negative' symptoms involve the impoverishment or loss of the capacity for pleasure (anhedonia), volitional impulses (abulia), interests (apathy), motivation (avolition), and the experience of restricted or flat affect. A restrictive focus on these features makes the idea of a link with creativity much less plausible. However, the concept of negative symptoms as the hallmark of schizophrenia is controversial and unresolved.

Moreover, studies on the cognition of bipolar disorders suggested that there are cognitive aspects in the bipolar spectrum akin to creative cognition (Holzman *et al.*, 1986). Overinclusive thinking was found to be present not only in schizophrenia but also in mania (Andreasen & Powers, 1974). The analysis of

---

[5] Thought disorder is differentiated in *content* and *form* or course. Disruptions in the content of thought primarily include false beliefs such as delusions. Disruptions in the form of thought (or *formal thought disorder*) refer to disturbances in the way that information is processed and is often indirectly assessed through decreases in the amount and coherence of speech.

cognition in hypomanic[6] states shows that it shares common aspects with creative cognition: a quantitative increase of ideational fluency, high mental speed and cognitive flexibility, and the enhanced capacity for combinatory thinking, that is, the association of old elements into new and original ideas (Jamison, 1993).

The link between bipolarity and creativity used to be attributed to the remarkable similarity between hypomania and creativity in terms of *motivational* and *emotional* features (Barrantes-Vidal & Vieta, 2001). For example, Jamison (1989) analysed the role of emotional states in the creative process in a study of 47 living eminent British writers and artists. More than one third had received psychiatric treatment due to affective disorders. Interestingly, artists and writers had only received treatment during depressive episodes, whereas poets had also required treatment due to hypomanic or manic phases. As many as 89% described the experience of having tremendously productive, creative and intensive periods in which there was a marked elation of mood, high energy, enthusiasm, self-confidence, speed in ideational association, sharpened and faster perception, higher mental fluency, and an intense sense of well-being. Indeed, all these experiences have a remarkable overlap with the affective and cognitive symptoms that constitute the diagnostic criteria for a hypomanic episode. Interestingly, the mood elation usually preceded the creative period rather than being a product of it and most subjects considered this emotional state fundamental for their creative work.

Among the spectrum of affective disorders, empirical data and theoretical formulations seem to support a specific association between creativity and *bipolarity* (e.g., Akiskal & Akiskal, 1988; Andreasen, 1987; Goodwin & Jamison, 1990). Depression alone is considered unlikely to be linked with enhanced creativity because it tends to slow and restrict cognitive processes to the prototypical ruminative depressive topics. Furthermore, it has been shown that those depressive patients with a family history of bipolar disorders are more creative than those without a positive family history of bipolarity (Richards *et al.*, 1992). The argument is that the cyclic and sometimes even juxtaposed experience of positive (manic) and negative (depressive) moods and their associated cognitive and biological features may give rise to a more complex mental organisation (Richards *et al.*, 1992; Jamison, 1993). This enhancement in the complexity of thought patterns may facilitate the usage of certain forms of creative cognition (Carreño & Goodwin, 1998), such as Janusian and homospatial thinking. *Janusian thinking* was defined by Rothenberg (1990) as the mental process by which multiple opposites or antitheses are conceived simultaneously. The person remains aware that the concepts are in opposition, which prompts the mental effort to generate original thoughts that provide reconciliation. *Homospatial thinking* operates later in the creative process and consists of conceiving two or more discrete entities occupying the same space, which leads to the articulation of a new identity (Rothenberg, 1990).

---

[6] Hypomania is a milder form of mania (e.g., an unmotivated elated mood, irritability, speeded mental processes, hyperaesthesia, etc.). It differs from mania in that it is less severe and never involves psychosis.

Jamison (1993) added to the argument of a specific link between creativity and bipolarity that the abrupt replacement of the melancholic experience by intense manic states of elation and expansiveness endows the bipolar subject with a special capacity for introspection and a heightened need to express it in a creative, mainly artistic, way. This connects with the classic theme of *inspiration* in artistic creation: the need to deepen or regress into the prerational or irrational while maintaining contact with reality. As Jamison (1993) puts it: 'The integration of these deeper, truly irrational sources with more logical processes can be a tortuous task, but, if successful, the resulting work often bears a unique stamp, a 'touch with fire' for what it has been through' (p. 104).

Given the current state of knowledge, the idea of an association between creativity and a unique form of psychosis is clearly untenable. Psychosis and its temperamental roots are highly heterogeneous domains of symptoms and traits. What seems more likely is that schizophrenia and bipolar *vulnerability* manifest in different creative advantages because of their possible differential personality and cognitive–perceptual characteristics. Actually, there is evidence indicating that people falling into the bipolar spectrum exhibit greater work-related than leisure-related everyday creativity, whereas the opposite is the case for schizophrenia spectrum subjects (Richards, 2000–2001). It may well be that the extraverted, competitive, driven, gregarious personality roots of bipolarity allow these subjects to display this creative advantage in the social contexts where professional activities take place, whereas the traits of introversion, social anxiety, or awkwardness, more common in the schizophrenia spectrum, may make it easier for these subjects to display their creative potential in more relaxed, less socially pressured and judged environments such as leisure and avocational activities (Richards, 2000–2001).

From a different angle, Sass (1992) argued that *artistic creativity* is probably much more likely to result from the psychological characteristics that define the bipolar spectrum, thus causing an overrepresentation of affective disorders in artistic fields, especially literature (e.g., Jamison, 1993; Post, 1994). However, other kinds of creativity present in fields such as sciences, philosophy, architecture may benefit from other psychological profiles that define the schizophrenia-spectrum, such as Storr (1972) suggested when analysing the schizoid personalities of Descartes, Newton, and Einstein. Sass (2000–2001) goes further by wondering whether the distinction between successfully creative and truly innovative, paradigm-breaking work, analogous to Kuhn's (1970) famous distinction between 'normal' and 'revolutionary' science, may be somehow connected to this issue. In most fields, creative work relies on a considerable degree of conventionality that allows the creation to be understood, accepted, and successful in its particular field. Only a minority attain a truly revolutionary creative production and abandon all previous canons. Sass' argument is that:

> what accounts for the higher proportion of persons with a connection to affective than to schizophrenic psychosis might, surprisingly enough, have as much to do with the greater conventionality of the former as with their superior originality or innovativeness *per se* (p. 70).

In favour of this hypothesis is the fact that the personalities comprised in the affective spectrum seem to be overly dependent on social approval and dependent on social norms (Barrantes-Vidal *et al.*, 2002a). Sass suggests that both depression and mania are not a source of radical innovation but a heightening of psychological states that are reasonably familiar to most that share a particular culture. On the contrary, schizotypy would be associated with a greater degree of eccentricity and an easy engagement in states of detachment from the 'given for granted' natural evidence of the world, thus enabling the subject to discover truly new perspectives or frameworks. Emotional detachment, loneliness and abstract thought is a combination that many studies have noted in the lives of many significant philosophers (Descartes, Locke, Hobbes, Pascal, Spinoza, Kant, Schopenhauer, Nietzsche, Kierkegaard, Wittgenstein), and scientists (Storr, 2000). Einstein, although married twice, described himself as 'a loner, who never belonged with his whole heart to the state, his country, his circle of friends, or even his closer family, but who felt with regard to all those ties a never overcome sense of being a stranger with a need for solitude' (p. 26; cf. in Storr, 2000). These features, far from the romantic concepts of creativity, are close to the hyper-self-consciousness and alienation that characterise *modernism* and *postmodernism* (Sass, 2000–2001).[7]

Claridge (1998) suggested that various types of creativity map on to different aspects of psychosis and that, even within each field and form of creative expression, there will be different creative processes and stylistic differences that will, at least in part, relate to the various cognitive and personality traits. Currently, some neurocognitive models attempt to account for these different psychopathology–creativity patterns.

Prentky (1980) argued that there are two distinct profiles characterised by cognitive, physiological, and clinical features, giving rise to different forms of creativity. The *A-type (abstract)* is cognitively characterised by a 'radar' type of functioning, with weak attentional focus, distractibility, easy attentional shifting, and a higher propensity for the loosening of ideational boundaries (i.e., overinclusion). Physiologically it is defined by high tonic arousal and overactivation of the right hemisphere or underactivation of the left hemisphere. Clinically it is more likely to present symptoms that range from depression, schizoid personality (e.g., solitary, emotionally cold, lack of close friends, anhedonic), and the before-mentioned schizophrenic negative symptoms (in which a higher activation of right hemisphere seems to occur). The creative output of this type is often relegated to the 'mystical' realm of intuition because there is not a sense of cognitive effort preceding it.

The *C-type (concrete)* is hypothesised to underinclude or constrict the attentional field, has low distractibility, and difficulty shifting attention. Clinically it is more related to the 'positive symptoms' of schizophrenia (e.g.,

[7] Sass uses *modernism* and *postmodernism* according to the standard usage of these terms in art history: the former refers to the formally innovative, avant-gardes period of the first half of the twentieth century, whereas the latter refers to the developments that took place after World War II (cf. Sass, 2000–2001).

hallucinations, delusions, bizarre behaviour, pressured speed), in which a higher left than right hemisphere activation is reported. The C-type creative style is characterised by an analytic dissection of the constitutive elements of a problem. Prentky (2000–2001) suggests that

> the normal range of input regulation is distorted by imbalances in hemispheric activity, resulting in two very different data processing strategies that facilitate creative solutions to problems. Because these imbalances are often associated with genetic predispositions to mental illness, there is a greater-than-chance probability that highly creative individuals may evidence signs associated with mental illness (p. 103).

VI: Answers From Psychometric Studies

As previously noted, the dimensional view of psychopathology states that psychotic disorders are continuous with normal personality dimensions. This has led to the development of psychometric instruments (i.e., questionnaires) that measure the degree to which these traits are present in normal subjects and disordered individuals. In a parallel fashion, creativity research has moved away from the sole analysis of eminent geniuses or artists to the assessment of psychometric or '*trait-creativity*', that is, the cognitive and personality factors considered to be the basis of creativity. Put in other words, creativity has also been 'dimensionalised' by distinguishing trait-creativity from creative achievements.

The first issue addressed by psychometric studies was to define the personality correlates of trait-creativity. It was found that creativity is significantly associated with a set of *normal personality traits* including individualism, originality, rebelliousness, independence, persistence, tolerance to ambiguity, motivation guided by internal rewards, and risk taking (McKinnon, 1961). Interestingly, normal subjects with high creativity scores tend to combine the presence of elevated levels of self-reported psychological deviance on various dimensions (e.g., narcissism, impulsivity, alcoholism, aggression, etc.) with high scores on the construct '*ego strength*' (Barron, 1969). Ego strength is characterized by resourcefulness, a proper sense of control, psychological well-being, good self-esteem, and self-realisation. Ego strength tends to be inversely related with psychopathology, although individuals defined as highly creative present with this peculiar combination of high ego-strength and high psychological deviance.

Another issue has been to examine whether creativity in normal individuals is related to the personality traits that are supposed to be the soft end of schizophrenia (schizotypic personality) and bipolar spectrum (hypomanic and depressive traits). Schuldberg *et al.* (1988) found in undergraduate students a positive and significant relation among several measures of positive schizotypy[8] and creativity tests, although a significant relationship between divergent thinking and

[8] Positive schizotypy is the personality foundation of positive psychotic symptoms (delusions and hallucinations). An example of the items used to measure the unusual experiences contained in positive schizotypy questionnaires would be: 'Have you felt that you might cause something to happen just by thinking too much about it?', 'Are your thoughts sometimes so strong that you can almost hear them?'. *Negative schizotypy* encompasses high introversion and social and physical anhedonia. An

positive schizotypy was not found. When scales of hypomanic and impulsive personality traits were added in a later study, results pointed to a stronger link between creativity and the affective/motivational sphere than with the schizotypy (Schuldberg, 1990). O'Reilly *et al.* (2001) also failed to find an association between schizotypy and divergent thinking, although schizotypy was related to engagement in creative pursuits.

It is important to note that positive schizotypy and hypomania correlate strongly and that their relative, perhaps differential, contribution can be difficult to disentangle. A study comparing 'pure' high scorers on hypomanic traits, 'pure' high scorers on positive schizotypy, and average scorers on both tests found that 'hypomanics' presented higher divergent thinking than 'schizotypals', and these were higher than average scorers (Barrantes-Vidal *et al.*, 1999; Barrantes-Vidal *et al.*, submitted). These results raise the possibility that creative cognition is more akin to manic 'flight of ideas' than to schizophrenic 'loose associations'.

Similarly, Schuldberg (2000–2001) concluded that there are positive associations between creativity and *both* schizophrenia-like positive schizotypy traits and hypomanic traits, with a slightly stronger association with the latter. Impulsivity, highly related to hypomania, also had a significant relation to creativity measures. Depressive traits and negative schizotypy traits (physical anhedonia) were not related to creativity, rather they had a negative correlation with creativity. It is interesting to note that this differential association of positive and negative schizotypal traits with creativity is consistent with the finding that normal subjects with high scores on positive schizotypy and low scores on negative schizotypy do not present with the subtle cognitive impairment that characterises high scorers on negative schizotypy (Barrantes-Vidal *et al.*, 2002b). As Claridge (1997) reviewed, *positive* schizotypy seems to predispose to a wide variety of both pathological (schizophrenia, obsessive–compulsive disorders, eating disorders) and *healthy* outcomes (profound spiritual experiences and out-of-the-body experiences).

This psychometric work has been complemented in recent years by studies associating creativity with new personality dimensions. For instance, *Openness to Experience* (OE), one of the dimensions of the dominating 'big five' personality model, seems to encompass many of the 'normal' personality traits that have been linked to creativity: intellectual curiosity, aesthetic sensitivity, liberal values, and emotional differentiation (McGrae, 1987). McGrae (1987) found that divergent thinking was significantly associated with self-reports and ratings of OE, and not with the remaining big five personality dimensions (extraversion, neuroticism, agreeableness, conscientiousness). Another personality variable, *Sensation Seeking*, has been also related to creativity (Zuckerman, 1979). Interestingly, this variable is significantly correlated to OE (McGrae, 1987), and both have been shown to be important influences in sophisticated forms of aesthetic judgement and preference (e.g., Rawlings *et al.*, 2000).

---

example would be: 'Are there very few things you have ever really enjoyed doing?', 'Is it true that your relationships with other people never get very intense?'.

One of the most elaborated and influential theories is that the personality dimension *psychoticism* underlies the link between trait-creativity and psychopathology (Eysenck, 1995). According to Eysenck, psychoticism (P) is genetically transmitted and reflects a general predisposition to all psychoses. A substantial bulk of studies have shown a positive and significant association between Eysenck's Psychoticism Scale (P)[9] and trait-creativity, whereas the other two dimensions of Eysenck's personality model, extraversion–introversion and neuroticism, have shown an inconsistent relationship with creativity (Eysenck, 1995).

Subjects high on P and on creativity tests present some common features: unusual patterns of word-sorting, more divergent thinking, and less degree of *cognitive inhibition* as measured by different attentional paradigms (e.g., latent inhibition, negative priming) (Eysenck, 1995). According to Eysenck, these common traits result from a shared biological profile, characterised by high dopamine and low serotonine levels. High dopamine would enhance creativity by decreasing cognitive inhibition, something that would make the subject more prone to divergent and combinatory thinking.

The relationship between dopamine levels and P has not been directly shown by molecular genetics, but there are several indirect evidences that link these variables, such as the elevation of dopamine receptors in post-mortem brains of schizophrenic patients (who score high in P), and the fact that high P scores are found in other disorders characterised by dopaminergic abnormalities (e.g., substance abuse, attention deficit hyperactivity disorder, etc.) (Martindale *et al.*, 2000). Further evidence comes from the genetic studies of a temperamental trait called *novelty seeking (NS)*. NS is defined as 'the tendency toward intense exhilaration or excitement in response to novel stimuli or cues for potential rewards or potential relief of punishment' (Cloninger, 1987, p. 575). NS is hypothesised in Cloninger's theory to depend on cortical dopaminergic activity. There is an association between NS and certain allelic variants of the dopamine receptor D4 (Ebstein *et al.*, 1996; Benjamin *et al.*, 1996), adding further indirect evidence to the link between creativity and dopaminergic function. New developments in this area point out the role of individual differences in other neurotransmitter systems as a common factor for creative cognition and vulnerability for psychosis (e.g., Folley *et al.*, in press).

Summary and Conclusions

This paper has revisited the ancient link between madness and creativity. The review of psychobiographical, psychometric and family studies supports that there is a consistent association between the two. The main argument defended in this paper is that *states* of true madness do not lead to creativity, but that both phenomena share common causative *traits* that make them go together. Substantial empirical work has shown that both creativity and the temperamental roots of

[9] The Psychoticism scale has been strongly criticised as a valid measure of a general predisposition towards psychosis because it is strongly contaminated by impulsivity and antisocial behaviour.

psychoses have common features at a biological (e.g., high levels of dopamine), cognitive (e.g., a brain organisation characterised by a weak inhibitory control that enables loosened or more flexible styles of mental activity), and emotional level (e.g., high openness to experience and phases of elation and intense enthusiasm).

The traditional interest of psychiatry has been to establish what particular form of psychosis, either schizophrenia or bipolarity, is truly related to creativity. Nowadays the effort has moved towards a more fruitful enterprise: to explore in detail what specific forms of creative endeavour are connected to the temperamental traits of the psychoses. There seems to be enough evidence to support that the prominent emotional changes and motivational features of affective psychosis would be especially suited to the 'romantic', inspirational, creativity more involved in writing and other sorts of artistic creation; whereas the personal detachment, prominent abstract thinking and cognitive peculiarities present in the schizotypic temperament, would have more in common with scientific or philosophical creativity. Obviously, this is not to say that creativity arises solely from such a temperamental basis, since many other factors should be included in the equation to give account of creativity.

Further empirical support to the idea that creativity may be a compensatory advantage to the vulnerability for psychosis will point out how our current medical and 'deficit' view of the psychotic spectrum is too simplistic and inadequate. One wonders if the relatively recent attention that academia is paying to this popular idea will support what the pioneer researchers in this field had already intuited:

> . . . it seems as though nature had intended to teach us respect for the supreme misfortunes of insanity; and also to preserve us from being dazzled by the brilliancy of those men of genius who might well be compared, not to the planets which keep their appointed orbits, but to falling stars, lost and dispersed over the crust of the earth (Lombroso, 1895).

Acknowledgments

I thank Thomas Kwapil for his very useful comments on the paper. I am indebted to Gordon Claridge for his many inspiring suggestions and guidance.

References

Akiskal, H.S. and Akiskal K. (1988), 'Reassessing the prevalence of bipolar disorders: clinical significance and artistic creativity', *Psychiatry and Psychobiology*, **3**, pp. 29–36.

Andreasen, N.J. and Canter, A. (1974), 'The creative writer: psychiatric symptoms and family history', *Comprehensive Psychiatry*, **15**, pp. 123–31.

Andreasen, N.C. and Powers, P.S. (1974), 'Overinclusive thinking in mania and schizophrenia', *British Journal of Psychiatry*, **125**, pp. 452–6.

Andreasen, N.C. (1987), 'Creativity and mental illness: prevalence rates in writers and first-degree relatives', *American Journal of Psychiatry*, **144**, pp. 1288–92.

Barrantes-Vidal, N., Caparrós, B. and Obiols, J.E. (1999), 'An exploratory study of sex differences in divergent thinking and creative personality among college students', *Psychological Reports*, **85**, pp. 1164–6.

Barrantes-Vidal, N. and Vieta, E. (2001), *Creatividad y Bipolaridad* (Barcelona: MRA Ediciones).

Barrantes-Vidal, N., Colom, F. and Claridge, G. (2002a), 'Temperament and personality in bipolar affective disorders', in: *Bipolar Disorders. Clinical and Therapeutic Progress*, ed. Vieta, E. (Madrid: Panamericana).
Barrantes-Vidal, N., Fañanás, L., Rosa, A., Caparrós, B., Riba, M.D. and Obiols, J.E (2002b), 'Neurocognitive, behavioural and neurodevelopmental correlates of schizotypy clusters in adolescents from the general population', *Schizophrenia Research*, **61**, pp. 293–302.
Barrantes-Vidal, N., Claridge, G. and Obiols, J.E., 'The relationship between schizotypal and hypomanic traits with creativity in normal subjects', (submitted for publication).
Barron, F. (1969), *Creative Person and Creative Process* (New York: Holt, Rinehart & Winston).
Becker, G. (1978), *The Mad Genius Controversy: A Study into the Sociology of Deviance* (Beverly Hills, CA: Sage).
Becker, G. (2000–2001), 'The association of creativity and psychopathology: Its cultural–historical origins', *Creativity Research Journal*, **13**(1), pp. 45–54.
Benjamin, J., Li, L., Patterson, C., Greenberg, B.D., Murphy, D.L. and Hamer, D.H. (1996), 'Population and familial association between the D4 dopamine receptor gene and measures of novelty seeking', *Nature Genetics*, **12**, pp. 81–3.
Bleuler, E. (1911/1950), *Dementia Praecox or the Group of Schizophrenias* (New York: International Universities Press).
Bowerman, W.G. (1947), *Studies in Genius* (New York: Philosophical Library).
Cameron, N. (1938), 'Reasoning, regression and communication in schizophrenics', *Psychological Monographs*, **50**, pp. 1–34.
Carreño, T. and Goodwin, P.J. (1998), 'Creativity and mood disorder', in, *Mania. Clinical and Research Perspectives*, ed. Goodnick, P.J. (Washington: American Psychiatric Press).
Claridge, G. (1995), *Origins of Mental Illness* (Cambridge, MA: Malor Books; re-edition of the original edition, 1985).
Claridge, G. (Ed.) (1997), *Schizotypy. Implications for Illness and Health* (Oxford: Oxford University Press).
Claridge, G., Pryor, R. and Watkins, G. (1998), *Sounds From the Bell Jar* (Cambridge, MA: Malor Books, re-edition of the original edition, 1990).
Claridge, G. (1998), 'Creativity and madness: clues from modern psychiatric diagnosis', in *Genius and the Mind. Studies of Creativity and Temperament*, ed. Steptoe A. (Oxford: Oxford University Press).
Cloninger, C.R. (1987), A systematic method for clinical description and classification of personality variants: A proposal. *Archives of General Psychiatry*, 44(6), 573–88.
Cox C. (1926), *The Early mental traits of three hundred geniuses* (Stanford: Stanford University Press).
Ebstein, R.P., Novick, O., Umansky, R., Priel, B., Osher, Y., Blaine, D. *et al.* (1996), Dopamine D4 receptor exon II polymorphism associated with the human personality trait of Novelty Seeking, *Nature Genetics*, **12**, 78–80.
Ellis, H. (1904), *A Study of British Genius* (London: Hurst and Blackett).
Eysenck, H.J. and Eysenck, S.B.G. (1976), *Psychoticism as a Dimension of Personality* (London: Hodder and Stoughton).
Eysenck, H.J. (1995), *Genius. The Natural History of Creativity* (Cambridge: Cambridge University Press).
Folley, B.S., Doop, M.L. and Park, S. (in press), 'Psychoses and creativity: Is the missing link a biological mechanism related to phospholipase metabolism?', *Journal of Prostaglandins, Leukotrienes and Essential Fatty Acids.*
Goodwin, F.K. and Jamison KR. (1990), *Manic-depressive Illness* (New York: Oxford University Press).
Greene, G. (1981), *Ways of Escape* (Harmondsworth: Penguin).
Guilford, J.P. (1970), 'Creativity: Retrospect and prospect', *Journal of Creative Behavior*, **4**, pp. 149–68.
Hasenfus, N. and Magaro, P. (1976), 'Creativity and schizophrenia: an equality of empirical constructs', *British Journal of Psychiatry*, **129**, pp. 346–9.
Heston, L.L. (1966), 'Psychiatric disorders in foster home reared children of schizophrenic mothers', *British Journal of Psychiatry*, **112**, pp. 819–25.
Holzman, P.S, Shenton, M.E. and Solovay, M.R. (1986), 'Quality of thought disorder in differential diagnosis', *Schizophrenia Bulletin*, **12**, pp. 360–72.
Jamison, K.R. (1989), 'Mood disorders and patterns of creativity in British writers and artists', *Psychiatry*, **52**, pp. 125–34.
Jamison, K.R. (1993), *Touched with Fire: Manic-Depressive Illness and the Artistic Temperament* (New York, Free Press).
Johns, L.C. and van Os., J. (2001), 'The continuity of psychotic experiences in the general population', *Clinical Psychology Review*, **21**(8), pp. 1125–41.
Juda, A. (1949), 'The relationship between highest mental capacity and psychic abnormalities', *American Journal of Psychiatry*, **106**, pp. 26–304.
Karlsson, J.L. (1970), 'Genetic association of giftedness and creativity with schizophrenia', *Hereditas*, **66**, pp. 77–182.

Kinney, D.K. and Matthysse, S. (1978), 'Genetic transmission of schizophrenia', *Annual Review of Medicine*, **29**, pp. 459–73.

Kinney, D.K., Richards, R.R., Lowing, P.A., LeBlanc, D., Zimblaist, M.E. and Harlan, P. (2000–2001), 'Creativity in offspring of schizophrenic and control parents: An adoption study', *Creativity Research Journal*, **13** (1), pp. 17–26.

Kraepelin, E. (1919), Dementia Praecox and Paraphrenia (Edinburgh: Churchill Livingstone).

Kuhn, T. (1970), *The Structure of Scientific Revolutions*, 2nd ed. (Chicago: University of Chicago Press).

Lange-Eichbaum W. (1932), *The Problem of Genius* (New York: Macmillan).

Lombroso, C. (1895), *The Man of Genius* (London: Walter Scott).

Ludwig, A.M. (1995), *The Price of Greatness* (New York: Guildford).

Ludwig, A.M. (1994), 'Mental illness and creative activity in female writers', *American Journal of psychiatry*, **151**, pp. 1650–5.

Lykken, D.T. (1998), 'The genetics of genius', in *Genius and the Mind. Studies of Creativity and Temperament*, ed. A. Steptoe (Oxford: Oxford University Press).

Martindale, C. (1999), 'Biological basis of creativity', in: *Handbook of Creativity*, ed. Sternberg, R.J. (New York: Cambridge University Press).

Martindale, C. (2000), 'Spiralling upward: A century of research on creativity and psychopathology', *Bulletin of Psychology of the Arts*, **1**(2), pp. 28–9.

Martindale, C., Vartanian, O. and Kwiatkowski, J. (2000), 'Disinhibition, dopamine, and creativity', *Bulletin of Psychology and the Arts*, **1**(2), pp. 49–53.

McConaghy, N. (1960), 'Modes of abstract thinking and psychosis', *American Journal of Psychiatry*, **117**, pp. 106–10.

McGorry, P.D., Bell, R.C., Dudgeon, P.L. and Jackson, H.J. (1998). 'The dimensional structure of first episode psychosis: An exploratory factor analysis', *Psychological Medicine*, **28**(4), pp. 935–47.

McGrae, R.R. (1987), 'Creativity, divergent thinking, and openness to experience', *Journal of Personality and Social Psychology*, **52**(6), pp. 1258–65.

McKinnon, D.W. (Ed.) (1961), *The Creative Person* (Berkeley: University of California Press).

Mednick, S.A. (1962), 'The associative basis of the creative process', *Psychological Review*, **69**, pp. 220–32.

Nettle, D. (2001), *Strong Imagination* (New York: Oxford University Press).

O'Reilly, T., Dunbar, R. and Bentall, R. (2001), 'Schizotypy and creativity: An evolutionary connection?', *Personality and Individual Differences*, **31**, pp. 1067–78.

Obiols, J.E. and Barrantes-Vidal, N. (1997), 'Arte, Creatividad y Espectro Bipolar', in: *Trastornos Bipolares*, ed. Vieta, E. and Gastó, C. (Barcelona: Springer-Verlag).

Post, F. (1994), 'Creativity and psychopathology. A study of 291 world-famous men', *British Journal of Psychiatry*, **165**, pp. 22–34.

Post, F. (1996), 'Verbal creativity, depression and alcoholism. An investigation of one hundred American and British writers', *British Journal of Psychiatry*, **168**, pp. 545–55.

Poulton, R., Caspi, A., Moffitt, T.E., Cannon, M., Murray, R., Harrington, H. (2000), 'Children's self-reported psychotic symptoms an adult schizophreniform disorder: A 15-year longitudinal study', *Archives of General Psychiatry*, **57**(11), pp. 1053–8.

Prentky, R.A. (1980), *Creativity and Psychopathology* (New York: Praeger).

Prentky, R.A. (2000–2001), 'Mental illness and roots of genius', *Creativity Research Journal*, **13** (1), pp. 95–104.

Rawlings, D., Barrantes-Vidal, N. and Furnham, A. (2000), 'Personality and aesthetic preference in Spain and England: Two studies relating Sensation Seeking and Openness to Experience to liking for painting and music', *European Journal of Personality*, **14**, pp. 553–76.

Richards, R.L. (1981), 'Relationship between creativity and psychopathology: an evaluation and interpretation of the evidence', *Genetic Psychology Monographs*, **103**, pp. 261–324.

Richards, R.L, Kinney, D.K, Benet, M. and Merzel, A.P.C. (1988), 'Assessing everyday creativity: characteristics of the Lifetime Creativity Scales and validation with three large samples', *Journal of Personality and Social Psychology*, **54**, pp. 476–85.

Richards, R.L, Kinney, D., Daniels, H. and Linkins, K. (1992), 'Everyday creativity and bipolar and unipolar affective disorder: preliminary study of personal and family history', *European Psychiatry*, 7, pp. 49–52.

Richards, R. (2000–2001), 'Creativity and schizophrenia spectrum: More and more interesting', *Creativity Research Journal*, **13** (1), pp. 111–32.

Rothenberg, A. (1990), 'A homospatial thinking in creativity', *Archives of General Psychiatry*, 33, pp. 17–26.

Sass, L.A. (1992), *Madness and Modernism: Insanity in the Light of Modern Art, Literature, and Thought* (New York: Basic Books).

Sass, L.A. (2000–2001), 'Schizophrenia, modernism, and the "creative imagination": On creativity and psychopathology', *Creativity Research Journal*, **13** (1), pp. 55–74.

Schildkraut, J.J., Hirschfeld, A.J. and Murphy, J.M. (1996), 'Depressive disorders, spirituality and early deaths in the abstract expressionist artists of the New York School', in: *Depression and the Spiritual in Modern Art*, ed. Schildkraut, J.J, and Otero, A. (Chichester: John Wiley).
Schuldberg, D., French, C., Stone, B.L. and Heberle, J. (1988), 'Creativity and schizotypal traits. Creativity test scores and perceptual aberration, magical ideation, and impulsive nonconformity', *Journal of Nervous and Mental Disease*, **176**, pp. 648–57.
Schuldberg D. (1990), 'Schizotypal and hypomanic traits, creativity, and psychological health', *Creativity Research Journal*, **3**, pp. 218–30.
Schuldberg, D. (2000–2001), 'Six subclinical spectrum traits in normal creativity', *Creativity Research Journal*, **13** (1), pp. 5–16.
Simonton, D.K. (1999), *Origins of Genius. Darwinian Perspectives on Creativity* (New York: Oxford University Press).
Spearman, C. (1931), *Creative Mind* (London: MacMillan).
Sternberg, R.J. (Ed.) (1999), *Handbook of Creativity* (New York: Cambridge University Press).
Storr, A. (1972), *The Dynamics of Creation* (New York: Atheneum).
Storr, A. (2000), 'Creativity and psychopathology', *Bulletin of Psychology of the Arts*, **1**(2), pp. 42–3.
Taylor, M.A. (1992), 'Are schizophrenia and affective disorder related? A selective literature review', *American Journal of Psychiatry*, **149**, pp. 22–32.
Terman, L.M. (1925), *Genetic Studies of Genius: vol. I. Mental and Physical Traits of a Thousand Gifted Children* (Stanford: Stanford University Press).
van Os, J. and Verdoux, H. (2003), 'Diagnosis and classification of schizophrenia: Categories versus dimensions, distributions versus disease', in: *The Epidemiology of Schizophrenia*, ed. Murray, R, and Jones, P.B. (New York: Cambridge University Press).
Zuckerman, M. (1979), *Sensation Seeking: Beyond the Optimal Level of Arousal* (New York: Erlbaum).

Ivar Hagendoorn

Some Speculative Hypotheses about the Nature and Perception of Dance and Choreography

I: Introduction

Ever since I first saw a dance performance I have wondered why it is that I am sometimes fascinated and touched by some people moving about on a stage, while at other times it leaves me completely indifferent. I will argue that an answer to this question has to be searched for in the way sensory stimuli are processed in the brain. After all, all our actions, perceptions and feelings are mediated and controlled by the brain. The thoughts and feelings evoked by a dance performance are no exception and thus they too have a neural substrate in the brain.

In music and the visual arts what has been called 'neuroaesthetics' (Zeki, 2001a) and 'neuromusicology' has already yielded some interesting insights. As one study showed, the aesthetic appeal of Mondrian's paintings can be related to certain psychophysical properties of the visual system (Latto *et al.*, 2000). Earlier studies had found that the perception of oblique lines is slightly inferior to the perception of horizontal and vertical lines. Making clever use of the fact that some of Mondrian's paintings have an oblique frame, the authors showed that people also *prefer* horizontal and vertical to oblique lines. Findings like this suggest that we have an aesthetic preference for those stimuli that are closely tuned to the respective sensory areas in the brain.

The present article draws an itinerary through various brain structures and shows how these may combine to ultimately give rise to the sensations we experience when watching a dance performance. Since watching dance is essentially a visual experience the present analysis concentrates on visual processing. This is not to deny that music is an integral part of most dance performances or that movements produce noise, which may influence visual processing and in the absence of a visual component elicit visual images. But, to state the obvious, if the stage lights go out the audience's experience of the dancers' movements will

Correspondence:Ivar Hagendoorn, Marnixstraat 18-A, 2518 PZ Den Haag, The Netherlands, *Email: ivar@ivarhagendoorn.com*

Journal of Consciousness Studies, **11**, No. 3–4, 2004, pp. 79–110

be impaired. I should emphasize that the itinerary chosen here is only one of many routes that participate in the processing of dance, although I believe it to be a main route. At the start of this itinerary lies the observation that neural processing delays interfere with both perception and action. This problem is at once illustrated and brought to the fore in both the perception and practice of dance. Several authors have proposed in various forms that the brain compensates for these delays by creating predictions of forthcoming sensory and motor events (e.g. Berthoz, 2000; Kawato *et al.*, 1987; Wolpert & Flanagan, 2001; Engel *et al.*, 2001). Based on these considerations I will advance two hypotheses. I will argue that the deviation from and correspondence between the actual motion trajectory of a moving object and the trajectory as predicted by the brain of the observer, gives rise to two distinct emotional responses, analogous to the euphoria and frustration of catching or missing a ball. Through their sequential interplay these responses may reinforce each other to give rise to the feelings one can experience when watching dance. As a corollary I will argue that in forming a prediction of a moving object's motion trajectory the brain engages in a form of motor imagery which, through a different route, may contribute to a state of arousal.

Much of the present article is devoted to a discussion of the brain regions involved in the above processes (Figure 1). The unsuspecting reader should therefore be warned of some tough neuroscience ahead. (Some readers may wish to jump straight to section VIII where I present my two main hypotheses and then read back to how I got there). I will argue that mirror neurons, which become active both when a movement is perceived and performed, may constitute a neural bridge between action and perception. Interestingly, as I will show, one of the brain regions where mirror neurons have been found has also been associated with perceptual anticipation. I will then relate these findings to the literature on prediction and reward and argue that brain regions associated with prediction errors may also account for at least some of the emotions we experience when watching dance.

Different people will have a different understanding of the word 'dance', some may recall a ballet or a musical they once saw, while others may think of

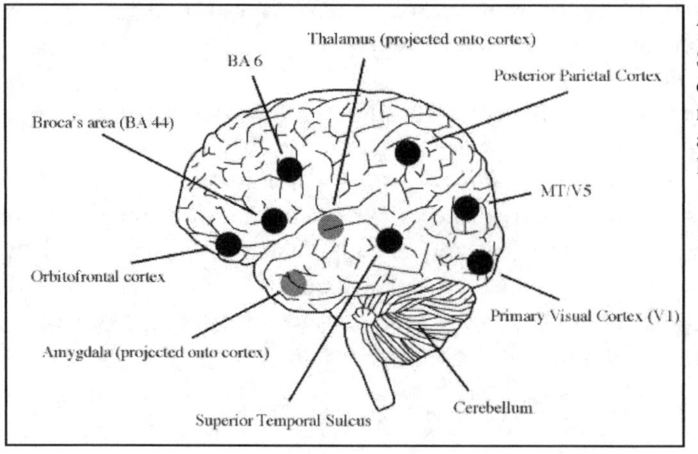

Figure 1.

Schematic representation of the main brain regions mentioned in the article and their approximate locations.

the movements they and others perform at a party. By dance or 'dance performance', I will here refer to a sequence of movements, not necessarily choreographed, of any length, from two seconds to two hours, whereby the goal of the movement is the movement itself. This is not so much a definition of dance, or dance as an art form, but an operational delimitation of the question I will be addressing here: why is it that it can be interesting to watch someone 'just dancing around' or, to avoid circular reasoning, going through a series of movements without any apparent goal, other than 'just' performing the movements? And what is it that choreographers *do* when they compose such a series of movements, with no other purpose than to be performed and seen? What goes on in their mind when they adjust a position or movement sequence? What are the neural processes that guide and constitute aesthetic judgment? My primary references here are works by choreographers such as George Balanchine, William Forsythe, Merce Cunningham and Jiri Kylián, often referred to as 'abstract' dance. However, movement sequences from martial arts when rehearsed 'as such' also fit the present description, so do Indian dances, Japanese butoh and various other dance traditions.

Having outlined how a movement sequence may bring about the feelings it does in certain dance performances, I will argue that choreographers like all other artists when creating a work, are implicitly led by the brain mechanisms underlying sensory experience and emotion. By making explicit some of these implicit considerations they may eventually be put to creative use, a proposition I will illustrate with some examples from my own choreographic work. I would like to emphasize from the outset that the ideas expressed here are tentative and not uncontroversial (e.g., Zeki, 2001b; Ione, 2001). However, it is only with their propagation and by inviting feedback from critics that they may be further developed.

II: From the Retina to the Brain

What we see is light and light reflected from surfaces. The difference between light hitting the eye or an arm, or a wall, is that inside the eye are light-sensitive receptors that transform the energy carried by the light into electrical signals. After some pre-processing these electrical signals are relayed along separate pathways to various specialized areas in the brain, where they are either used to form a visual representation of the stimulus or immediately translated into an action such narrowing the pupil.

Of the various pathways emanating from the retina only two are directly involved in processing visual information for perception. One conveys information contributing primarily to the perception of movement, while the other is associated with the processing of colour and shape. Before reaching the visual areas of the brain, both pathways pass through the thalamus, the brain's central relay centre. From thereon the visual information is relayed to the primary visual cortex, where, after some intermediate processing, it is once more separated into different paths, each leading to a more specialized area. In all there are over 30 regions performing such tasks as determining colour, shape, solidity, size and motion of whatever hits the eye. It is currently believed that motion is processed

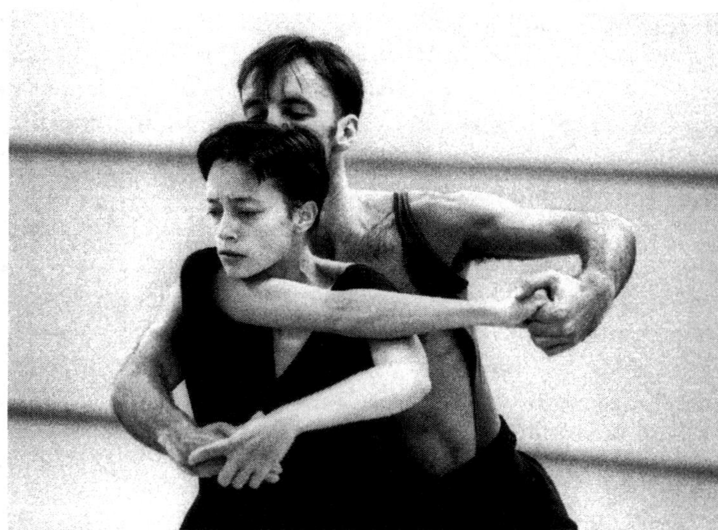

Figure 2.

Which limb belongs to which body? Jiri Kylian, *As if never been* (1992). Dancers: Nancy Euverink and Patrick Delcroix.

Photo: © Dirk Buwalda.

in two areas, one of which, the middle temporal gyrus, often referred to as MT or V5, is involved in processing an object's speed and direction, while the other, the medial superior temporal area or MST, is specialized for detecting its dynamical properties, like rotation and tilting.

It seems likely that all connections between these higher visual processing areas are reciprocal. What's more, information may re-enter a given area after it has been processed in any number of other areas (Martin, 2002). It is difficult to see how the different attributes of a scene that are analysed in specialized areas would otherwise be integrated into a visual image, a feature of the visual system often referred to as the 'binding problem', a 'problem' since its workings are still largely unknown (Robertson, 2003). With respect to motion perception the binding (or maybe we should say 'unbinding') problem, comes down to determining what is moving and what is stationary, and distinguishing between the motion of different parts of a single object and the motion of different objects, something choreographers like to play with (Figure 2). Already we catch a glimpse of how aspects of the visual system can be employed artistically. By keeping the background and some attributes of an object constant, a choreographer can create a setting which, in terms of brain processing, leaves more resources available for processing one salient feature — movement, for instance.

Not all visual information passes from the thalamus to the primary visual cortex. One pathway leads straight to MT, one of the areas specialized in visual motion processing. This may be why some people with damage to the primary visual cortex are nevertheless able to perceive movement, a condition called blindsight (e.g., Schoenfeld *et al.*, 2002). Another pathway projects from the thalamus to the amygdala, a brain structure associated with emotional behaviour, in particular in relation to danger (LeDoux, 1996). The direct pathway from the thalamus to the amygdala ensures that the brain can already begin to respond before an object has been identified, for instance by modulating the processing in the visual cortex, with which it is reciprocally connected, or by initiating withdrawal. Even though theatres tend to be relatively safe environments, by emulating the perceptual characteristics of potentially dangerous events, the brain will respond in much the same way as in the case of a real threat, as every movie director knows. A possible explanation for this is that from an evolutionary point of view it is better to retreat ten times too often than once too few. A related explanation is that in these circumstances the emotional system overrules cognition. We are carried away even though we know 'it's only a movie'. The opposite, by the way, may also occur: we may cognitively value something we don't enjoy, for instance an avant-garde dance performance with little or no movement.

Interestingly, the amygdala also appears to play a role in attributing emotions to movements. When watching animation movies featuring simple geometric figures like circles, squares and triangles, people tend to attribute emotions such as joy, anger and frustration to the figures based on the nature of their movements (Heider & Simmel, 1944). Patients with damage to the amygdala, however, fail to assign emotions to the movements of such figures (Heberlein *et al.*, 1998). It would therefore be interesting to investigate how these patients respond to dance, especially if the dancers were to wear single-coloured costumes and masks or hoods covering both head and face so as to create a purely graphic display.

III: Motion Anticipation and Smooth Pursuit

Having hit the retina it takes between 50 and 100 milliseconds before the information carried by a light particle reaches the visual cortex. Some simple arithmetic shows that a car driving at 100 km/h will have covered an additional 2 to 3 metres by the time the light activates the appropriate regions in the brain. To make up for this delay it has been conjectured that the brain somehow forms a prediction of the path of a moving object (Nijhawan, 1994). According to this view the brain forms an internal simulation of the trajectory covered so far, on the basis of which the object's movement is extrapolated into the future. Such an extrapolation would ensure that its perceived position coincides with its actual position.

Perceptual anticipation and prediction are likely to involve both low- and high-level brain processes. It has been proposed that a rudimentary prediction in the form of a forward shift of the image occurs as early as the retina (Nijhawan, 1997; Berry *et al.*, 1999; for a review, see Nijhawan, 2002). At the level of object representations, learned characteristics of the behaviour of target objects (e.g., the bouncing of a ball) bias the processing of its speed and direction of motion (the second bounce is lower than the first). Getting to the roots of this phenomenon, an intriguing study, which compared the performance of astronauts catching a ball on earth and under zero gravity, recently suggested that the brain uses an internal model of gravity-induced acceleration when predicting the trajectory of a falling ball (McIntyre *et al.*, 2001).

Various other experimental findings support the hypothesis that motion perception is predictive. It has been found that, if a moving target suddenly disappears, its last position is remembered as being slightly ahead of its actual final position, a phenomenon technically known as representational momentum, which suggests that the percept is shifted forward (Freyd & Finke, 1984). What's more, even still images of an object in motion, such as that of a falling glass, exhibit 'representational momentum', in that they convey information about the motion implied in the picture (Freyd, 1983). This, of course, is nothing new to dance audiences. While many dance photos could also have been posed, some 'capture' the dance (see Figure 3, as well as Figures 6 and 9). They extend the movement frozen by the camera forward in time. Interestingly it has been demonstrated that watching still photographs with implied motion yields increased neural activity in MT/MST, the part of the visual cortex involved in the processing of visual motion (Senior *et al.*, 2000; Kourtzi & Kanwisher, 2000).

Perhaps some of the most compelling evidence for the predictive nature of motion perception has come from the study of fast ball sports like tennis, baseball and cricket. In baseball, outfielders run to where they expect to be able to catch a fly ball, which implies that the brain forms a prediction of the ball's trajectory (McBeath *et al.*, 1996; McLeod *et al.*, 2001). Land and McLeod (2000) recorded the eye movements of batsmen in cricket as they prepared to hit an approaching ball. They found that the batsmen's eyes monitored the ball shortly after its release, then made a predictive saccade to where they expected it to hit the ground, waited for it to bounce and then tracked its trajectory for 100–200 ms afterward. As the authors argue 'information provided by these fixations may allow precise prediction of the ball's timing and placement'. If this is true for moving balls, why wouldn't it also be the case for human movements such as dance?

The study by Land and McLeod (2000) demonstrates that the central nervous system employs two types of eye movements to track a moving target: saccades

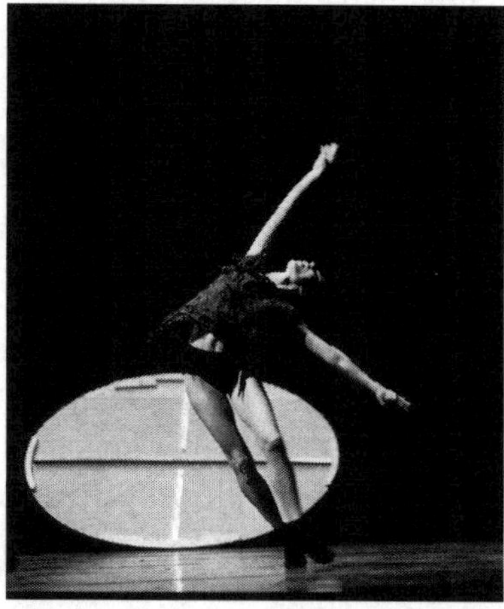

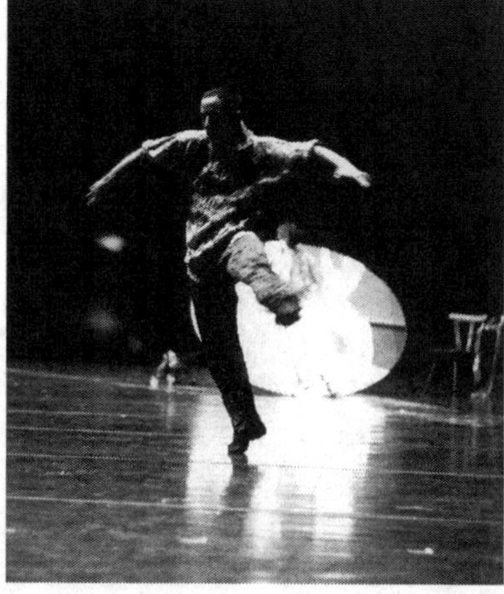

Figure 3. Implied motion. A good dance photo 'captures' the dance. The movement appears to continue in the direction of motion. Indeed, photos such as these yield increased activity in MT/MST, the part of the visual cortex involved in the processing of visual motion (Senior *et al.*, 2000; Kourtzi & Kanwisher, 2000). William Forsythe, *As a Garden in this Setting* (1992). Dancer: Regina van Berkel (l), Tony Rizzi (r). Photo: © Dominik Mentzos.

and smooth pursuit. Saccades direct the fovea, the high-acuity region at the centre of the retina, towards a target in discrete jumps. Smooth pursuit eye movements stabilize the image of the object on the retina by smoothly rotating the eyes in congruence with the motion of the target. Sometimes, however, moving the eyes alone is not enough and the head, and if necessary other parts of the body, are integrated into the smooth pursuit movement. In tennis, the heads of the umpire and the public can often be seen to move from side to side as they track the ball. What's more, when tracking an object with binoculars or a camera, the eyes are fixed and the body adjusts to keep the object within view. I would therefore like to suggest that the mechanisms for tracking a moving target — eyes, head or attention — form a continuum and as such share a common neural network, which predicts the trajectory of the moving target.

While many studies have investigated the properties of neurons in visual motion area MT and the neural mechanisms of smooth pursuit eye movements and saccades, surprisingly few have analysed the functional neuroanatomy of visual motion anticipation. Ando (2002) recently reported the results of a functional neuroimaging experiment using fMRI, in which participants had to predict the motion trajectory of a virtual three-dimensional object. The data revealed activity in the intraparietal sulcus, the inferior and superior parietal lobules (BA 40 and BA 7), the dorsal premotor cortex (BA 6), the inferior frontal gyrus (BA 44, Broca's area) and the lateral cerebellum. These findings are in congruence with recent experiments by Schubotz and Von Cramon (2001; 2002a; 2002b). They found increased activity in the right ventrolateral premotor cortex (BA 6) and the right intraparietal sulcus, as subjects predicted the last in a series of 12 sequentially displayed circles of different size, which created the illusion of regularly pulsing motion (Schubotz & Von Cramon, 2002b). What is perhaps most interesting about these results is the activation of premotor regions, as in all experiments the task was purely perceptual.

Catching a ball, hitting a moving object or tracking a target with a camera, all require a form of sensorimotor integration. Visual information about the object's motion trajectory has to be instantaneously transformed into movement of the body, whether the eye, finger, hand or arm. The results by Ando (2002) and Schubotz and Von Cramon (2002b) indicate that even in the absence of a motor task, attending to and predicting the trajectory of a moving target activates premotor regions. On a speculative note Schubotz and Von Cramon suggest that

> when we try to predict how a target will move, the motor system generates a 'blueprint' of the observed motion that allows potential sensorimotor integration. In the absence of any motor requirement, this blueprint appears to be not a by-product of motor planning, but rather the basis for target motion prediction (Schubotz and Von Cramon, 2002b).

What's more, since the lateral premotor cortex is also activated when predicting a colour or pattern transition or a change in auditory pitch, Schubotz and Von Cramon (2002a) suggest that the lateral premotor cortex is involved in the prediction of any kind of sequential event, with human movement as a special case.

Additional evidence for the involvement of motor areas in perceptual anticipation comes from the study of handwriting movements. It has been shown that when writing an 'l' followed by another 'l', the first 'l' is written down faster than when it is followed by an 'n' (Orliaguet *et al*., 1997). Further experiments demonstrated that, when watching a dot as it traces the curve of an 'l', observers are able to use information about its kinematics to predict the upcoming letter, 'l' or 'n' (Kandel *et al*., 2000a; 2000b). Chaminade *et al*. (2001) used positron emission tomography (PET) to measure brain activity as observers predicted the continuation of the motion trajectory of a dot produced by mechanical, pointing and writing movements. All three conditions were associated with a common neural network comprising the orbitofrontal and right frontal cortex. However, unlike Schubotz and Von Cramon (2002b), activation of the premotor cortex and the right intraparietal sulcus was found only when the trajectory had been produced by a pointing movement. The authors also report increased activity in the superior parietal lobule and Broca's area (BA 44) during the anticipation of writing movements, two of the areas that were also activated in the fMRI study by Ando (2002). Some caution in interpreting the findings by Chaminade *et al*. (2001) is warranted though, since the baseline condition required subjects to indicate whether they expected the dot to move up or down. This, however, is itself a prediction task and can therefore not be properly used to test for perceptual anticipation. In summary, while the results are not unequivocal they do partially reinforce each other, suggesting that (pre-)motor areas are involved in predicting visual motion, which obviously would include the movements of a dancer or group of dancers.

IV: Apparent Motion

It frequently happens that a moving object is temporarily occluded from view, an arm which briefly moves behind the body, a car entering a tunnel or a dancer who disappears behind one of the other dancers. In principle almost anything can happen while we are unable to see the object, but in practice most objects continue along their track and we are able to accurately predict where and when it will reappear.[1] Indeed, we tend to be surprised if the object does not reappear or at a different location. Conversely, once the object has reappeared the brain is able to infer the motion trajectory between the points where it vanished and resurfaced. The latter is a specific example of what is known as 'apparent motion', since we did not really see the object move, we merely saw it dis- and reappear.

The term apparent motion is commonly used to refer to the illusory perception of motion from the rapid sequential display of static images as in a film or 'motion picture'. Consider a prototypical film consisting of two frames, one with two vertically aligned dots on the left, the other with two vertically aligned dots on the right. If the two frames are rapidly interchanged, the dots are perceived as

[1] A choreographer aware of this phenomenon could manipulate dancers, movements and stage props such that part of the audience sees what is occluded from the rest of the audience as in William Forsythe's *Enemy in the Figure* (1987), which features a wavy-shaped wooden panel positioned diagonally on the middle of the stage.

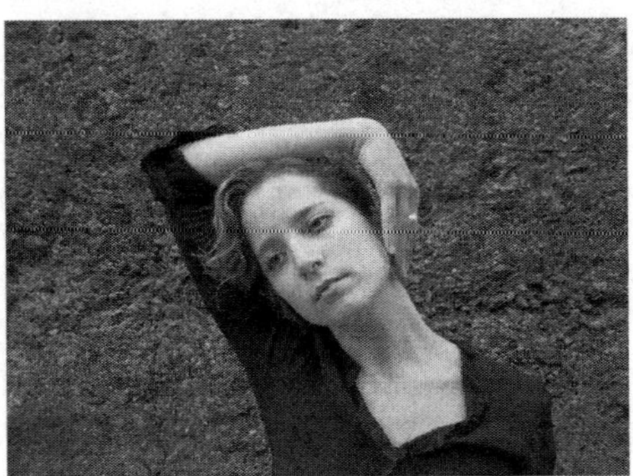
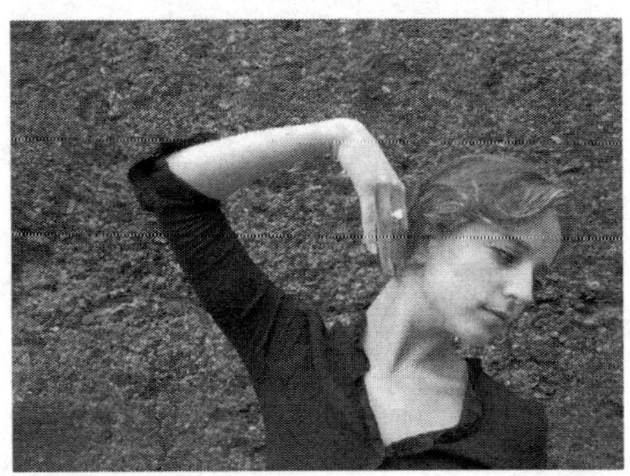

Figure 4. Apparent motion of the human body. When alternately shown two body positions the brain chooses a biomechanically feasible path to connect them. The example used in most experimental studies shows a hand behind and in front of a knee, the idea being that the hand cannot move through the leg. If the hypothesis is correct in the above example the brain will simulate a movement of the head underneath the arm, a movement most people are unlikely to have previously performed. Dancer: Ester Natzijl. Photo: © Ivar Hagendoorn.

jumping from left to right and back. However, this is only one of several *logical* possibilities, the upper and lower dots could in principle have swapped positions. This classic example illustrates that given a point A and B, the visual system selects the shortest path to connect both points, that is, to describe the movement needed to go from A to B (e.g., Dawson & Pylyshyn, 1988). However, as shown by Shiffrar and Freyd (1990; 1993), if A and B are *body* positions, perception follows an anatomically feasible path, even though a physically impossible route may be shorter (Figure 4).

A recent PET study in which subjects were briefly presented with two body positions and subsequently had to choose between a direct impossible and an indirect possible connecting movement, yielded selective activation of regions in the primary motor and superior parietal cortex, but only if the connecting movement was biomechanically possible (Stevens *et al.*, 2000). On the basis of these findings the authors suggest that

> we might expect an absence of motor executive activations during the visual perception of actions that an observer interprets as beyond his/her motor capabilities, e.g., *a technically challenging ballet movement.* In such cases, the impossibility of completing the action is determined within the context of the observer's own motor experience rather than in terms of the general movement limitations of the human body [emphasis mine].

This hypothesis could be tested empirically by first showing two positions unlikely to be the beginning and end of a continuous movement and subsequently the movement that connects them.

Stevens *et al.* (2000) suggest that, when connecting two body positions, the brain engages in a form of motor imagery to create the motion percept. Motor imagery refers to the mental performance of a movement, or, more formally 'a dynamic state during which the representation of a given motor act is internally rehearsed within working memory without any overt motor output' (Decety & Grèzes, 1999). It is the experience of seeing and feeling oneself executing a movement, a kinaesthetic feeling of speed, effort and changing body configuration. As Jeannerod (1994) explains 'visual images are experienced by the self in the same way as a spectator who watches a scene, motor images are experienced from within as the result of a first-person process where the self feels like an actor rather than a spectator'. Thus, according to this view, if within a movement sequence part of the body is temporarily occluded, the brain will either extrapolate the movement from the last visible position or interpolate between the positions before and after the occlusion, by covertly performing the movement itself.

V: Biological Motion

Most of the experimental studies discussed so far dealt with the movement of abstract stimuli like dots or virtual balls. If we want to learn more about dance we will have to consider movements of the (whole) human body. As it turns out there is a large body of evidence which shows that humans have a special ability for recognizing what has become known as biological motion, the visual motion patterns of humans and animals. In the early 1970s Gunnar Johansson developed a now classic technique whereby an actor was filmed as he moved through a darkened room with small light bulbs attached to the head and key joints such as the shoulders, elbows, wrists, hips, knees and ankles. When the actor was sitting in a chair people watching the film reported seeing nothing but a random collection of lights. But as soon as the actor started moving they instantly identified the pattern as that of a moving person. In a second experiment a dancing couple was filmed under the same conditions and again observers had no difficulty in identifying the moving pattern of lights as that of a dancing couple (Johansson, 1973).

This technique has since been replicated in a variety of experimental settings.[2] The lights, or their more contemporary motion capture equivalents, were placed on other parts of the body, actors were instructed to perform a range of activities, from hammering to greeting to climbing a staircase, and the display as a whole has been turned upside-down or masked with a cloud of random noise (for a review, see Pinto & Shiffrar, 1999). One experiment demonstrated that people are able to recognize acquaintances and even themselves from a point-light display of their movements. In fact in this particular experiment the probability of correct self-recognition was even higher than all other probabilities (Beardworth & Bukner, 1981). The latter is particularly striking since apart from dancers, most people don't often see themselves moving. Not only does this rule out the possibility that recognition was due to perceptual learning, as might be suspected if the phenomenon only showed up in the perception of other persons, it also suggests once more a possible link between motor and perceptual processes. Another experiment showed that people are able to extract an emotional state from motion characteristics alone (Dittrich *et al.*, 1996). For this experiment the

[2] Given the number of experimental studies, it may surprise that only recently, some 25 years after the original experiments, the potential of this technique has been explored in a ballet (video projected on a scrim covering the full stage height as part of the set design), Merce Cunningham, *Biped* (1999), in collaboration with multimedia artists Paul Kaiser and Shelley Eshkar.

researchers asked two dancers to portray fear, anger, grief, joy, surprise and disgust. The movements were recorded as such and using a point-light display. Participants in the study then had to judge which emotion was being portrayed. Interestingly they got 88% right from the full display and 63% from the point-light display.

In recent years various neuroimaging studies have examined the brain regions associated with the recognition of biological motion from point-light displays (Bonda *et al.*, 1996; Grossman *et al.*, 2000; 2002; Vaina *et al.*, 2001; Grezès *et al.*, 2001; Servos *et al.*, 2002). A common area found in all studies is a region on the (posterior) superior temporal sulcus (STS). In addition, perhaps not unexpectedly, Grossman *et al.* (2000), Vaina *et al.* (2001) and Grezès *et al.* (2001) report activity in MT/MST. Other areas that were found to be significantly activated were the cerebellum (Grossman *et al.*, 2000; Vaina *et al.*, 2001), the lingual gyrus (Servos *et al.*, 2002), the ventral premotor cortex (Grezès *et al.*, 2001) and the amygdala (Bonda *et al.*, 1996). The activation in STS is consistent with neurophysiological studies in monkeys (Oram & Perrett, 1994). Using single cell recordings it was shown that some neurons in the superior temporal cortex are selectively activated by arm movements and the direction of walking. The posterior STS therefore appears to be a key area for the recognition of biological motion.

Neurological case studies provide further evidence for this hypothesis. Howard *et al.* (1996) and Vaina *et al.* (1990) report patients who, because of a lesion in the visual motion processing areas MT/MST, are practically motion blind, but are still able to perceive biological motion. This led Beintema and Lappe (2002) to re-examine the stimuli used in point-light studies. They observed that the standard point-light displays exhibit what they call 'local image motion': each individual dot, for instance the dot tied to the right elbow or the left ankle, traces a stationary trajectory through space and thus not only contains motion information but also information about its location on the (implied) body. They therefore developed an alternative technique in which the location of the light points changes from frame to frame and position and motion information are dissociated (e.g., the point that was on the elbow in the first frame moves somewhere between elbow and shoulder in the second frame, then changes again in the third frame, etc.). Even though Beintema and Lappe's 'sequential position walker' as they call it, is somewhat more difficult to recognize, observers' performance is comparable with standard point-light displays. Based on these findings they suggest that the perception of biological motion relies on the sequential analysis of body postures.

Point-light displays were originally intended to show how little information is needed for the human brain to recognize human motion. There is a danger that explaining this phenomenon, which is essentially a laboratory condition, becomes an end in itself. Real-life motion stimuli are often imperfect, due to differential lighting conditions and partial occlusion, but as the study by Beintema and Lappe (2002) shows, standard point-light displays may be 'perfect in their imperfection'. It may surprise that only few neuroimaging studies have been performed using real human movements as stimuli, rather than point-light displays. Decety *et al.* (1997) and Grèzes *et al.* (1998) conducted a PET study using video filmed pantomimes of opening a bottle, hammering a nail, sewing a button or turning the pages of a book as stimuli, as well as movements from American Sign Language. Participants were instructed to memorize the movements so that they could either imitate or recognize them after the scanning session or to just watch the movements. Since the subjects were unfamiliar with American Sign Language the authors were able to make a distinction between the observation of meaningful and meaningless movements. In the absence of a goal, observation of both meaningful and meaningless movements activated the occipital–temporal junction, which corresponds to MT/V5, the superior occipital gyrus, the middle temporal gyrus and the inferior parietal lobe. Meaningful movements also activated the dorsal precentral gyrus (BA 6), the inferior frontal gyrus (BA 44/45) and the fusiform gyrus, whereas meaningless movements resulted in stronger activation in the inferior parietal lobe, the superior parietal lobule and the cerebellum. If the goal was to imitate, both meaningful and meaningless movements led to activation in the cerebellum and the occipital–parietal ('dorsal') pathway extending to the premotor cortex, while meaningful movements additionally activated the supplementary motor area (SMA) and orbitofrontal cortex.

The differences in activated areas between observing point-light figures and the experiments by Decety *et al.* (1997) and Grèzes *et al.* (1998) may be due to the fact that the former represented full body motion, whereas the latter were confined to movements of the hand and arm. It would therefore be interesting to replicate the study by Decety *et al.* (1997) with the higher spatial resolution that can be obtained with today's fMRI and using full body movements rather than movements of the arm and hand alone. In combination with a point-light version of the same movements, it could then be tested whether real human movements and their point-light representation do indeed rely on the same neural mechanisms.

Of course it would go too far to straightforwardly extrapolate any of these findings to the perception of dance. The motion stimuli in the study by Decety *et al.* (1997) were very short, lasting for as little as 4 seconds and were restricted to movements of the hand and arm, with only the upper limbs and trunk being shown on a computer display. What is perhaps most interesting about these two studies is that differences between the observation of meaningful and meaningless movements on the one hand and cognitive strategy on the other can actually be detected at the level of neural processing. Translated to dance one may therefore speculate about a difference in neural processing already at the level of perception between watching the abstract ballets of for instance George Balanchine and the expressionist more gestural based dance theatre of Pina Bausch.

VI: Mirror Neurons

Above I have briefly outlined some of the brain regions involved in (biological) motion perception and perceptual anticipation. Although the evidence is as yet inconclusive, it appears that motor regions contribute to action perception. What is missing is a possible mechanism or a common computational framework linking these scattered reports.

Some years ago neuroscientists discovered a population of neurons in the premotor cortex of a monkey that discharge both when the monkey performs a movement and when it observes the same action performed by someone else (Rizzolatti *et al.*, 1996; Gallese *et al.*, 1996). These so-called 'mirror neurons' could therefore provide a neurophysiological bridge between perception and action. At first sight mirror neurons appear to respond in much the same way as the neurons in the superior temporal cortex that respond to the sight of a moving hand, face or body (Oram & Perrett, 1994). What is striking about mirror neurons, though, is that they also fire when the monkey *performs* a movement. Therefore they cannot be exclusively visual. A recent study showed that mirror neurons in the premotor cortex also respond to auditory stimuli, making them not just bi- but multimodal (Kohler *et al.*, 2002).

At present there is much speculation about the role of mirror neurons in perception and behaviour. Rizzolatti *et al.* (1996) have suggested a role in the understanding of motor events. The brain has an implicit knowledge of the immediate consequences of its own actions, that is, of the movements it generates, both in terms of its changing relation to the external world, as in terms of a change in body state and body configuration. This knowledge is the result of an association between the representation of a movement and its consequences, in other words,

> the movement has a meaning (e.g., 'grasp') and this meaning is represented by a specific cortical activation pattern. Mirror neurons show that this movement knowledge can be attributed to actions made by others. When an external stimulus evokes a neural activity similar to that which, when internally generated, represents a certain action, the meaning of the observed action is recognized because of the similarity between the two representations, the one internally generated during action and that evoked by the stimulus (Rizzolatti *et al.*, 1996).

This account, if correct, might explain why people understand not only mime, but also non-imitative movements in dance, which have a more abstract 'meaning'. The back of the hand is more vulnerable than the palm, so leaning on the back rather than the palm of the hand may exude a sense of 'vulnerability'. It may also explain why a dancer balancing in a virtuoso position may inspire awe and be

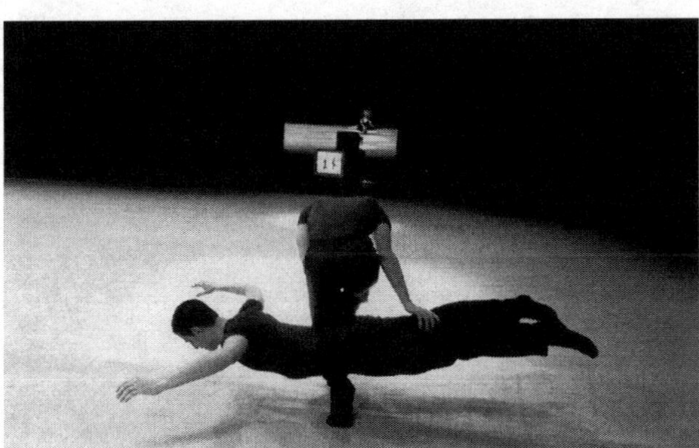

Figure 5.

Is he actually? To understand what is going on the brain virtually performs the movement and body configuration. Jirí Kylián, *Click–Pause–Silence* (2001). Dancers: Patrick Marin and Stefan Zeromski.

Photo: © Joris-Jan Bos.

literally breathtaking: we hold our breath as we internally simulate the movement (see Figures 5, 6 and 8).

Jeannerod (1994; 1997) has suggested a role for mirror neurons in the learning of new motor skills. There is now a growing body of literature linking mirror neurons to imitation learning (Meltzoff & Prinz, 2002; Hurley & Chater, 2004), which of course is the basis of not only dance education but also much choreography. Jeannerod (1994) gives the example of a pupil learning a motor skill such as playing a musical instrument, but we could also think of a choreographer demonstrating a new movement sequence to a dancer. Although the dancer remains immobile during the demonstration, he or she must somehow internalise the movement, that is, he or she must form an image of the movement sequence as it unfolds. The choreographer in turn will compare the movements of the dancer with what he himself had in mind and in the words of Jeannerod '[will] experience a strong feeling of what should be done and how'. As Jeannerod continues,

> Similar feelings may be experienced by sports addicts watching a football game on television. They mentally perform the appropriate action to catch the ball (and indeed, they express frustration when the ball has been missed by the player). The vividness of the imagined action can induce in the watchers changes in heart and respiration rates related to the degree of their mental effort (Jeannerod, 1994; 1997).

Although mirror neurons have only been directly demonstrated in monkeys, there is accumulating evidence that similar cells or a similar *mirror system* exist in humans. As one experiment showed, the observation of human movement facilitates the same muscle groups and motor circuits as when the movements are executed (Fadiga *et al.*, 1995). Neuroimaging studies also suggest the existence of a human mirror system. Iacoboni *et al.* (1999) performed an fMRI experiment in which participants were instructed to imitate a finger movement, lift a finger in response to a spatial cue or to just watch either the finger movement or the spatial cue. Activation in the left inferior frontal cortex (BA 44, Broca's area), the right anterior parietal cortex and the right parietal operculum was significantly higher during imitation than in the other tasks. Of particular interest is the activation in Broca's area, since this area has been proposed to be the human homologue of area F5 in the monkey premotor cortex (Rizzolatti & Arbib, 1998), where mirror neurons were first discovered. To directly test the involvement of Broca's area in imitation Heiser *et al.* (2003) used transcranial magnetic stimulation (TMS) to temporarily disrupt processing in the left inferior frontal cortex as subjects imitated a finger movement or alternatively, performed a finger movement in response to a visual cue. It was found that while simple key presses were unaffected, imitation was significantly impaired during the application of TMS, thus providing evidence for the involvement of Broca's area, or at least the region comprising Broca's area, in imitation. However, Manthey *et al.* (2003) recently reported that the ventrolateral part of the premotor cortex (BA 6) and *not* Broca's area (BA 44) was predominantly activated when subjects observed 36 short movies of simple goal-directed actions. This is in congruence with findings by Decety *et al.* (1997) for the observation of meaningful movements, but at odds with the observation-only condition in, for instance, Iacoboni *et al.* (1999). If Broca's area is associated with imitation one would expect it to be activated during all instances of action observation, as indeed in the observation only task in an experiment similar to Iacoboni *et al.* (1999) by Carr *et al.* (2003), which used facial expressions instead of finger movements. It may therefore be too early to draw firm conclusions about the precise role of Broca's area in the perception of action or about the location of a brain region subserving the function of matching action observation and execution.

Subsequent experiments by Iacoboni *et al.* (2001) also revealed increased activity in the superior temporal sulcus (STS). While this is consistent with findings that report activation during the perception of point-light displays of human motion (see references above), interestingly and somewhat unexpectedly activation was greater during the imitation task. This could of course be due to increased attention, but Iacoboni (2003) offers an intriguing alternative explanation, suggesting that

> the increased STS activity may be due to efferent copies of motor commands originating from fronto-parietal mirror areas. These efferent copies would allow a prediction of the sensory consequences of the planned imitative action that would be compared with the description of the observed action provided by STS.

Although Iacoboni *et al.* (2001) provide some evidence in favour of the latter hypothesis it may be difficult to show that this is indeed what is happening.

Gallese (2002) also interprets mirror activity in premotor regions in terms of efference copies of motor commands, but places premotor mirror neurons at the receiving rather than the sending end, suggesting that they perform a simulation of the planned movement, allowing for the prediction of its sensory consequences. Interestingly this hypothesis is in line with findings reported above, that suggest a role for the lateral premotor cortex (BA 6/44) in predicting perceptual events (Schubotz & Von Cramon, 2002a; b). This raises the question whether the same neural mechanism underlies *either* perceptual anticipation and imitation *or* the computations of the lateral premotor cortex.

VII: A Common Representational Framework

Neural processing delays interfere not only with the sensory system, but also with motor control. As various computational studies have shown, sensorimotor loops are too slow to allow feedback control of fast coordinated movements (e.g., Kawato, 1987). To overcome this problem it has been proposed within the motor control literature that the brain uses what are known as internal models to calculate a feed-forward motor command from the desired motion trajectory (for a review, see Kawato, 1999). An internal model in general is a system that mimics the behaviour of a natural process. Internal models come in two types. An *inverse* model provides the motor commands necessary to perform a movement. A *forward* model captures the forward or causal relationship between the input to a system and its output, by predicting the next state of the system, given its current state. Thus the *forward* model predicts how the pointer will move if the mouse is moved. The *inverse* model estimates how the mouse should be moved so that the pointer moves in the desired direction. In the context of motor control, forward models could compensate for delays in sensory feedback, anticipate and cancel out the sensory effects of self-produced movements or transform the errors between the desired and actual outcome of a movement into the corresponding errors in the motor command (Wolpert, 1997; Wolpert *et al.*, 1995). It seems reasonable to suppose that, when tracking a rapidly moving target with a cursor, as controlled by a mouse or joystick — think of a computer game — the brain also forms a forward model of its motion trajectory. From here it is only a small step to the hypothesis that the brain forms a forward model of a target's motion trajectory regardless of whether it tracks the target with a mouse, the eyes, a camera or attention, and whether the target is a dot on a screen, a ball, a limb or a dancer. Indeed the term forward model is just a technical notion for the predictive function referred to in previous sections.

There is accumulating evidence that the brain does indeed employ internal models. Above we already encountered one instance in the form of catching a ball on earth and in outer space (McIntyre *et al.*, 2001). Of relevance to the present context is a recent study by Mehta and Schaal (2002). Comparing the output of various computational models with actual performance of a visuomotor task requiring subjects to balance a pole on a finger, a task which depends crucially on visual feedback, they conclude that the data are best described by a forward model at the sensory processing stage. Given the nature of this task, it seems reasonable to extend these results to the visual tracking of a moving target, whether with the eyes or head.

In recent years various authors have proposed a role for internal models, more in particular forward models, in the perception of action and the understanding of behaviour (Blakemore & Decety, 2001; Jeannerod, 2001; Gallagher & Jeannerod, 2002; Gallese, 2002; Rizzolatti *et al.*, 2001; Iacoboni, 2003; Wolpert *et al.*, 2001; 2003). In its most intriguing and also most speculative form, it is hypothesized that, when watching human movement, the predictions of a forward model are compared, not with sensory feedback from the own body, but with the next movement of the person performing the movement (Wolpert *et al.*, 2003). This extends the computational logic of internal models far into the realm of understanding intentions (Blakemore & Decety, 2001) and social cognition (Gallese, 2002; Iacoboni, 2003; Wolpert *et al.*, 2003).

To illustrate this hypothesis it may be instructive to go back to the example of a choreographer demonstrating a movement sequence to a dancer and interpret it in the context of forward and inverse models. When the choreographer performs the movement, along with the motor commands that innervate the musculoskeletal system, efference copies of the motor commands are fed into a corresponding forward model, which simulates the sensory consequences of the movement. These predictions can be compared with visual and proprioceptive feedback and used to update the movement in real-time or to improve its future performance. The possible role of forward models in perception becomes most apparent when we consider what happens the moment the choreographer watches the dancer imitate the movement sequence. The relevant inverse models are now run 'off-line', without acting on the musculoskeletal system, and their output is sent directly as input to the corresponding forward models. The output of the forward models is now compared with the movements of the dancer and in case of an error give rise to the 'feeling of what should be done and how' referred to by Jeannerod (1994; 1997).

It should be emphasized that, while attractive for reasons of its theoretical appeal, this framework is speculative. For instance, the present scenario does not specify how and where visual information is transformed into a format that can be used as input to a forward model. Iacoboni (2003) speculates that, when imitating a movement, the STS forms an inverse model of the movement to be imitated. It then sends a visual description of the movement to the mirror areas in the parietal and premotor cortex, which generate the motor commands necessary to perform the movement, a copy of which is send back to the STS as input to a forward model, which predicts the sensory consequences of the planned movement. However, there is no experimental evidence that the computations of the STS do indeed constitute an internal model, whether inverse or forward model or both. What's more, whereas Gallese (2002) suggests that mirror neurons in premotor cortex act as a forward model, an interpretation recently put forth by Schubotz and Von Cramon for ventral lateral premotor cortex as a whole[3], Blakemore and Decety (2001) propose the cerebellum as a possible repository of internal models. This need not be contradictory though, since internal models may be located in all brain regions having synaptic plasticity, as pointed out by Kawato (1999).

VIII: Two Hypotheses

I would now like to propose two hypotheses. First of all I would like to speculate that, when watching dance, the brain is submerged in motor imagery. If this hypothesis is correct when watching dance the observer is in a sense virtually dancing along. Above I have reviewed some lines of evidence in support of a role for motor areas in the perception of human movement. Using magnetoencephalography (MEG) it has recently been demonstrated that, when listening to piano music, pianists exhibit involuntary motor activity in the unilateral primary motor cortex (Haueisen & Knösche, 2001). Since this requires auditory information to be mapped onto motor areas it is not improbable to assume that watching dance also activates motor areas.

It is also *plausible* that watching dance involves a form of motor imagery. To state the obvious, with the exception of some avant-garde performances that question the assumptions of other performances, dance has a high movement density. Movements are at once fast and slow and often intertwine without any clear beginning or end. Even within a solo the next movement may already have started before a motion percept of the previous movement has been formed. It also frequently happens that some limbs are temporarily occluded from view or that a dancer briefly disappears behind another dancer. As argued above the brain will complement the movement by interpolating between the *positions* it

[3] Poster presented at the CNS meeting in New York, March 2003.

did perceive, which in case of body positions means choosing a biomechanically feasible path. Stevens *et al.* (2001) have provided tentative evidence that this task involves motor areas. In dance the brain has to work overtime in this respect, as it is confronted not only with a flood of movement, but also with movements not part of the brain's own movement repertoire. And just as actual movement when exercised to excess produces a state of arousal, so may virtual movement.

It would be interesting to directly test the hypothesis put forth here, for instance by recording the brain activity of someone watching a short dance sequence. Since this is likely to activate a variety of brain areas the results may be difficult to interpret. However, in principle the stimuli would not be very different from those used in biological motion studies or the experiments of Decety and Grèzes (1997) or Manthey *et al.* (2003).

In the example adapted from Jeannerod (1994; 1997) it was said that a choreographer watching a dancer imitate a movement 'experiences a strong feeling of what should be done and how', yet it was not explained how and where this *feeling* arises. Jeannerod also remarked that spectators who see a player miss a ball will experience a sense of frustration. This however depends which side they are on. The same event, hitting a target, whether in soccer, basket ball, golf or combat, can be a reward for one person and a punishment for another. Rewards and punishments are the technical notions for the positive respectively negative value ascribed to a stimulus. Rewards, like all sensory stimuli, can be both anticipated and unanticipated. At the level of neural processing single cell recordings from monkeys indicate that dopamine neurons respond to the delivery of an unexpected reward. What's more, if the monkey learned that a certain stimulus always preceded delivery of the reward, dopamine neurons would respond to the predictive stimulus rather than the reward itself. The output of dopamine neurons therefore appears to encode reward expectation. Another way of saying this is that dopamine neurons code for an error in the prediction of reward, the discrepancy between the occurrence of reward and the *predicted* occurrence of reward (Schultz, 2000).

Dopamine neurons are not the only neurons that respond to prediction errors. Neurons in the orbitofrontal cortex, a brain region that has been implicated in the processing of emotion (Rolls, 1999), have also been found to be activated when stimuli deviate from their expected value. Nobre et al. (1999) asked subjects to respond as quickly as possible to visual targets appearing at peripheral locations in the visual field. Immediately preceding the target a visual cue was presented that either correctly or incorrectly predicted the location of the upcoming target. This experiment is particularly interesting since the network of activation in the latter condition comprised regions associated with sensory prediction (the lateral premotor cortex, BA 6), attention (the posterior parietal cortex) and emotion (the orbitofrontal cortex). Janata and co-workers (2002) recently reported significant activity in the orbitofrontal cortex as eight musically experienced listeners performed a perceptual discrimination task requiring them to respond whenever they heard a note played by a flute instead of a clarinet, or when a note violated local tonality. Similar results had previously been reported in a task whereby participants were asked to respond to the degree of dissonance or consonance in the chords accompanying a melody (Blood *et al.*, 1999). Goel and Dolan (2001) finally found the orbitofrontal cortex (BA 10/11) to be associated with the appreciation of humour in the form of semantic and phonological jokes of the kind 'Why did the golfer wear two sets of pants?... He got a hole in one,' which are based on the juxtaposition of expectation and its resolution.

The function of the orbitofrontal cortex may therefore be to evaluate the reward value of environmental stimuli and to attach an emotional 'tag' to a prediction error. In support of this hypothesis in a fascinating fMRI study Anderson *et al.* (2003) recently showed that, with respect to olfaction, stimulus intensity was associated with activation in the amygdala, regardless of whether the odour was pleasant or unpleasant. Activity in the right medial orbitofrontal cortex by contrast correlated with pleasantness, but not intensity, while a region in the left lateral orbitofrontal cortex responded to both unpleasantness and intensity. Even though these results cannot be straightforwardly extended to other than olfactory stimuli, the fact that the same event, a goal in sports, as noted above, almost instantly brings about two opposite responses, suggests that a similar dissociation may underlie visual processing.

I would now like to propose the following scenario. When watching dance, to keep track of the movement, which may require a visuomotor transformation in order to move the eyes or head, the brain makes an internal prediction of its motion trajectory and dynamics. As argued in the previous section this task is described by the computational logic of forward models. A deviation from the expected path results in a prediction error. If the same movement sequence were to be repeated, the prediction error would be used to adjust the next prediction so that the visual representation of the motion trajectory and dynamics would be learned and the prediction error would converge to zero.[4] Since in dance the following movements are usually different, the brain will put a premium on increasing the likelihood of getting the next movement right. It does so by focussing attention on processing the motion stimuli. Interestingly dopamine neurons have also been proposed to play a role in the regulation of attention (Nieoullon, 2002) and could control a 'nonselective form of attention or arousal, which is dependent on uncertainty and designed to aid the learning of predictive stimuli and actions' (Fiorillo *et al.*, 2003). Furthermore, if within a sequence of movements the predicted path of a given section *corresponds* to the actual path, the orbitofrontal cortex awards a positive tag, if it *deviates* it awards a negative tag. The almost instant sigh an audience gives out if in a ballet a dancer suddenly falls, a radical deviation from the expected continuation of the movement, may be regarded as the physical manifestation of such a negative tag.

---

[4] The activity of dopamine neurons has been shown to resemble a class of reinforcement learning algorithms known as temporal difference models, in which prediction errors are used to adjust the model's parameters (Schultz *et al.*, 1997). What is most interesting in the present context is that the standard temporal difference model can be extended to incorporate internal models, whereby dopamine neurons code for the difference between the actual reward and the reward predicted by a forward model (Suri, 2001). This could, with the emphasis on could, bring the observed activity of dopamine neurons in line with the computational logic of forward models.

Thus in dance there is a double route to pleasure, one operates through the increased allocation of attention and by promoting a general state of arousal if a movement deviates from its predicted path, the other by rewarding the correct prediction of the motion trajectory. It follows that *without* the interplay of correct and incorrect predictions the brain may as it were 'lose interest'[5]: if the movements are too predictable attention wanes and we feel bored; if they are too erratic and unpredictable there is no positive reinforcement, which ultimately leads the brain to focus attention on something else. Anecdotal evidence for this hypothesis can be gathered both from audience responses and dance reviews.

Now dopamine neurons respond to errors in the prediction of reward, so the question is, where is the reward in watching dance? And how does the above scenario lead to the conscious experience of pleasure? It could be that the mechanisms that evolved to facilitate avoiding and catching moving objects are also activated in the absence of immediate threats or rewards. When pursuing a goal the final reward may only occur after considerable effort and so the brain may have evolved a motivational mechanism, which signals to the person whether he is on or off track, analogous to the childhood pastime whereby the distance from a hidden object is indicated by 'cold', 'warm' and 'hot'. There may also be an evolutionary advantage in correctly predicting the motion trajectory of a moving target (think of trying to hit it or having to avoid it). Even though this, of course, is only speculative, it means that correctly predicting the unfolding of a movement is by its very nature rewarding: after all, how could doing something *wrong* be rewarding?[6]

Everyday experience tells us that there is an asymmetry between positive and negative tags: we are not thrilled every time our perceptual expectations are met, even though we tend to be surprised if they aren't. On the other hand, we can ascribe a goal to almost any movement, for example which of two cars will reach the traffic lights first, and rejoice if our prediction is correct. Thus it appears that the emotional tag, when juxtaposed to a goal, gives rise to a feeling of pleasure or frustration, which is consistent with the distinction between emotions and feelings put forth by Damasio (1994; 2001). An emotion according to Damasio is 'a patterned collection of chemical and neural responses that is produced by the brain when it detects the presence of an emotionally competent stimulus' whereas feelings are 'the mental representation of the physiological changes that characterize emotions' in juxtaposition to the mental images that caused them (Damasio, 1994; 2001). This may also explain why we can be puzzled by our own emotions, for instance, when for the first time in our life, we attend a dance performance. The act of going to a theatre to watch someone perform a series of movements may be enough to establish the sort of goal that is a necessary but not sufficient condition for deriving pleasure from watching movement. Indeed, as I myself have witnessed, the same people who will cheer if a dancer performs on

[5] Properly speaking it is the person who loses interest.

[6] I would like to thank Ricarda Schubotz for drawing my attention to this possible explanation.

stage, will ignore her if she performs on the street in front of the theatre, an artistic and behavioural experiment I one day hope to formalize.

The idea that the elicitation, undermining and fulfilment of expectations underlie our affective response to dynamic stimuli is well established in music theory (e.g., Meyer, 1956; Tramo, 2001) and has also been proposed as a possible explanation for humour (Deacon, 1997; Goel & Dolan, 2001). Interestingly a recent fMRI study investigating the neural correlates of listening to Western tonal music showed a similar network of activation as has been hypothesized here, comprising the precentral gyrus (BA 6), inferior frontal gyrus (BA 44), the cerebellum, all three of which may be associated with perceptual prediction, and the orbitofrontal cortex (BA 11), in addition to regions associated with auditory processing (Janata *et al.*, 2002). A PET study whereby neural activity was measured as subjects listened to pre-selected music which elicited an intense emotional response, often referred to as 'chills' or 'shivers-down-the-spine', yielded increased activity in the ventral striatum and midbrain, both sources of dopaminergic signals, the orbitofrontal cortex, the medial supplementary motor area (BA 6), the insula and the cerebellum (Blood & Zatorre, 2001). These studies therefore not only add to the hypothesis put forth here, they also suggest that one reason music and dance go together so well is that both stimuli share the same neural mechanisms.

With respect to humour, Marc Jeannerod recently gave an interesting interpretation in terms of internal models of why we laugh when we see a clown pretending to make a huge effort to lift a seemingly heavy object, fall on his back. 'We laugh', according to Jeannerod, 'because we have created in ourselves an expectation by simulating the effort of the clown, and we see something that is very different from the expectation. The effect we see is at discrepancy with respect to our internal model, and this is the source of comedy' (Gallagher & Jeannerod, 2002).

IX: The Beautiful and the Sublime

The second hypothesis has a remarkable resemblance with the aesthetic theory of the German philosopher Immanuel Kant (1724–1804). In his analysis of aesthetic judgment Kant draws a distinction between the beautiful and the sublime. Beauty, according to Kant, is the feeling we experience and subsequently endow upon the object of our experience, when we discover a harmonious order, whether in art or in nature, that appeals to the mind's own drive towards creating order. The sublime also refers to a feeling, or perhaps better, a state of mind, but differs quite markedly from the beautiful in that it is characterized by disorder and internal conflict. Faced with an immense object, a skyscraper or a Boeing 747, or a powerful phenomenon like a hurricane, the faculty of imagination, in Kantian terms, is overwhelmed, unable to form an adequate representation of the phenomenon at hand. This in itself would not be much of a problem if it were not for the faculty of reason, which demands that every object be captured in its totality. It is at this moment of conflict that, again in Kantian terms, the subject realizes that even though it cannot represent this grand object, it can conceive of it as such. That is, the subject

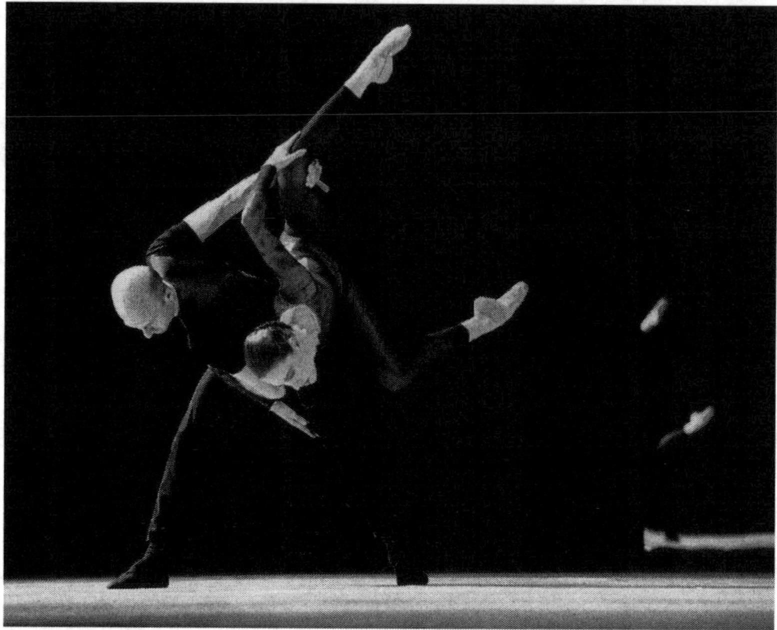

Figure 6. Before the brain has figured out what it sees, the dancers have already moved into a different body configuration. What remains is the memory of something seemingly impossible, here captured on a photo. Notice also the symmetry and extension of lines in the body. This is what, in combination with the fluidity and effortlessness with which the movements are performed, creates a sense of beauty, the virtuosity of the positions and movements fills us with awe and keeps our attention span at peak level. At the back of the stage a mirror doubled the image of the dancers. Jirí Kylián, *Click–Pause–Silence* (2001). Dancers: Stefan Zeromski and Elke Schepers. Photo: © Joris-Jan Bos.

becomes aware of the 'presence' of something that exceeds 'representation'. The sublime is the feeling which accompanies the resolution of this conflict. In a more contemporary terminology we could say that the sublime refers to a moment of intense awareness, following an initial moment of disorientation, during which attention peaks and the self is filled with awe.

It is this feeling or state of mind that can be said to characterize the thrill of watching dance. It is triggered by the failure of the brain to correctly predict the unfolding of a movement sequence and maintained by its effort, through increased attention, to keep up with the movement.[7]

Following the same logic we can also account for beauty, which may be defined as the feeling that arises when the movement trajectory as simulated by the brain, and the actual perceived movement as it unfolds in front of our eyes, coincide. In the event of human motion, this feeling is intensified if the perceived movement is performed seemingly without effort (Figure 6).

It follows that slow and fluid movements are more likely to be considered beautiful than fast, jerky movements. This prediction appears to agree

[7] Surprisingly it is not only neural processing delays that pose a challenge to the perception of (fast) moving objects, the human brain also takes a long time to respond to *slow* visual target motion (Kawakami *et al.*, 2002), possibly because it requires increased attention.

remarkably well with audience responses and dance reviews, although of course familiarity with a particular style or movement aesthetic influences the ability to predict the unfolding of movements, as can be concluded from the above. Here is, for instance, what one dance critic wrote when *Firstext*, a ballet by William Forsythe, was first performed in London at the Royal Ballet in 1995.

> [the dancers] have come up with astonishing ways of coordinating their limbs and timing their interconnections — but they are no match for Sylvie Guillem. She has the reactions of a racing driver, the hyper-agility of a computer-generated figure: hardly a pretty sight, but we're not here to watch pretty (Parry, 1995; my emphasis).

Within a proper conceptual framework the feelings experienced when watching dance can thus be called 'aesthetic'. It should be emphasized though that the distinction between the beautiful and the sublime made here is purely conceptual, and that actual experience is a mixture of a variety of feelings. The beautiful and the sublime are best seen as two moments of an otherwise indeterminate feeling or experience. Just how indeterminate and conflicting aesthetic experience can be is exemplified by the many words we use to describe our feelings, or indeed our struggle to find the words that carry exactly the right subtleties. This does not attest to the inadequacy of language, but rather to the complexity of the feelings involved.

XI: From Perception to Principles of Aesthetic Experience

Movement proper is only one aspect of dance and for a complete picture we will also have to look into other features of the visual system than motion processing. In their seminal paper, *The science of art: A neurological theory of aesthetic experience*, Ramachandran and Hirstein (1999) introduced eight, as they claim universal, laws of aesthetic experience. In short these laws are: enhancement of features that deviate from average; grouping of related features; isolation of a particular visual clue; contrasting of segregated features; a dislike of unnatural perspectives; perceptual problem solving, which refers to the pleasure the brain takes in deciphering ambiguous scenes; metaphor; and symmetry. The elicitation and resolution of expectations can be considered a principle specific to dance, music and cinema. Ramachandran and Hirstein continue where Rudolf Arnheim, in *Art and Visual Perception. A Psychology of the Creative Eye*, first published in 1954, had stopped, providing it with the neurobiological foundations made possible by recent advances in cognitive neuroscience.

The main law or aesthetic principle, according to Ramachandran and Hirstein, is what they call a peak-shift effect. By accentuating traits that are otherwise considered to be distinctive, perception can be intensified. What are characteristic features of women? Breasts, hips and waists. And thus, from Indian art to cartoons, manga and computer games such as Tomb Raider, we find women with large breasts, tight waists and pronounced hips. The visual system immediately recognizes these features as belonging to a woman and, because of the exaggeration, gives off a quicker and stronger than usual response. One problem with the peak-shift effect as defined by Ramachandran and Hirstein is that it may be difficult to apply to landscapes and still lives or the work of artists like Rogier van der Weyden. Another problem is that, as Wittgenstein (1953) showed in his *Philosophical Investigations*, it is at least doubtful whether there is such a thing as an essence or an essential feature. Rather than saying that an artist emphasizes essential features, I would therefore like to suggest that he emphasizes *some* features. Whether they are essential or not is irrelevant, they *become* essential in his work. Art is leaving out and emphasizing what remains, hoping that what is left is essential and says something definite, albeit fleetingly. Following this line of thought, dance can be seen as a reverse-engineered peak-shift effect in human movement perception.

The second principle suggested by Ramachandran and Hirstein concerns the grouping of related features. The brain constantly searches for patterns, structures and other regularities in the environment. Since patterns tend to signal an object or an underlying regularity that the brain can use to its advantage, it pays to be apt at recognizing patterns, even if from time to time it means being lured into seeing things that aren't there. It follows that by adding structure and pattern an artist can please the viewer or audience. The frame acceleration in the movie *Koyaanisqatsi* (1983), for instance, revealed the implicit patterns in traffic. In dance synchronizing the movements of limbs belonging to different bodies teases the brain into seeing a kind of moving hyperbody. Having patterns evolve in time creates tension and suspense, both synonymous with anticipation. Consequently it may not be necessary to perfectly organize everything in a ballet, since the brain of the observer will do part of the job all by itself. However, as in *La Bayadère* or Balanchine's *Symphony in Three Movements*, razor-sharp and perfectly synchronized lines create a peak-shift effect in pattern perception, at which Ramachandran and Hirstein (1999) and Ramachandran (2001) also hint.[8]

As to the other principles introduced by Ramachandran and Hirstein, symmetry of course is a principle that is very popular, both in classical ballet and

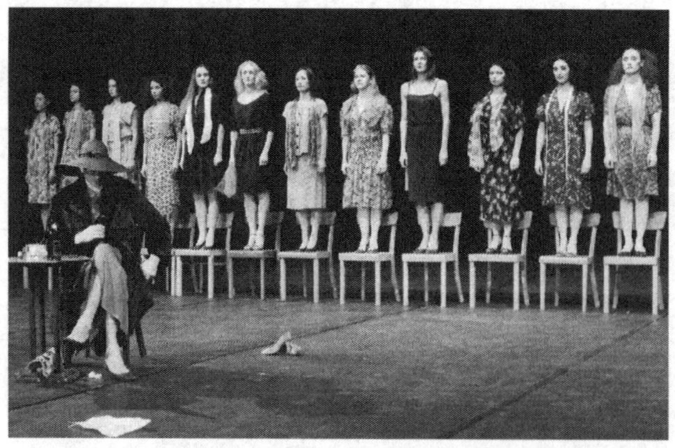

Figure 7.

Grouping and contrast. Count with me: group vs. individual, sitting vs. standing, front vs. back stage, hat vs. bare head. The scene and its subsequent unfolding are perfectly composed. Pina Bausch, *Viktor* (1986).

Photo: © Jochen Viehoff.

[8] I disagree with Ramachandran (2001) that introducing a postural peak-shift in a point-light display would create a stronger response than real movement and be more pleasing to watch. As argued above, point-light displays show how little information is needed to recognize biological motion. Enhancing the outcome of this process of subtraction is not necessarily a postural peak-shift. Distorting the point-light display may even make the movements more difficult to observe.

modern dance, whereas contrast can be achieved by the opposition of a group and an individual, male and female, left and right, front and back, global movements involving the whole body and local movements confined to one limb, etc. It should be noted that none of these principles specify how they are to be applied. Apart from that, the application of one principle may coincidentally

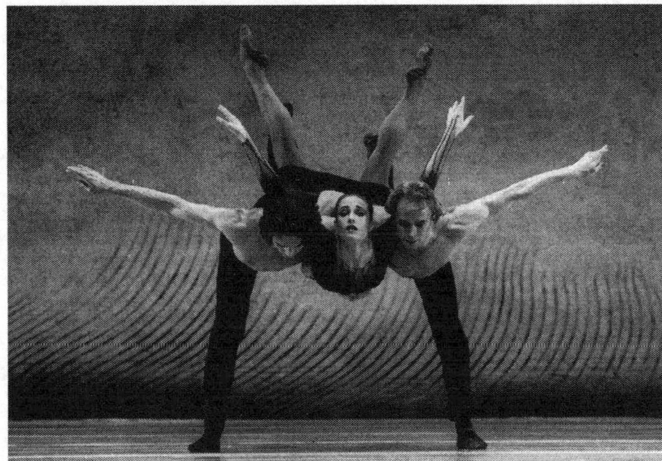

Figure 8.

Symmetry and perceptual problem solving. How do they do it? Notice also how arms and legs align and extend into space. Jirí Kylián, *Dreamtime* (1983). Dancers: Gaby Baars, Elke Schepers and Johan Inger.

Photo: © Dirk Buwalda.

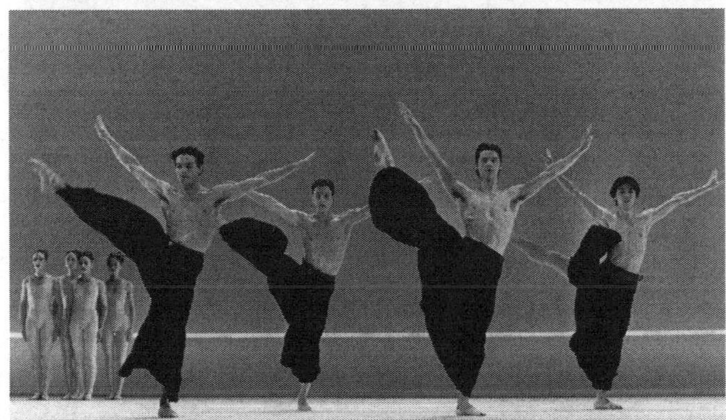

Figure 9.

Grouping, symmetry, contrast. Hans van Manen, *Große Fuge* (1971). Dancers: Netherlands Dance Theatre 2.

Photo: © Joris-Jan Bos.

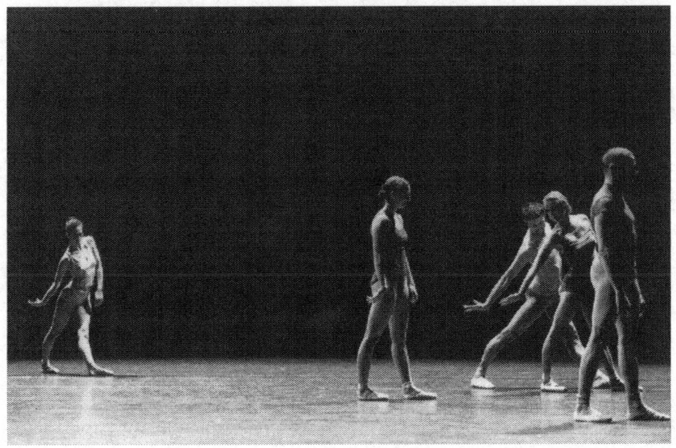

Figure 10.

Grouping in combination with isolation of a particular visual clue. The photographer clicked at the right moment, but the fact that he could make the photo means that the moment was already implicated by the choreographer. William Forsythe, *Workwithinwork* (1998). Dancers: Ballett Frankfurt.

Photo: © Dieter Schwer.

implicate another, which is why even a formal analysis like this remains ambiguous as to what produces which effect to what extent (Figures 7–10).

XII: Conclusion. The Nature of Dance and Choreography?

The feelings we experience when watching dance are the product of a myriad of sensory, cognitive and emotional brain processes. As such they are not accidental but depend on the properties of the brain processes involved in the analysis of sensory stimuli and on the interaction of expectations, associations and personal preferences as laid down in the brain. The present analysis has been limited to only one aspect, that of sensory processing, which itself has been largely narrowed down to one feature. Nothing was said about the functional organization of visual motion processing areas MT and MST in relation to dance, which many will no doubt see as a grave omission. However, I would be happy if as a result of the present article others will be encouraged to correct my errors and omissions.

In so far as sensory processing is concerned there is no difference between an audience watching the finished work and a choreographer watching a work in progress. A choreographer will continue adjusting a piece until every aspect has been fine-tuned to its desired perceptual and emotional effect. The feelings experienced by the audience are therefore in part prefigured by the choreographer. From this it follows that the feelings embedded in a choreography can be regarded as a function of the properties of the brain mechanisms that give rise to these feelings. I would therefore like to suggest that what is composed in a choreography is at once the material — movement — and the sensation it entails, first and foremost a sensation of movement, but extending to other feelings, events and contingencies.[9] Choreography could thus be defined as the two-way merger of movement and sensation, whereby movement passes into sensation and vice versa. When creating or rehearsing a ballet both choreographer and dancers are as much spectator as they are author and composer. It may be said that what are exercised during rehearsals are movements, but they are exercised to learn the moves as much as to craft the sensations they entail. The art of dancing is as much 'moving' as it is knowing the effect a movement sequence has on the

[9] The philosophically inclined reader may see in this hypothesis the resonance of what French philosophers Gilles Deleuze (1925–1995) and Félix Guattari (1930–1992) in *What is Philosophy?* argue is the aim of art, 'by means of the material, to wrest the percept from perceptions of objects and the states of a perceiving subject, to wrest the affect from affections as the transition from one state to another: to extract a bloc of sensations, a pure being of sensations.' (Deleuze & Guattari, 1994). Their notion of percept is somewhat idiosyncratic and differs from its common usage in cognitive neuroscience. For Deleuze and Guattari, percepts are no longer perceptions, any more than affects are feelings or affections. 'They are independent of a state of those who experience them' (Deleuze & Guattari, 1994), they have an existence of and in themselves. What Deleuze and Guattari are trying to say is that the artist has enveloped into the work of art the perceptual and emotional effect it has on the observer. Why are we moved, thrilled or delighted by a ballet, a novel or a movie? We are because what is caught and preserved in a work of art is not only an act or a situation, but also the emotional affect it entails. The interested reader is also referred to *Les Muses* (1994) by the French philosopher Jean-Luc Nancy who argues that a work of art opens up a realm of perceptual qualities beyond the traditional definition of the senses. For instance music is more than 'sound' and encompasses such qualities as melody, rhythm, timbre, tonality, consonance, dissonance and chroma.

observer. It is knowing where to put an accent, which phrase to emphasize, when to accelerate or when to release. Most of this knowledge is implicit and dancers like to refer to it as 'the body's knowledge', but this is just metaphor, it all resides in the brain. It encompasses the principles of perception and motor control and what is summed up by experience, the product of years of training, itself shaped by tradition, that is, the choices and aesthetic preferences of past generations.

In this article I have attempted to make explicit some of the implicit principles that govern the perception of dance and thereby its creation. Perception, of course, is only the springboard leading up to the judgement involved in creating a work of dance. Nonetheless a better understanding of the brain mechanisms involved in perceiving dance may help dancers and choreographers in fine-tuning their material to its perceptual effect, after all, this is what they already do, implicitly.

What is true for dance may also hold for cognitive neuroscience. As cognitive neuroscientists probe deeper into the neural mechanisms for recognizing human movement, they devise ever more complex and subtler motion stimuli. Effectively this means *choreographing* appropriate movement sequences. A meeting of cognitive neuroscience and choreography could therefore tell us more about both perception and dance.

In my own work I try to translate what I have here referred to as 'principles of perception' into techniques dancers can use when they are improvising (Hagendoorn, 2003). One such technique is based on the principles of a mechanism not discussed here: attention. Movements can be distinguished into *global* movements involving the whole body or an arm or leg and *local* movements involving a hand, shoulder or finger. Now whatever is global or local depends to a large extent on the preceding and subsequent movements. By switching between global and local movements a dancer can bring structure into her dancing and 'expand' or 'contract' the attention of the audience into space or onto a focal point. Indeed one could say that this is what choreographers do: they compose movements such that they draw and maintain attention. Several other of my improvisation techniques address the tendency of the brain to extrapolate a movement. Knowing this tendency a dancer can consciously play with it by either continuing a movement into its 'natural' or 'most likely' direction or by what one of my dancers once called 'going against the logic of the movement'. A simple example is to undo a body configuration not by withdrawing or re-moving the limb that gave rise to it, but by moving another limb. If this sounds complicated just stick your right arm between your legs and instead of removing your arm move your right leg around your arm.[10] Practice these techniques and surprise your friends and colleagues at the next party you attend.

The real test for any theory is whether it explains existing and predicts new experimental findings. In the present case these 'experimental findings' take the shape of ballets and dance performances. The problem with 'explaining' why something is 'good', or is generally considered as such, even when concentrating

[10] Examples can be found on my website, http://www.ivarhagendoorn.com.

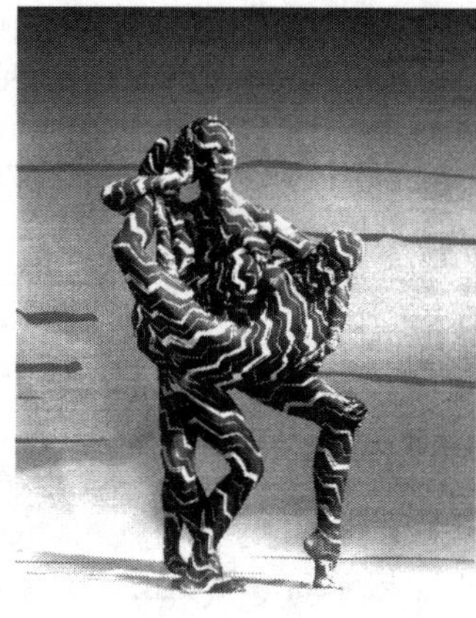

Figure 11

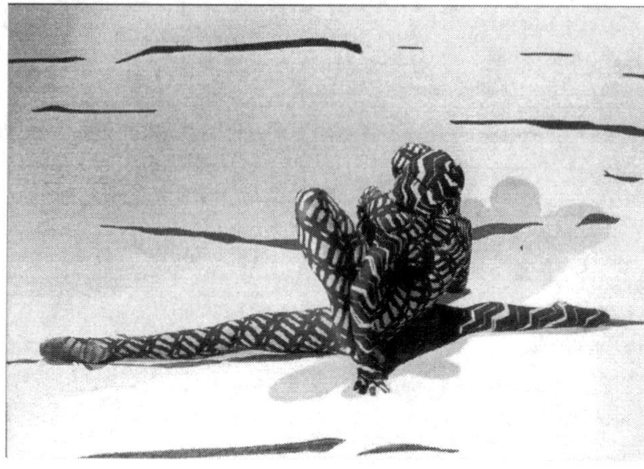

Figure 12

Figures 11 and 12. Find the dancer(s). Great photos, but on stage costumes of dancers and background merge, as they do in these stills, making it difficult to discern the movement. This, of course, was the original concept, but it worked much better than intended. Ed Wubbe, *Perfect skin.* (1993). Dancers: Charlotte Baines, Mariëlle de Jong and Rinus Sprong (l). Mariëlle de Jong and Rinus Sprong (r). Photo: © Hans Gerritsen.

on perceptual effects, is that there may be several competing and equally valid explanations. This follows from the fact that the aesthetic principles mentioned above can only be isolated in theory, in practice some or all combine and reinforce each other, as the illustrations show. An interesting aspect of the present account is that it also explains why some things *don't* work (e.g., Figures 11 and 12).

But, as I once heard a voice say in *The Vile Parody of Address*, a ballet by William Forsythe, 'Despite what I keep saying it doesn't have to be this way'.

Acknowledgements

I would like to thank William Forsythe, Michael Arbib and Ricarda Schubotz for many thought-provoking discussions about dance, the brain and aesthetic experience, and Sarah-Jayne Blakemore and the anonymous referees for their comments on an earlier version of this article. I would also like to thank the dancers of the Frankfurt Ballet, both past and present, for their friendship and hospitality as well as the dancers I myself have had the pleasure of working with, especially Andrea Mitschke, Raphaëlle Delaunay and Ester Natzijl.

References

Anderson, A.K., Christoff, K., Stappen, I., Panitz, D., Ghahremani, D.G., Glover, G. *et al.* (2003), 'Dissociated neural representations of intensity and valence in human olfaction', *Nature Neuroscience* **6**, pp. 196–202.

Ando, H. (2002), 'Human Brain Regions Involved in Visual Motion Prediction', *NeuroImage* S20054.

Arnheim, R. (1974), *Art and Visual Perception. A Psychology of the Creative Eye. The new version* (Berkeley, CA: University of California Press).

Beardworth, T., Bukner, T. (1981), 'The ability to recognize oneself from a video recording of one's movement without seeing one's body', *Bulletin of the Psychonomic Society* **18**, pp. 19–22.

Beintema, J.A., Lappe, M. (2002), 'Perception of biological motion without local image motion', *Proceedings of the National Academy of Science USA 99,* **pp**. *pp. 5661–3.*

Berry, M.J., Brivanlou, I.H., Jordan, Th.A., Meister, M. (1999), 'Anticipation of moving stimuli by the retina', *Nature* **398**, pp. 334–38.

Berthoz, A. (2000), *The Brain's Sense of Movement* (Cambridge, MA: Harvard University Press).

Blakemore, S.-J., Decety, J. (2001), 'From the perception of action to the understanding of intention', *Nature Reviews Neuroscience* **2**, pp. 561–7.

Blood, A.J., Zatorre, R.J., Bermudez, P., Evans, A.C. (1999), 'Emotional responses to pleasant and unpleasant music correlate with activity in paralimbic brain regions', *Nature Neuroscience* **2**, pp. 382–7.

Blood, A., Zatorre, R.J. (2001), 'Intensely pleasurable responses to music correlate with activity in brain regions implicated in reward and emotion', *Proceedings of the National Academy of Sciences* 98, pp. 11818–23.

Bonda, E., Petrides, M., Ostry, D., Evans, A. (1996), 'Specific involvement of human parietal systems and the amygdala in the perception of biological motion', *The Journal of Neuroscience* **16**, pp. 3737–44.

Carr, L., Iacoboni, M., Dubeau, M.-C., Maziotta, J.C., Lenzi, G.L. (2003), 'Neural mechanisms for empathy in humans: A relay from neural systems for imitation to limbic areas', *Proceedings of the National Academy of Sciences USA*, early edition.

Chaminade, Th., Meary, D. Orliaguet, J-P., Decety, J. (2001), 'Is perceptual anticipation motor simulation? A PET study', *NeuroReport* **12**, pp. 3669–74.

Damasio, A. (1994), *Descartes' Error. Emotion, Reason and the Human Brain* (New York: Avon).

Damasio, A. (2001), 'Fundamental feelings', *Nature* **413**, p. 781.

Dawson, M.R.W., Pylyshyn, Z.W. (1988), 'Natural constraints on apparent motion', in: Pylyshyn, Z.W. (Ed.), *Computational Processes In Human Vision* (Norwood, NJ: Ablex), pp. 99–120.

Deacon, T. (1997), *The Symbolic Species. The Co-Evolution of Language and the Human Brain* (London: Penguin).

Decety, J., Grezes, J., Costes, N., Perani, D., Jeannerod, M., Procyk, E. *et al.* (1997), 'Brain activity during observation of actions. Influence of action content and subject's strategy', *Brain* **120**, pp. 1763–77.

Decety, J., Grèzes, J. (1999), 'Neural mechanisms subserving the perception of human actions', *Trends in Cognitive Sciences* **3**, pp. 172–8.

De Duve, Th. (1996), *Kant after Duchamp* (Cambridge MA: MIT Press).

Deleuze, G., Guattari, F. (1994), *What is Philosophy?* [transl. H. Tomlinson and G. Burchell] (New York: Columbia University Press).

Dittrich, W.H., Troscianko T., Lea, S.E., Morgan, D. (1996), 'Perception of emotion from dynamic point-light displays represented in dance', *Perception* **25**, pp. 727–38.

Engel, A.K., Fries, P., Singer, W. (2001), 'Dynamic predictions: oscillations and synchrony in top–down processing', *Nature Reviews Neuroscience* **2**, pp. 704–16.

Fadiga, L., Fogassi, L., Pavesi, G., Rizzolatti, G. (1995), 'Motor facilitation during action observation: a magnetic stimulation study', *Journal of Neurophysiology* **73**, pp. 2608–11.

Fiorillo, C.D., Tobler, P.N., Schultz, W. (2003), 'Discrete coding of reward probability and uncertainty by dopamine neurons', *Science* **299**, pp. 1898–902.

Freyd, J. (1983), 'The mental representation of movement when static stimuli are viewed', *Perception and Psychophysics* **33**, pp. 575–81.

Gallagher, S., Jeannerod, M. (2002), 'From action to interaction', *Journal of Consciousness Studies* **9** (1), pp. 3–26.

Gallese, V. (2002), 'The Shared Manifold Hypothesis', *Journal of Consciousness Studies* **8** (5–7), pp. 33–50.

Gallese, V., Fadiga, L., Fogassi, L., Rizzolatti, G. (1996), 'Action recognition in the premotor cortex', *Brain* **119**, pp. 593–609.

Goel V., Dolan R.J. (2001), 'The functional anatomy of humor: segregating cognitive and affective components', Nature Neuroscience **4**, pp. 237–8.

Grèzes, J., Costes, N., Decety, J. (1998), 'Top–down effect of strategy on the perception of human biological motion: a PET investigation', *Cognitive Neuropsychology* **15**, pp. 553–82.

Grèzes, J., Fonlupt, P., Bertenthal, B., Delon-Martin, Ch., Segebarth, Ch., Decety, J. (2001), 'Does perception of motion rely on specific brain regions?', *NeuroImage* **13**, pp. 775–85.

Grossman, E.D., Donelly, M., Price, R., Pickens, D., Morgan, V., Neighbor, G. *et al.* (2000), 'Brain areas involved in perception of biological motion', *Journal of Cognitive Neuroscience* **12**, pp. 711–20.

Grossman, E.D., Blake, R. (2002), 'Brain areas active during visual perception of biological motion', *Neuron* **35**, pp. 1167–75.
Hagendoorn, I.G. (2003), 'Cognitive dance improvisation. How study of the motor system can inspire dance (and vice versa)', *Leonardo* **36**, pp. 221–7.
Haueisen, J., Knosche, T.R. (2001), 'Involuntary motor activity in pianists evoked by music perception', *Journal of Cognitive Neuroscience* **13**, pp. 786–92.
Heberlein, A.S., Adolphs, R., Tranel, D., Kemmerer, D., Anderson, S., Damasio, A. (1998), 'Impaired attribution of social meanings to abstract dynamic visual patterns following damage to the amygdala', *Society for Neuroscience Abstracts* **24**, p. 1176.
Heider, F., Simmel, M. (1944), 'An experimental study of apparent behavior', *American Journal of Psychology* **57**, pp. 243–9.
Heiser, M. Iacoboni, M, Maeda, F., Marcus, J., Mazziotta, J.C. (2003), 'The essential role of Broca's area in imitation', *European Journal of Neuroscience* **17**, pp. 1123–8.
Howard, R.J., Brammer, M., Wright, I., Woodruff, P.W., Bullmore, E.T., Zeki, S. (1996), 'A direct demonstration of functional specialization within motion-related visual and auditory cortex of the human brain', *Current Biology* **6**, pp. 1015–19.
Huettel, S.A., Mack, P.B., McCarthy, G. (2002), 'Perceiving patterns in random series: dynamic processing of sequence in prefrontal cortex', *Nature Neuroscience* **5** (5), pp. 485–90.
Hurley, S., Chater, N. (2004), *Perspectives on Imitation: From Cognitive Neuroscience to Social Science* (Cambridge, MA: MIT Press).
Iacoboni, M., (2003), 'Understanding others: Imitation, language, empathy', in *Perspectives on Imitation: From Cognitive Neuroscience to Social Science,* ed. Hurley, S., Chater, N. (Cambridge, MA: MIT Press).
Iacoboni, M., Woods, R.P., Brass, M., Bekkering, H., Mazziotta, J.C., Rizzolatti, G. (1999), 'Cortical mechanisms of human imitation', *Science*, **286**, pp. 2526–8.
Iacoboni, M., Koski, L.M., Brass, M., Bekkering, H., Woods, R.P., Dubeau, M-C. *et al.* (2001), 'Reafferent copies of imitated actions in the right superior temporal cortex', *Proceedings of the National Academy of Sciences USA*, **98** (24), pp. 13995–9.
Ione, A. (2001), 'Innovation in art and science. Reply to Semir Zeki', *Trends in Cognitive Sciences* **5**, p. 140.
Janata, P., Birk, J.L., Van Horn, J.D., Leman, M., Tillmann, B., Bharucha, J.J. (2002), 'The cortical topography of tonal structure underlying Western Music', *Science* **298**, pp. 2167–70.
Jeannerod, M. (1994), 'The representing brain: Neural correlates of motor intention and imagery', *Behavioral and Brain Sciences* **17**, pp. 187–245.
Jeannerod, M. (1997), *The Cognitive Neuroscience of Action* (Cambridge, MA: Blackwell).
Jeannerod, M. (2001), 'Neural simulation of action: A unifying mechanism for motor cognition', *NeuroImage* **14**, pp. S103–9.
Johansson, G. (1973), 'Visual perception of biological motion and a model for its analysis', *Perception and Psychophysics* **14**, pp. 202–11.
Kandel, S., Orliaguet J.P., Viviani, P. (2000), 'Perceptual anticipation in handwriting: the role of implicit motor competence', *Perception and Psychophysics* **62**, pp. 706–16.
Kant, I. (1987), *Critique of Judgment* [transl. W.S. Pluhar] (Indianapolis: Hackett).
Kawakami, O., Kaneoke, Y., Maruyama, K., Kakigi, R., Okada, T., Sadato, N. et al. (2002), 'Visual detection of motion speed in humans: spatiotemporal analysis by fMRI and MEG', *Human Brain Mapping* **16**, pp. 104–18.
Kawato, M. (1999), 'Internal models for motor control and trajectory planning', *Current Opinion in Neurobiology* **9**, pp. 718–27.
Kawato, M., Furukawa, K., Suzuki, R. (1987), 'A hierarchical neural-network model for control and learning of voluntary movement', *Biological Cybernetics* **57**, pp. 169–85.
Kohler E., Keysers C., Umilta M.A., Fogassi L., Gallese V., Rizzolatti G., (2002) 'Hearing sounds, understanding actions: action representation in mirror neurons', *Science* **297**, pp. 846–8.
Kourtzi, Z., Kanwisher, N. (2000), 'Activation in human MT/MST by static images with implied motion', *Journal of Cognitive Neuroscience* **12**, pp. 48–55.
Land, M.F., McLeod, P. (2000), 'From eye movements to actions: how batsmen hit the ball', *Nature Neuroscience* **3**, pp. 1340–5.
Latto, R., Brain, D., Kelly, B. (2000), 'An oblique effect in aesthetics: Homage to Mondrian', *Perception* **29**, pp. 981–7.
LeDoux, J. (1996), *The Emotional Brain. The Mysterious Underpinnings of Emotional Life* (New York: Simon & Schuster).
Manthey, S., Schubotz, R.I., von Cramon, D.Y. (2003), 'Premotor cortex in observing erroneous action: an fMRI study', *Cognitive Brain Research* **15**, pp. 296–307.
Martin, K.A.C. (2002), 'Microcircuits in visual cortex', *Current Opinion in Neurobiology* **12**, pp. 418–25.
McBeath, M.K., Shaffer, D.M., Kaiser, M.K. (1995), 'How baseball outfielders determine where to run to catch fly balls', *Science* **268**, pp. 569–73.

McIntyre, J., Zago, M., Berthoz, A., Lacquaniti, F. (2001), 'Does the brain model Newton's laws?', *Nature Neuroscience* **4**, pp. 693–4.

McLeod, P., Reed, N., Dienes, Z. (2001), 'What we do not know about how people run to catch a ball', *Journal of Experimental Psychology: Human Perception and Performance* **27**, pp. 1347–55.

Mehta, B., Schaal, S. (2002), 'Forward models in visuomotor control', *Journal of Neurophysiology* **88**, pp. 942–53.

Meltzoff, A.N., Prinz, W. (2002), *The imitative mind: Development, evolution and brain bases*. (Cambridge: Cambridge University Press).

Meyer, L.B. (1956), *Emotion and meaning in music* (Chicago: University of Chicago Press).

Nancy, J.-L. (1994), *Les muses* (Paris: Galilée).

Nieoullon, A. (2002), 'Dopamine and the regulation of cognition and attention', *Progress in Neurobiology* **67**, pp. 53–83.

Nijhawan, R. (1994), 'Motion extrapolation in catching', *Nature* **386**, pp. 256–7.

Nijhawan, R. (1997), 'Visual decomposition of color through motion extrapolation', *Nature* **386**, pp. 66–9.

Nijhawan, R. (2002), 'Neural delays, visual motion and the flash-lag effect', *Trends in Cognitive Sciences* **6**, pp. 387–93.

Nobre, A.C., Coull, J.T., Frith, C.D., Mesulam, M.M. (1999), 'Orbitofrontal cortex is activated during breaches of expectation in tasks of visual attention', *Nature Neuroscience* **2**, pp. 11–12.

Oram, M.W., Perrett, D.I. (1994), 'Responses of anterior superior temporal polysensory (STPa) neurons to "biological motion" stimuli', *Journal of Cognitive Neuroscience* **6**, pp. 99–116.

Orliaguet, J.P., Kandel, S., Boe, L.J. (1997), 'Visual perception of motor anticipation in cursive handwriting: influence of spatial and movement information on the prediction of forthcoming letters', *Perception* **26**, pp. 905–12.

Parry, J. (1995), 'Out on a limb', *The Observer*, 30 April 1995.

Pinto, J., Shiffrar, M. (1999), 'Subconfigurations of the human form in the perception of biological motion displays', *Acta Psychologica* **102**, pp. 293–318.

Ramachandran, V.S. (2001), 'Sharpening up "The Science of Art". An interview with Anthony Freeman', *Journal of Consciousness Studies* **8** (1), pp. 9–29.

Ramachandran, V.S., Hirstein, W. (1999), 'The science of art: A neurological theory of aesthetic experience', *Journal of Consciousness Studies* **6** (6–7), pp. 15–51.

Rizzolatti, G., Arbib, M.A. (1998), 'Language within our grasp', *Trends in Neurosciences* **21**, pp. 188–94.

Rizzolatti, G., Fadiga, L., Gallese, V., Fogassi, L. (1996), 'Premotor cortex and the recognition of motor actions', *Cognitive Brain Research* **3**, pp. 131–41.

Rizzolatti, G., Fogassi, L., Gallese, V. (2001), 'Neurophysiological mechanisms underlying the understanding and imitation of action', *Nature Reviews Neuroscience* **2**, pp. 661–70.

Robertson, L.C. (2003), 'Binding, spatial attention and perceptual awareness', *Nature Reviews Neuroscience* **4**, pp. 93–102.

Rolls, E.T. (1999), *The Brain and Emotion* (Oxford: Oxford University Press).

Schoenfeld, M.A., Noesselt, T., Poggel, D., Tempelmann, C., Hopf, J.M., Woldorff, M.G. *et al.* (2002), 'Analysis of pathways mediating preserved vision after striate cortex lesions', *Annals of Neurology* **52**, pp. 814–24.

Schubotz, R.I., von Cramon, D.Y. (2001), 'Functional organization of the lateral premotor cortex: fMRI reveals different regions activated by anticipation of object properties, locatio and speed', *Cognitive Brain Research* **11**, pp. 97–112.

Schubotz, R.I., von Cramon, D.Y. (2002a), 'Predicting perceptual events activates corresponding motor schemes in lateral premotor cortex: an fMRI study', *NeuroImage* **15**, pp 787–96.

Schubotz, R.I., von Cramon, D.Y. (2002b), 'A blueprint for target motion: fMRI reveals perceived sequential complexity to modulate premotor cortex', *NeuroImage* **16**, pp. 920–35.

Schultz, W. (2000), 'Multiple reward signals in the brain', *Nature Reviews Neuroscience* **1**, pp. 199–207.

Schultz, W., Dayan, P., Read Montague, P. (1997), 'A neural substrate of prediction and reward', *Science* **275**, pp. 1593–9.

Senior, C., Barnes, J., Giampietro, V., Simmons, A., Bullmore, E.T., Brammer, M. et al. (2000), 'The functional neuroanatomy of implicit-motion perception or representational momentum', *Current Biology* **10**, pp. 16–22.

Servos, Ph., Osu, R., Santi, A., Kawato, M. (2002), 'The neural substrates of biological motion perception: an fMRI study', *Cerebral Cortex* **12**, pp. 772–82.

Shiffrar, M., Freyd, J.J. (1990), 'Apparent motion of the human body', *Psychological Science* **1**, pp. 257–64.

Shiffrar, M., Freyd, J.J. (1993), 'Timing and apparent motion path choice with human body photographs', *Psychological Science* **4**, pp. 379–84.

Suri, R.E. (2001), 'Anticipatory responses of dopamine neurons and cortical neurons reproduced by internal model', *Experimental Brain Research* **140**, pp. 234–40.

Stevens, J.A., Fonlupt, P., Shiffrar, M., Decety, J. (2000), 'New aspects of motion perception: selective neural coding of apparent human movements', *NeuroReport* **11**, pp. 109–15.
Tramo, M.J. (2001), 'Music of the hemispheres', *Science* **291**, pp. 54–6.
Vaina, L.M., Lemay, M., Bienfang, D.C., Choi, A.Y., Nakayama, K. (1990), 'Intact "biological motion" and "structure from motion" perception in a patient with impaired motion mechanisms: a case study', *Vision Neuroscience* **5**, pp. 353–69.
Vaina, L.M., Solomon, J., Chowdhury, S., Sinha, P., Belliveau, J.W. (2001), 'Functional neuroanatomy of biological motion perception in humans', *Proceedings of the National Academy of Sciences* **98**, pp.11656–61.
Wittgenstein, L. (1953/19993), *Philosophical Investigations* [transl. G.E.M. Anscombe], (New York: Prentice Hall).
Wolpert, D.M. (1997), 'Computational approaches to motor control', *Trends in Cognitive Sciences* **1**, pp. 209–16.
Wolpert, D.M., Flanagan, J.R. (2001), 'Motor prediction', *Current Biology* **11**, pp. R729–32.
Wolpert, D.M., Ghahramani, Z., Jordan, M.I. (1995), 'An internal model for sensorimotor integration', *Science* **269**, pp. 1880–2.
Wolpert, D.M., Ghahramani, Z., Flanagan, J.R. (2001), 'Perspectives and problems in motor learning', *Trends in Cognitive Sciences* **5**, pp. 487–94.
Wolpert, D.M., Doya, K., Kawato, M. (2003), 'A unifying computational framework for motor control and social interaction', *Philosophical Transactions of the Royal Society London B* **358**, pp. 593–602.
Zeki, S. (2001a), 'Artistic Creativity and the Brain', *Science* **293**, pp. 51–2.
Zeki, S. (2001b), 'Closet reductionists', *Trends in Cognitive Sciences* **5**, pp. 45–6.

Erich Harth

Art and Reductionism

All thinking is done by our brains. They are also responsible for our feelings of love and hate, and for our ability to make and appreciate art. But there is a popular reluctance to credit the brain with some of these so-called *higher* functions. We have difficulty associating our appreciation of beauty with electrical impulses propagating down nerve fibres. We don't see love as residing in the organ that is hidden away inside the skull, where it sits, shaped like a boxing glove, grey, motionless, and seemingly inert. Instead, the icon of love is that fist-sized muscle in your chest.

We have learned that the three pounds of grey mass in the head is the most delicate and liveliest object we know of in the universe, and that below its quiet, non-assuming, exterior, billions of nerve cells are constantly tending to our many needs.

Four years ago, The *Journal of Consciousness Studies* devoted two issues to the question, how art relates to what goes on in the brain. In his editorial introduction, Joseph Goguen (1999) states that the larger question confronted in this volume is, 'what does it mean to be human?'

The lead article, *The Science of Art*, by Ramachandran & Hirstein (1999) listed eight *universals,* or 'laws of artistic experience', and assigned neural mechanisms to some of these. In a follow-up interview, Ramachandran (2001) responds to frequent criticisms of his paper, by (correctly) calling reductionism the 'most powerful strategy known to science'. He defines reductionism (wrongly) as 'explaining a phenomenon in terms of the behaviour of its constituent components', which in this case means the specialized signalling cells in the brain, the *neurons.* The same misunderstanding causes Donnya Wheelwell (2000), the harshest critic of the paper by Ramachandran and Hirstein(1999), to cite the word *reductive* along with such pejorative adjectives as *superficial, tawdry, debasing, offensive,* and *anti-human.*

I wish to address this very common misunderstanding in this brief note.

Correspondence:
Erich Harth, Department of physics, Syracuse University, Syracuse, NY 13244-1130, USA.
Email: harth@physics.syr.edu

Journal of Consciousness Studies, **11**, No. 3–4, 2004, pp. 111–16

Reductionism in Physics

Physics is often considered to be a difficult subject, mainly because of its extensive use of mathematics. At the same time it is conceptually one of the simplest structures, as it attempts to weave a seamless fabric of cause and effect that takes us from the smallest and most elementary to the most complex. Drastically different sets of phenomena are shown to rest on the same underlying principles and laws. The classic case of this *unification* brought together Newtonian mechanics and the theory of heat through the work of Clerk Maxwell and Ludwig Boltzmann. Here, the *macroscopic* science of thermodynamics is *reduced* to a statistical treatment of atomic collisions.

This type of reductionism, which takes us from the large (and complex) to the small (and elementary), is almost the rule in physics. It has to do with the fact that — with inanimate matter — causality works more strongly from the small to the large than in the opposite direction. Reductionism seeks out the roots of this causality. It is the nature of the atom that determines how bulk matter behaves, but there is little effect going the other way. We *understand* what makes an ice crystal by tracing its structure to the known properties of water molecules and the forces between them, and we understand the water molecule as resulting from the binding between atoms of oxygen and hydrogen. It would seem foolish to proceed in the opposite direction. The atom of oxygen in a water molecule is no different from one in the molecular oxygen we breathe, and the molecule of water *doesn't know* whether it is part of an icicle, a waterfall, or chicken noodle soup. If we wanted to, we could continue to *descend* to the constituent electrons, protons, and neutrons, and to the *ultimate* elementary units, the quarks and gluons. Because of the search for the smallest, elementary causes, I will call this process *atomistic reductionism.*

But reductionism does not always seek understanding of the large by looking for causes in the small. Large-scale structures *do* affect phenomena on a smaller scale: the mass of a chunk of U235 determines the local cascade of fission events.

Nagel's Definition of Reductionism

The Latin root *reducere* means to *lead back* (not necessarily toward smaller scales). The *reductio ad absurdum* demonstrates a faulty argument by *leading back* to the original assumption and showing it to be untenable. In physics, as we have seen, reduction most often seeks explanation in elementary events. But there are exceptions. What, then, do we mean by a reductionist explanation?

The philosopher of science Ernest Nagel, who defined reductionism (1961), sees it as the unification of two distinct fields of inquiry. One he calls the *primary science* which has the virtue of greater range of applicability, and a generally more elegant, intellectually satisfying, structure. According to Nagel, reductionism consists of expressing the laws and rules of the secondary science in terms of those of the primary science. In this way, the secondary science of thermodynamics was shown to be expressible in terms of the concepts and laws of the primary science of Newtonian mechanics. Often the elements of the primary science are smaller, more elementary; but not always. Nagel is careful not to state this as a general rule. The field of optics was reduced to the more all-encompassing electrodynamics. Both are macroscopic theories.

Nagel set down some formal, and very stringent, conditions for the process of reduction.

> It is an obvious requirement that the axioms, special hypotheses, and experimental laws of the sciences involved in a reduction must be available as explicitly formulated statements, whose various constituent terms have meaning unambiguously fixed by codified rules of usage or by established procedures appropriate to each discipline. To the extent that this elementary requirement is not satisfied, it is hardly possible to decide with assurance whether one science (or branch of science) has in fact been reduced to another.

Later, Nagel admits that this 'ideal demand' is not always realizable in practice. Certainly, Ramachandran's eight 'laws of artistic experience' fall far short of that ideal.

Causality in Living Matter

There is a quantitative difference between living and inanimate matter in the relative strengths of the up and down streams of causality. Just as in inanimate matter, so in an organism, the properties of molecules still determine what happens on a larger scale. The details of our bodily structure and its elaborate chemistry are determined by the microstructure of DNA. The control is delicate and extends over several orders of magnitude in scale. But here, unlike in inanimate systems, the stream of causal events from the large to the small is powerful and ever-present. Bertrand Russell remarked that 'No part of any living entity and no single process of any complex organic unity can be fully understood in isolation from the structure and activities of the organism as a whole'.

This kind of unity is only occasionally seen in inanimate matter. We mentioned the case of chain reactions in fission. Also, the integrity and size of a star are required to sustain the nuclear fires at its core. When they cease, we speak of the *death of the star*. An extreme case of *top-down control* was proposed about a hundred years ago by the German physicist Ernst Mach. He attributed the inertia of every object to its being embedded in a universe of objects.

In living things, the source of such *top-down* control is not confined to lie within the boundaries of the individual, but includes all of the ecological environment and extends backwards in time. Over millions of years, countless members of the species carried the DNA through their brief lives and, with their struggles for survival, helped shape the molecule to make the individual better able to evade predators, outwit prey, and achieve dominance among its own kind.

To *understand* the contents of a particular DNA molecule and their significance, it is therefore not sufficient to trace the physics and chemistry of its component groups and the valence bonds and hydrogen bonds that link them together, and how it is synthesized from its parent structure by codon–anticodon bonding. We must search the past history of the species and analyse how the environment *selected* the genes that gave today's individuals the best chance to live and reproduce.

Reductionism and the Brain

The human brain is shaped not just by the *bottom-up* influences of our genes, but also by a wealth of *top-down* effects of past experiences, including what we generally refer to as *culture*. Accordingly, what we perceive through our senses is determined not just by the 'upstream' transport of information — Ramachandraan refers to it as a sensory 'bucket brigade', but by a wealth of events stored and anticipated by the brain. What is more, almost any macroscopic physical event that involves the intervention by a human brain cannot be fully understood by just following the chain of cause and effect beginning with elementary neural events (Burns & Engdahl, 1998). There is no mystery involved in this.

To illustrate, consider this scenario set in a supermarket in the State of New York. Among the different items selected by the shoppers, there will be an occasional six-pack of beer. But not on Sundays. To explain that phenomenon, which is evidently controlled by the brain of the shopper, one could resort to one of the powerful new means of monitoring brain activity. An fMRI may show that certain activities in the motor cortex that have to do with the retrieval of six-packs of beer are absent on Sundays. The investigator might then be encouraged to look for a selective motor inhibitor with a seven day cycle. If we are lucky and find one, this will only raise more questions. The approach appears hopeless. But there is a simple and very satisfactory explanation: The State of New York has a law that forbids the sale of alcoholic beverages on Sundays. The shoppers know it.

The point I am making here is twofold: 1) To arrive at an *understanding* of a phenomenon, especially one involving the human brain, it is often necessary to go beyond *atomistic reductionism* and consider top-down causation: 2) A satisfactory explanation may involve *non-physical* factors, such as the knowledge of laws, in the above example, and the anticipation of being stopped at the checkout counter when in violation. Simply stated, events in the mind (knowledge, desires, etc.) 'can have the status of scientific entities', as Brown has stated (1999), that is, they can be part of an intellectually satisfying causal framework. This is not to deny the existence of a seamless chain of *physical* causes, but the details of these may be both inaccessible and uninteresting.

Beyond the Reflex

A possible division between what is understandable in brain functions in terms of elementary neural mechanisms (atomistic reductionism), and what is not, may be found in the different time scales on which these processes take place. Fast perception, including discrimination and selective motor function, sometimes called cortical reflexes, can be completed in just a few tenths of a second. Thus,

Thorpe and Fabre Thorpe (2001) have shown how a visual discrimination task involves propagation of information from the retina via LGN to the primary visual cortex, then along one of the branches of the visual pathway, to the prefrontal cortex, then from there to the pre-motor and motor cortex, then down the spinal cord to the motoneurons that enervate the appropriate muscles. In the animals tested, this whole process, from eye to action, takes place in something like two tenths of a second, from which the authors concluded that no feedback loops are involved. It is strictly *feed-forward,* or what Ramachandran characterized as the *bucket brigade*.

By contrast, the duration of relevant neural mechanisms in most thought processes, including the creation and contemplation of works of art, is many times the time required for neural signals to traverse the entire brain. We conclude that this involves sustained, reverberatory activity which touches on a panoply of stored information and releases a wealth of associations, memories and emotions. I want to suggest that such brain functions — like those of the supermarket shopper — generally do not allow a detailed analysis in terms of a seamless chain of microscopic neural events.

Reductionism and Art

We appreciate and enjoy artistic expression. Some of us also try to understand its roots and phenomenology. The approach by Ramachandran and Hirstein (1999) and Ramachandran (2001), in which the causes of artistic rules are sought in the microworld of neural mechanisms, while 'ignoring the complexities imposed by culture', offers little hope for any significant insight and invites the common criticism of what is sometimes called a 'reductionist approach'. That is why most of us derive greater intellectual satisfaction from a good art history (such as E.H. Gombrich, 1960), than from a theory of art that attempts to apply atomistic reductionism while neglecting the 'complexities imposed by culture'.

Is knowledge of our brain irrelevant in relation to art? Of course not, though Zeki (1999) overstates the case saying that 'no theory of aesthetics is likely to be complete, let alone profound, unless it is based on an understanding of the workings of the brain'. Many mental states have known correlates in neural activities. The science of seeing has much to tell us about how we make and view images. Vision in the human brain is a system of loops and recurrent pathways (Yingling & Skinner, 1977; Felleman & Van Essen, 1991) that link peripheral images and central symbols, the specific and the general, sensation and knowledge. I have stressed the significance of these structures in our use of *internal sketchpads* in reasoning and imagery (Harth, *et al*., 1987; Harth, 1993; 1995), and the natural extension of this process to the creation of external images (Harth, 1999).

Ultimately, a profound evaluation of artistic expression must involve both the world at large, which is its inspiration, and the human brain, which is capable of being inspired.

References

Brown, J.W. (1999), 'On aesthetic perception', *Journal of Consciousness Studies,* **6** (6–7), pp.144–60.

Burns, T.R. & Engdahl, E. (1998), 'The social construction of consciousness', *Journal of Consciousness Studies*, **5**, pp. 67–85.

Felleman, D.J., & Van Essen, D.C. (1991), 'Distributed hierarchical processing in the primate cerebral cortex', *Cerebral Cortex*, **1,** pp. 1–47.

Goguen, J. A. (1999). 'Art and the Brain' *Journal of Consciousness Studies*, **6**, pp. 5–14.

Gombrich, E. H. (1960), *Art and Illusion* (New York: Pantheon)

Harth, E. (1993), *The Creative Loop. How the Mind Makes a Brain* (Reading: Addison-Wesley).

Harth, E. (1995), 'The sketchpad model', *Consciousness and Cognition,* **4**, pp. 346–68.

Harth, E. (1999), 'The emergence of art and language in the human brain', *Journal of Consciousness Studies*, **6** (6–7), pp. 97–115.

Harth, E., Unnikrishnan, K.P., & Pandya, A.S. (1987), 'The inversion of sensory processing by feedback pathways: A model of visual cognitive functions', *Science*, **237**, pp. 184–87.

Nagel, E. (1961), *The Structure of Science* (New York: Harcourt).

Ramachandran, V. S. (2001), 'Sharpening up the "science of art". An Interview with Anthony Freeman', *Journal of Consciousness Studies*, **8**, (1), pp. 9–29.

Ramachandran, V.S. & Hirstein, W (1999), 'The science of art'. *Journal of Consciousness Studies*, **6**, (6–7) , pp. 15–51.

Thorpe, S. J. & Fabre-Thorpe, M. (2001), 'Seeking categories in the brain'. *Science*, **291**, pp. 260–3.

Yingling, C.D. & Skinner, J.E. (1977). 'Gating of thalamic input to cerebral cortex by nucleus reticularis thalami', in *Progress in Clinical Neurophysiology*, Vol. 1, ed. J.E. Desmedt (Basel: Karger).

Zeki, S. (1999), 'Art and the Brain', *Journal of Consciousness Studies*, **6** (6–7), pp. 76–96.

Joseph A. Goguen

Musical Qualia, Context, Time and Emotion

Abstract: *Nearly all listeners consider the subjective aspects of music, such as its emotional tone, to have primary importance. But contemporary philosophers often downplay, ignore, or even deny such aspects of experience. Moreover, traditional philosophies of music try to decontextualize it. Using music as an example, this paper explores the structure of qualitative experience, demonstrating that it is multi-layer emergent, non-compositional, enacted, and situation dependent, among other non-Cartesian properties. Our explanations draw on recent work in cognitive science, including blending, image schemas, and sensory memory, as well as on phenomenology. A hierarchical structure transformation based complexity theory is applied to obtain a non-linear dynamical systems explanation of qualia and emotion that respects phenomenological insights about time, including retention and protention. The complexity measure provides both a metric structure and a potential function, on spaces of pieces that are constructed using given elements and transformations, with weights that reflect their cognitive difficulty. However, the approach is not reductionist; using improvisation and the evolution of musical notation as data, we argue that situatedness, especially enactment and social context, are key aspects of musical consciousness.*

I: Introduction

This paper addresses issues in the philosophy, cognitive science, and sociology of music, clustered around the notion of *qualia*,[1] which (roughly speaking) are the qualitative aspects of conscious experience. In particular, we consider the structure of qualia, that is, their parts, and how those parts combine. Other concerns include contextuality, memory, saliency, time and emotion.

Correspondence:
Professor J.A. Goguen, Dept of Computer Science & Engineering, University of California at San Diego, 9500 Gilman Drive, La Jolla, CA 92093-0114, USA. *Email: Goguen@cs.ucsd.edu*

[1] The singular form of this word is '*qualé*'.

Sections II and III focus on the philosophy of music, with Section II.1 devoted to a very quick historical survey, and with Section II.2 exploring some notions of context and situatedness, including the 'fourth person' methodology that is used in this paper. Section III focuses on qualitative aspects of music, sketching some positions that philosophers have taken, including the separation of subjective from objective aspects, treating mainly the latter, and dubbing the former 'qualia'. We propose an alternative approach, supported by examples[2] demonstrating some curious properties of musical qualia, such as having heterogeneous components with multiple levels, combining non-compositionally, and appropriating temporally prior qualia (thus violating some naive ideas about temporal linearity of perception). These phenomena are interesting in themselves, and they also contribute to scepticism about the ontological status of qualia. Section III.1 discusses time consciousness, including Edmund Husserl's notions of fresh memory, retention, and protention.

Section IV.1 discusses some cognitive science of music, arguing for the relevance of recent developments in cognitive linguistics, including image schemas and blending. Section IV.2 extends these ideas to handle structure more effectively, while Section IV.3, which is the technical heart of the paper, develops a hierarchical structural complexity theory with transformations, which is used to model qualia, and then extended to construct a dynamical systems model of musical comprehension. Section V concerns the sociology of music, arguing that many phenomena discussed in previous sections, including qualia, have a significant social component. It takes as data an improvisation by Ryoko Goguen (which is documented in Appendix A), and some observations on the evolution of musical notation. Section VI draws some conclusions about cognitivism, and about the origin, structure, and study of emotion and consciousness.

The study of music is usually the study of representations of music, mostly scores, in fact, mostly formal properties of eighteenth and nineteenth century scores in the European classical tradition. But scores are not music, and digital recording technology makes possible much more detailed representations of a much broader range of styles, including those for which scores do not exist and/or would not be very helpful even if they did exist. However, this still leaves us dealing with representations. Actually, I do not think it desirable to banish representations; the problem is with the 'objective' third person approach usually taken to representations, rather than with their existence or their use. Our proposed alternative is the 'fourth person' method sketched in Section II.2, which requires *listening* to be taken much more seriously, including its social situatedness. We do this not only through close attention to our responses to music, but also in Section IV.3, by constructing *models* of listening, and comparing their responses with our own, with results from experimental psychology, and with relevant philosophical and musicological literature.

[2] The lecture version of this material featured short piano segments performed by Ryoko Goguen as illustrations.

II: Some Philosophy of Music

Following a brief overview of some traditional Western philosophical views of music, some alternatives based on recent developments in sociology and cognitive science are discussed.

1. Some traditional western views

The earliest influential views on music in the Western tradition come from Pythagoras, who claimed that music is essentially mathematical, based on his discovery that the ratios of the tones in musical intervals are simple rational numbers. Attempts to reduce music to mathematics are by no means confined to antiquity; for example, the great contemporary Greek composer Yannis Xenakis has written extensively (though not always coherently) in this mode. Returning to antiquity, Plato, in his *Republic* (Plato, 1993), wrote that 'music education is of paramount importance. More than anything else, rhythm and melody find their way straight to the deepest parts of our being,' which is consistent with what many musicians and educational psychologists think today. But Plato also seems aligned with many contemporary political conservatives, in wishing to 'clean our republic of depravity [in the arts] ... connected with vulgarity, insolence, madness, or other evils.' Thus, Plato was not a musical Platonist, believing that musical objects exist in some ideal realm, independently of humans; on the contrary, Plato's view is focused on the moral character of musicians.

A common view during the Romantic era was that good music is an accurate representation of the emotions of its composer. Although still common among the general public, this view is rarely accepted by professionals.[3] Perhaps the earliest persuasive arguments against it are due to the Viennese critic Eduard Hanslick (1986), who ascribed the emotional responses of listeners to analogies between dynamic patterns of music and emotions. Despite this apparently cognitivist view, Hanslick seems to have been a kind of Platonist, asserting that the beauty of music exists independently of any listener. Although Nelson Goodman is also interested in musical patterns, he identifies a musical work with its score and with the class of its authentic performances (Goodman, 1968). We argue against this 'score nominalism' by noting that scores often do not exist, and for styles such as ambient music, would make little sense even if they did exist. More recent thinkers, e.g., Peter Kivy (1980), take a cognitivist approach, defining music in terms of conscious patterns in the minds of listeners. Although music theory rather than philosophy, and written before the rise of cognitivism, the pioneering work of Leonard Meyer (1956) takes a cognitive approach, defining musical experience instead of music, and emphasizing structure, anticipation, and emotion, in ways related to those in Section IV.3 below. Interestingly, Meyer's three distinguishing characteristics of musical experience (Meyer, 1956, p. 23) do not mention sound, and (assuming the omission is deliberate) are so abstract as to encompass sequences of non-referential visual stimuli; I like

[3] Leonard Meyer (1956) suggests that this is in part because emotional responses often become denatured through intellectual analysis and professional training.

this, and note its consistency with some postmodern views that music has an inherent multimedia character.

Theodor Adorno (2002) takes a neo-Marxist social critical view of music, focusing on its roles in consumerism, class difference, etc. Despite this, one of his more philosophical statements, that 'music is gesture', embraces abstraction, and many recent composers, including Igor Stravinsky, support stronger views, in which music has only abstract musical content. Such views resemble those of modernist movements such as logical positivism, which attempts to reduce all 'meaningful' information to abstract logic, as well as with psychological behaviourism, and with 'eliminitivist' trends which attempt to delete all mention of consciousness (see Section III below). Modernist Anglo-American analytic philosophy in general downplays or ignores the qualitative aspects of experience, despite strong experimental evidence of its importance, e.g., for motivation and recall (Damasio, 1999). Section III.1 discusses some ideas from phenomenology, an approach that takes consciousness as central, and Section VI includes a critique of cognitivism.

What seems clear from all this is that music is one of the least settled areas of philosophy. And of course Western views are not the only ones available; deep and interesting ideas can be found in many non-Western traditions, including those of China, Japan, and Bali. Moreover, even within the Western tradition, much of value can be learned from such often ignored genres as avant garde jazz, Delta blues, hip-hop, folk music, gospel, and heavy metal rock.

2. *Context, situatedness, and embodiment*

Traditional philosophical approaches like those discussed in the previous subsection tend to decontextualize music. A common approach is to identify a musical object with some purely formal entity, which necessarily omits an enormous amount of relevant information. For example, no transcription, not even a spectral analysis, let alone a score, can capture all the nuances of an actual performance, which will include particular mediations by particular musicians, musical instruments, listeners, and rooms. The philosophical error that underlies such mistakes resembles that of mathematical Platonism, in which a transcendental ontological status is claimed for mathematical objects. Moreover, an emphasis on formal notation necessarily downgrades traditions, such as contemporary jazz, in which improvisation has great importance.

One approach to avoiding such problems is to reify the notion of context. But researchers in what we may call phenomenological sociology, for example, in ethnomethodology (Suchman, 1987; Garfinkel, 1967), emphasize that context is dynamically emergent from activity, rather than fixed, definable in advance, formally representable, or separable from activity. Thus one should speak of *situated actions*, or *occasions of action*, rather than of *contextualized representations*, because neither situations nor their contexts are specifiable, representable, stable, or separable from their actual uses. For example, when a contemporary composer like Toru Takemitsu quotes Debussy, even if some measures are identical, the effect is radically different from the original; and similarly when Hans Werner Henze quotes Cuban folk songs or Monteverdi. Even in a Mozart piano sonata, the second entrance of a theme can have a very different effect from the first.

Paul Dourish (2003) gives an insightful discussion of context in connection with current trends towards ubiquitous or 'context aware' computing; the problem addressed by this field is how to use powerful new sensor technologies to make computational systems more responsive to their users' physical and social settings, as those users move through and modify these settings. This has turned out to be unexpectedly difficult, and Dourish claims this is essentially for reasons like those described above.

Musical Platonism, score nominalism, cognitivism, and modernist approaches in general, all assume the primacy of representation, and hence all flounder for similar reasons. Context is crucial to interpretation, but it is determined as part of the process of interpretation, not independently or in advance of it. Certain elements are recognized as the context of what is being interpreted, while others become part of the emergent musical 'object' itself, and still others are deemed irrelevant. Moreover, the elements involved and their status can change very rapidly. Thus, every performance is uniquely situated, for both performers and listeners, in what may be very different ways. In particular, every performance is *embodied*, in the sense that very particular aspects of each participant are deeply implicated in the processes of interpretation, potentially including their auditory capabilities, clothing, companions, musical skills, prior musical experiences, implicit social beliefs (e.g., that opera is high status, or that punk challenges mainstream values), spatial location, etc., and certainly not excluding their reasons for being there at all (this is consistent with the cultural historical approach of Lev Vygotsky, 1985). More than that, participants *enact*, or actively construct, the context of musical experience, sometimes quite visibly so, as in rock concerts and karaoke parties, e.g., with shouts of encouragement or disparagement. David Sudnow gives an insightful ethnomethodological description of learning to play jazz piano, emphasizing the role of the body (hence its title, *Ways of the Hand*, Sudnow, 1979).

Most scientific studies of art are problematic for similar reasons. In particular, the third person, objective perspective of science requires a stable collection of 'objects' to be used as 'data', which therefore become decontextualized, with their situatedness, embodiment, and interactive social nature ignored. Moreover, any choice of a fixed dataset necessarily makes some arbitrary presuppositions about the nature of what is analysed. For example, typical textbooks on harmony deal exclusively with traditional Western classical music, e.g., Aldwell & Schachter (1989), as do typical artificial intelligence projects, e.g., Gerhard Widmer (2003) uses electronic transcriptions of performances of Mozart piano sonatas as data. In the visual arts, Ramachandran & Hirstein (1999) use optical illusions and classical Indian erotic art as data, while Zeki (1999) uses mainly Renaissance and early modern art, and Taylor (2000) classifies the drip art of Jackson Pollock using fractal dimension. Although certainly valuable in their own domains, one should be cautious about generalizing the conclusions of such studies, particularly for contemporary art, a major theme of which has been to question what art is, and to explore its boundaries (Goguen, 2000).

This paper draws on data from both science and phenomenology, in a spirit similar the 'neurophenomenology' of Francisco Varela (1996), as a way to reconcile first and third person perspectives, by allowing each to impose constraints upon the other. Such approaches acknowledge that the first and third person perspectives reveal two very different domains, neither of which can be reduced to the other, but they also deny that these domains are incompatible. It is important to note that phenomenology is *not* merely a more disciplined form of introspection, but rather attempts to enhance sensitivity to ordinary experience, without distortion caused by separation from its natural context.[4] The approach of this paper goes beyond that of Varela in the following ways: (1) it admits not just neuroscience, but also the third person perspectives of other sciences, especially evolution, as well as of critical studies in the arts and humanities; (2) it takes account of the 'second person' perspective of society, in the style illustrated by Section V; and (3) it places greater emphasis on the lived experience and personal transformation of scientists, technologists, critics, etc.[5] The intention of this approach is to advance scientific knowledge, technical practice, personal awareness, and the health of society. I propose to call it the *fourth person method* or *perspective*, since it encompasses the first, second, and third person perspectives, and because of an analogy with the 'fourth moment', which is described at the end of Section VI. This paper illustrates the application of this approach to music, in which all three perspectives play an important role. It seems to me that such an approach is quite natural, since it is what many of us do anyway, and hence it does not require any elaborate methodological justification. However, the fact that it challenges some deeply entrenched strictures of conventional science, does raise issues that require further discussion, although this paper is not the right place to do it.

III: Musical Qualia

Listeners generally consider the qualitative feel of music to be its essence and its chief attraction, emotion of course being a prime example. But as noted in the previous section, many philosophers ignore the qualitative aspect of experience, and some even deny its existence. When it is admitted that experience is not just perceptual and conceptual, a common approach is to 'bracket' or exile the qualitative aspects, and concentrate attention on aspects that are reducible to scientific analysis, which for music would include duration in milliseconds, intensity in decibels, and spectral analysis of timbres; the recalcitrant residua are then

[4] Since training in phenomenological observation is difficult to obtain, Buddhist meditation is often mentioned as an alternative, which moreover has a good track record in anticipating results from cognitive science (see Section VI).

[5] Our method also differs from the 'heterophenomenology' of Dennett (1991), though this discussion lies outside the scope of this paper.

dubbed 'qualia' and thereafter largely ignored. Under this view, qualia are what's left after the objective aspects are subtracted (a variant is that qualia are what's left after intentionality is subtracted — see Crane (2003) for a relatively clear exposition of this and related issues). The resulting residual category[6] could include non-conceptual associations, emotional content, etc. Examples from perception are often given, since what we perceive often differs significantly from what physical instruments reveal as objective. Perhaps the most commonly used example is the 'redness of red'; some others are the special qualities of a slowly bent major to minor third, the smell of onion, and the blueness of sky. Of course any piece of music is an example, although the philosophical literature tends to shy away from examples having strong emotional connotations.

A difficulty with qualia advocacy is that it tends to reify qualia, giving them independent existence as Platonic entities, and introducing a fundamental ontological distinction between subjective and objective aspects of experience. For example, David Chalmers (1996) claims there are two fundamental 'world substances', matter and information. It seems to me that such approaches are what Daniel Dennett (1988) argues against, although he is sometimes accused of arguing against the existence of qualitative experience as such. A genuine eliminitivist is Francis Crick (of DNA fame), who wrote 'You're nothing but a pack of neurons' (Crick, 1994, p. 3); see also Churchland (1996). One motivation for qualia is to challenge dominant reductionist paradigms of neuroscience, analytic philosophy, and experimental psychology. For example, Chalmers (1996) poses what he calls 'the hard problem', which is to explain qualia in the language of the hard sciences, his presumption being that this may not be possible. We argue that cognitive and qualitative aspects of experience are inseparable, even though first and third person approaches artificially separate them.

Whatever approach is taken, qualia are often considered to be *atomic*, i.e., non-reducible, or without constituent parts, in harmony with doctrines of logical positivism, e.g., as often attributed to Wittgenstein's *Tractatus* (1922). Though I have never seen it stated quite so baldly, the theory (but perhaps 'belief' is a better term, since it is so often implicit) seems to be that qualia atoms are completely independent from elements of perception and cognition, but somehow combine with them to give molecules of experience. For example, this view can be inferred from standard musical notation, where the qualitative, or 'expressive', aspects are given in natural language, typically Italian (e.g., *dolorisimo*, *fantastico*, *con spirito*), whereas pitch and duration are given in an abstract symbolic language.[7] Interestingly, tempo occupies an intermediate position, with both kinds of notation in active use, though musicians often interpret even quite precise tempo markings (in beats per minute) as if they were qualitative. Moreover, volume (intensity) markings are also intermediate, the notation used consisting of contractions of natural language (again from Italian) rather than

[6] Residual categories often have a special sociological flavour, as 'the other', which is partially unknown, partially feared, partially valorized, and always ambiguous. Examples less esoteric than qualia include racial and ethnic minorities, new diseases, and in some circles, consciousness itself.

[7] But this notation is somewhat iconic, in the technical sense of Charles Sanders Peirce (1965).

precise decibel levels. Contemporary classical music elaborates these conventions in numerous ways, with varying degrees of success, usually to give composers more control over performers; for example, the Italian contemporary classical composer Luigi Nono distinguishes numerous kinds of fermata[8] in some of his scores. It is easy to find examples of non-atomic musical qualia, having a feeling tone that are not simple combinations of the feeling tones of their constituents; this means that qualia are non-compositional. For example, a minor triad has a feeling that cannot be inferred by listening to its three notes on three sufficiently separated occasions.

The view of this paper, which is influenced by phenomenology, especially that of Edmund Husserl (1964) and Martin Heidegger (1962), is that qualia are not separable from experience, and that experience is primary. Given this view, it is convenient to use the word 'quale' to emphasize that we address this primary experiential dimension, rather than objective measurements, and to informally define '*qualia*' as conscious experiences having unity[9] and duration. This definition does not separate 'subjective' aspects from some other, allegedly 'objective' aspects: we could perhaps say that it views everything as subjective, but it would be much better to say that we consider the distinction meaningless at this level of analysis. This approach to qualia escapes criticisms like those advanced by Dennett (1988). Actually, our view of the nature of qualia is such that it is more appropriate to *model* the production of qualia than it is to define qualia; see the developments in Section IV.3.

Musical practice confirms that separation of quantitative and qualitative aspects is illusory, a matter of notational convenience and tradition, not an inherent property of music itself. For example, the same written phrase is performed in a very different way if it occurs in a Mozart score or a Count Basie score, and experienced listeners can easily detect many variants even within a single genre, as well as very many genres, realized for example through small variations in timing (e.g., Kansas City swing, Mersey beat, and Afro-Cuban bebop).

Here are some further curious properties of musical qualia: Small changes can have huge effects, e.g., changing one note of a traditional diatonic melody by a quarter tone. Also, the same quale may have components of many different kinds; for example, the uplifted feeling of the final chorus in the Gloria of Bach's *B Minor Mass* arises from a very complex interaction of melody, harmony, voicing/orchestration, tempo changes, key changes, and dynamics.[10] Moreover, temporally prior qualia may be appropriated (depending on saliency), thus violating overly simple ideas about the temporal linearity of perception; for example, in a rapid chromatic run, most notes will lose their identity, except (potentially) the first and last. Ambiguities are very possible, and are often exploited by composers, e.g., in false endings. There are also important large grain effects, such as

[8] These are rests of free duration.

[9] In the sense of being experienced as whole, even though possibly also experienced as having distinguishable parts.

[10] In music, 'dynamics' usually refers mainly to amplitude, even though all parameters are constantly changing.

similarity and contrast in the development section of a classical sonata. A particularly interesting phenomenon is when some material 'jumps' from being a sequence to being the operation of a process; my favourite example occurs in the third piece of Anton Webern's *Five Pieces for Orchestra*, opus 10, when a sequence of irregular percussive sounds is suddenly perceived as the erratic operation of some malfunctioning device, such as a broken clock; however, qualia within the cycles still retain individuality. Such phenomena demonstrate that qualia are far from being atomic or compositional, and hence far from being Cartesian, in the sense of Descartes' *Discourse on Method* (1956), which recommends analysing phenomena into 'as many parts as possible', each of which is 'clear and distinct', and then 'gradually and by degrees reaching towards more complex knowledge'.[11]

Musical qualia provide concrete counter-examples to certain philosophical positions, including Brentano's thesis on intentionality, which (under some interpretations, e.g., Crane, 2003) holds that every thought has an intentional component, some 'thing' that it is about. For, although some musical thoughts are 'about' something (e.g., Roman fountains), most are not, unless perhaps a very broad notion of 'about' is allowed, which includes intra-musical relationships, since most musical thoughts are only about other aspects of music. In addition, the end of Section III.1 refutes some of Hume's views on time (Hume, 1986). Section VI discusses some further disconfirmations and implications.

1. Time consciousness

The subjective perception of time, which is clearly crucial for music, has been investigated deeply by phenomenologists, especially Edmund Husserl, whose work makes explicit use of music, at least as a metaphor.[12] Husserl describes some important ways in which our actual subjective experience of the three-fold division into past, present, and future differs from the usual physical scientific analysis. He observes that the flow of time is a continual 'sinking away' into the past, and that experience can only occur in the present. Thus, the past can be experienced in the present, but in a different *mode* from that in which it was originally experienced. Husserl names this mode *retention*; it allows us to distinguish present experience from past experience, even though both are experienced in the now. In addition, while listening to music, we are constantly anticipating what may come next, a mode that Husserl names *protention*; this is what makes it possible for us to experience qualia of surprise. Note that protention is not symmetrical with retention: it does not provide a single 'image'

---

[11] Although Descartes did not treat qualia as such, nor did he name his smallest parts atoms, it seems fair to say that his clear description of his method, and his very impressive application of it in reducing geometry to arithmetic with Cartesian coordinates, were enormously influential for all subsequent philosophy of science, which often impose a stricter interpretation than was probably intended by Descartes.

[12] Given the methods of phenomenology, it is likely that Husserl actually used music in these investigations (Husserl, 1964).

of what is coming, but rather a complex network of expectations about what might come.

Husserl's observations on retention are confirmed by recent research on temporal cognition of music (Sams *et al.*, 1993), identifying a pre-conscious buffer of about 10 seconds. This buffer corresponds to what Husserl calls *fresh memory*,[13] and it differs from the more familiar short term memory and long term memory in that it is not conscious, i.e., it works whether or not we are aware of it (though conscious attention may make it work better). Of course, the traditional short and long term memories also play important roles in music, allowing us to recognize themes that recur in a piece, and pieces that we have previously heard. Note that reification through repetition of a sequence to a process works best if the sequence is short enough to fit into the fresh memory buffer, especially if there are continual variations, as in the third piece of Webern's opus 10. There do not yet appear to be any neuro-cognitive studies of protention.

For Husserl, 'objective moments' of time are not pre-determined, but rather, objects-in-time arise through processes of retention and protention. His goal was to discover the origin of time, and these processes are his answer. Our observations on musical qualia demonstrate that only certain salient configurations of objects and relations become so solidified, and that it is this solidification that creates apparent 'moments' in time; other less salient configurations are less solidified, and less likely to be retained or 'objectified' as events. Moreover, these moments, unlike those of physics, have duration, or are 'temporally thick', since they relate to real events which take time to process (the processing time is about one tenth of a second, but varies considerably with conditions). In addition, relationships that hold a salient configuration together are retained in memory with their salient constituents, and their qualia. Indeed, there is much experimental evidence that qualia, at least emotional qualia, function as 'indices' for the retrieval of memories, as well as playing important roles in many other mental processes, including reasoning, e.g., see Damasio (1994; 1999). Husserl does not discuss qualia, but our musical observations show that only salient perceptions become phenomenological events, and that only these have an associated qualia; we will argue in Section IV.3 that this has to do with protention and anticipation.

These observations also disconfirm aspects of David Hume's pointilist theory of time (Hume, 1986). Hume was right that time consists of discrete episodes, but wrong that these are discrete point-like instants, since musical qualia are clearly 'temporally thick', i.e., have durations that cannot meaningfully be broken into points; moreover, it is easy to find musical examples in which an event has ill-defined or gradual onset and/or conclusion (e.g., in group improvisations by the Art Ensemble of Chicago). Alfred North Whitehead (1985) is another philosopher in this category. His notions of prehension and concrescence, and his 'epochal' theory of time, have similarities with Husserl and with the theory of

[13] A usual term for it in psychology is 'sensory memory'. Note also that short term auditory memory is about 30 seconds (unless refreshed by repetition), and thus is quite distinct from sensory memory.

qualia in this paper. Nor should we fail to mention William James (1950), whose prescient ideas are further briefly discussed in Section VI.

Jun Tani (forthcoming) observes that during a sensory-motor learning task, a simulated robot with a certain hierarchical neural net architecture exhibited transitions between phases of coherence and incoherence in its anticipation of perceptions, where the resulting coherent chunks correspond to the structure of the task. Tani relates this to Husserl's phenomenology of time, in that the chunks are 'immanent' for the robot. Varela (1999) also studied some connections between cognitive neuroscience and Husserl's phenomenology of time, in part as an illustration of the neurophenomenological method introduced in Varela (1996).

IV: New Models for Understanding Music

This section suggests that we can better understand what it means to understand music by constructing models of *how* we understand music. Like all models, ours will be partial descriptions constructed for particular purposes, but also, since they are mathematical models, they can be more precise, and more falsifiable, than more traditional philosophical or musicological theories. Our approach is intended to apply to contemporary musical manifestations, such as noise music, digital multimedia productions, free jazz improvisation, music sculptures, environmental music, etc. Though more rigorous, the theory has many points of contact with the innovative work of Leonard Meyer (1956), particularly regarding the importance of anticipation in music, and can even be seen as an attempt to update Meyer's work; however, our approach also differs in some significant ways, particularly its technical machinery for handling structure and hierarchical complexity. There are of course many other mathematical approaches to music, e.g., see the collection (Assayag *et al.*, 2002}, though usually they are limited to classical music, and often have a Platonist philosophy.

1. Metaphor and blending

Research in cognitive linguistics by George Lakoff and others under the banner of 'conceptual metaphor theory' (abbreviated 'CMT') has greatly deepened our understanding of metaphor (Lakoff & Johnson, 1980; Lakoff, 1987), showing that many metaphors come in families, called *image schemas*, that share a common pattern. One example is BETTER IS UP, as in 'I'm feeling up today,' or 'He's moving up into management,' or 'His goals are higher than that.' Some image schemas, including this one, are grounded in the human body[14] and are called *basic image schemas*; they tend to yield the most persuasive metaphors. Such image schemas do occur in music; for example, an angelic choir with high voices instantiates the BETTER IS UP schema.

[14] The source UP is grounded in our experience of gravity, and the schema itself is grounded in everyday experiences, such as that when there is more beer in a glass, or more peanuts in a pile, the level goes up, and that this is a state we often prefer; therefore the image schema MORE IS UP, discussed in Lakoff (1987), is even more basic.

Fauconnier and Turner (1998; 2002) have studied *blending*, or *conceptual integration*, claiming it is a basic human cognitive operation, invisible and effortless, but nonetheless fundamental and pervasive, appearing in the construction and understanding of metaphors, as well as in many other cognitive phenomena, including grammar and reasoning. Many simple examples are blends of two words, such 'houseboat', 'roadkill', 'jazz piano', 'computer virus', 'classical composer' and 'melodramatic conductor'. To explain such phenomena, blending theory (abbreviated 'BT') posits that concepts come in clusters, called *conceptual spaces*, which consist of certain items and certain relations that hold among them. Such spaces are relatively small, transitory constructs, selected on the fly from larger domains, to meet an immediate need, such as understanding a particular phrase or sentence. However, we do not assume that they are necessarily the *minimal* such spaces needed to understand a given blend, since that can only be determined after the blend has been understood. Moreover, different blends may omit different elements of the input spaces, and it may also be necessary to recruit additional information from other spaces in order to understand a blend. The abstract mathematical structure of a conceptual space consists of a set of atomic elements together with a set of relation instances among those elements (Goguen, 1999b); of course, such a representation necessarily omits the qualitative, experiential aspects of what is represented (the qualia). *Conceptual mappings* are partial functions from the item and relation instances of one space to those of another, and *conceptual integration networks* are networks of conceptual spaces and mappings that are to be blended together.

The simplest blends[15] have the form of Figure 1, where I_1 and I_2 are called the *input spaces*, B is called the *blend space*, and G the *generic space*; the latter contains conceptual structure that is shared by the two input spaces.[16] A *blendoid* of I_1, I_2 *over* G consists of a space B together with conceptual mappings $I_1 \to B$, $I_2 \to B$, and $G \to B$. There may be many such blendoids, but relatively few are likely to be interesting. Therefore additional principles are needed for identifying the most interesting possibilities, so that we can define a *blend* to be a blendoid that is

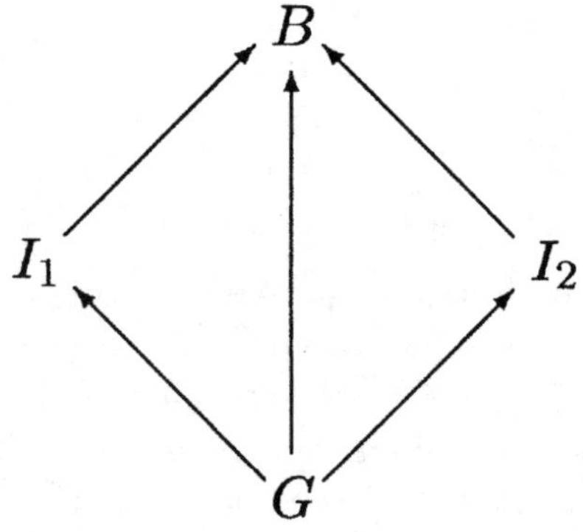

Figure 1. A Blend Diagram

[15] This diagram is 'upside down' from that used by Fauconnier and Turner, in that our arrows go up, with the generic G on the bottom, and the blend B on the top. This is due to a pervasive and natural duality between theories and models, in the sense that these terms are used in mathematical logic; see Section IV.2 for further discussion. Our convention is also consistent with the way that such diagrams are usually drawn in mathematics, as well as with the image schema MORE IS UP (since B is 'more'). Also, Fauconnier and Turner do not include the map $G \to B$.

[16] However, Goguen (1999b) uses the term '*base space*', because it is more descriptive of how this space is used in applications to user interface design.

optimal with respect to these principles. Fauconnier and Turner (2002, ch. 16) suggest a number of 'optimality principles' that serve this purpose, but they are too vague to be easily formalized. A tentative and difficult but precise mathematical approach is given in Goguen & Malcolm (1996), Appendix B, based on a modification of the category theoretic notion of 'pushout' (MacLane, 1971); this modification takes advantage of an ordering relation on morphisms, with respect to their quality, as discussed in Goguen (1999b). The intuition is that nothing can be added to or subtracted from such an optimal blendoid without violating consistency or simplicity in some way. However, there can still be more than one blend in this sense, as an example discussed below will make very clear. It should also be noted that this notion of blend easily generalizes to any number of semiotic spaces, and even to arbitrary diagrams of semiotic spaces and morphisms, for which there are many significant applications. Thus, the emphasis on double scope blending in Fauconnier and Turner (2002) seems somewhat out of place in algebraic semiotics, because its major applications typically involve multiple 'scopes' arising from multiple spaces and morphisms among them.

It has perhaps not been sufficiently emphasized in the BT literature that blending does not always give a unique result. For example, the following are four different blends of conceptual spaces for 'house' and 'boat': houseboat; boathouse; amphibious RV; and boat for moving houses. The last may be a bit surprising, but I once saw such a boat in Oban, Scotland, transporting prefabricated homes to a nearby island. There are also some other, even less obvious blends (Goguen & Harrell, in preparation).

The CMT view of metaphor associates aspects of one domain to another, and describes this association using a mapping, of which the target domain concerns what the metaphor is 'about'. On the other hand, BT views metaphors as 'cross-space mappings' that arise from blending conceptual spaces extracted from the domains involved. For example, the metaphor 'my love is a rose' arises from blending conceptual spaces for 'my love' and 'rose', such that the identification of the two items 'love' and 'rose' in the blend space gives rise to a correspondence between certain items in the rose space and the target love space. Such *metaphoric blends* are *asymmetric*, in that as much as possible of the target space is imported into the blend space, whereas only key aspects from the source space, associated with elements that have been identified with elements of the target space, are imported, e.g., sweet smell and attractive colour; moreover, names from the top space take precedence over those in the source space, so that relations in the source space become 'attributed' to items in the target space. Our approach differs from orthodox BT not only in that we allow many more kinds of structure in our spaces (as discussed below in Section IV.2), but also in that we do not first construct a minimal image in the blend space and then 'project' that same material back to the target space, but instead, we build the entire result structure in the blend space. Thus it is not the case for us that, in forming the blend, elements are preferentially omitted from the target space, only to be restored upon projection, as with the procedure described in Grady *et al.* (1999).

Since CMT has been mainly concerned with families of metaphors having a shared pattern, whereas BT has been more concerned with how novel metaphors can be understood, the two theories are compatible, and can both play a role in understanding complex language. This and related issues are discussed with many interesting details in Grady *et al.* (1999).

The conceptual spaces, mappings and blending of cognitive linguistics seem well adapted for treating many aspects of literature, as in Turner (1997), as well as some recent trends in art, including the (very aptly named) conceptual art movement, and with the conceptual aspects of works in many other styles, which are often designed to provoke conceptual conflicts or to force unusual conceptual blends. One important application is the combination of music and lyrics, as skillfully studied using cross-domain mappings by Lawrence Zbikowski (2002). However, the framework seems too restricted for studying blending *within* music, e.g., harmony, polyphony, polyrhythm, etc., because musical structure is inherently hierarchical, and hence cannot be adequately described using only atomic elements and relation instances among them. Understanding how a particular melody, chord sequence, and rhythm can work together requires close attention to the component notes, phrases, chords and beats, as well as to their subcomponents. Fortunately, it appears that the added generality of semiotic spaces and semiotic morphisms, as sketched in the next subsection, is adequate for such purposes. In the UCSD Meaning and Computation Lab, Fox Harrell and I have an experimental blending algorithm, which has generated novel metaphors, which in turn were used in generating poems (Goguen & Harrell, in preparation).

2. *Semiotic spaces and structural blending*

Before introducing algebraic semiotics and structural blending, it is good to be clear about their philosophical orientation. The reason for taking special care with this is that, in Western culture, mathematical formalisms are often given a status beyond what they deserve. For example, Euclid wrote, 'The laws of nature are but the mathematical thoughts of God.' Similarly, the 'situations' in the situation semantics of Barwise and Perry, which resemble conceptual spaces (but are more sophisticated — perhaps *too* sophisticated), are considered to be actually existing, ideal Platonic entities (Barwise & Perry, 1983). Somewhat less grandly, one might consider that conceptual spaces somehow already exist in the brain. However, the point of view of this paper is that all formalisms are constructed in the course of some task, such as scientific study or engineering design, for the heuristic purpose of facilitating consideration of certain issues in that task. Under this view, all theories are situated social entities, mathematical theories no less than others; of course, this does not mean that they are not useful.

Classical semiotics was founded by Charles Sanders Peirce (1965) and Ferdinand de Saussure (1976) in the late nineteenth century. Peirce was an American logician concerned with problems of meaning and reference, who concluded that these are relational rather than denotational, and who also made an influential distinction among modes of reference, as symbolic, indexical, or iconic (see footnote 7). Saussure, a Swiss linguist, wanted to understand how features of languages relate to meanings, and he emphasized binary features and denotational meaning. More recent thinkers, such as French literary theorist Roland Barthes (1968), combined and extended these theories, creating a powerful language for cultural and media studies, which in various versions has been called semiotics, semiology, structuralism, and finally post-structuralism. However, this body of theory lacks the mathematical precision needed for scientific analysis, and also does not address dynamic signs, social issues such as arise in collaboration, or the systematic mapping of signs in one system to signs in another; moreover, many versions tend towards a Platonist view of signs. Algebraic semiotics, which was originally developed as a foundation for user interface design, attempts to overcome these problems. We now give an intuitive introduction to the way that it treats the structure of complex signs, such as musical scores, books, and graphical user interfaces. Details omitted here can be found in Goguen (1999b; 2003) and Goguen & Harrell (2003); this theory originated in an early experimental study of multimedia learning (Goguen & Linde, 1984), and was adapted to user interface design in Goguen (1996).

A *semiotic system* or *semiotic theory* consists of: a *signature*, which gives names for sorts,[17] subsorts, and operations; some *axioms*; a *level ordering* on sorts having a maximum element called the *top* sort; and a *priority ordering* on the constructors at each level, where constructors are operations that build new signs from given parts. Sorts classify the parts of signs, among which data sorts provide values for attributes of signs (such as colour and size). Axioms are constraints on the possible signs of a system. Levels express the whole–part hierarchy of complex signs, whereas priorities express the relative importance of constructors and their arguments; social issues play an important role in determining these orderings. This approach has a rich mathematical foundation, e.g., Goguen & Malcolm (1996); Goguen *et al.* (1978; 2002), since a signature plus equational axioms is an algebraic theory, on which there is a large literature. A theory-based approach is preferable to a more concrete set-based approach, because it allows both multiple models and open structure, both of which are important for applications. The first means, for example, there are many ways to play a score, while the second means that additional structure (such as another movement) or constraints (e.g., on tempo) can be imposed at a later time. In addition, it is more natural to treat levels and priorities in theories. Conceptual spaces correspond to the very special case of semiotic theories where there is only one sort, there are no operations except those representing atomic elements and relations, and axioms only assert that a relation holds of certain constants.

Associated with any theory are all the structures (called *models* or *algebras*) that provide *interpretations* for the things in the signature of the theory: sorts are interpreted as sets; operation symbols are interpreted as functions on these sets, with constant symbols interpreted as elements; all in such a way as to satisfy the

[17] The word 'sort' is used to avoid the ambiguities of the word 'type'.

axioms in the theory. The theory is thus a formal language for talking about such models. For example, the space of models for a theory of books consists of all books having the structure specified in the theory. Models and theories are *dual* ways of looking at the same thing, since associated with any class of structures is a unique most restrictive theory that has the given ones among its models.

Mappings between structures became increasingly important in twentieth century mathematics and its applications; examples include linear transformations (and their representations as matrices), continuous maps of spaces, differentiable and analytic functions, group homomorphisms, and much more. Mappings between sign systems are only now appearing in semiotics, as uniform representations for signs in a source space by signs in a target space. Since we formalize sign systems as algebraic theories with additional structure, we should formalize *semiotic morphisms* as mappings of theories that preserve the additional structure; however, these mappings must be partial, because in general, not all of the sorts, constructors, etc., are preserved in real examples. For example, the semiotic morphism from the rose space to the blend space for the metaphor 'My love is a rose' (most likely) omits fertilizer and insects, while (possibly) preserving at least one of perfume and thorns. In addition to the structure of algebraic theories, semiotic morphisms should also (partially) preserve the priorities and levels of the source space. The extent to which a morphism preserves the various features of semiotic theories is an important determinant of its quality (Goguen & Malcolm, 1996). Semiotic morphisms can also be used to relate music to extra-musical elements. For example, letters of an alphabet can be associated with notes, so that sequences of notes can spell names, about which some information could be given, e.g., that 'BACH' is the name of a composer who likes such tricks.

The simple form of blend in Figure 1 applies just as well to semiotic spaces and semiotic morphisms. In this generalization, the diagram is called a *structural blend diagram* and *B* a *structural blend*. Moreover, this also extends to diagrams with any number of semiotic spaces, and even to arbitrary diagrams of semiotic spaces and morphisms, in which case one may speak of a *structural integration network*.

3. Structural complexity, protention and qualia

This section develops a model for the understanding of music, based on a complexity theory for hierarchical structures that are constructed through sharing and transformation.[18] The resulting theory appears to capture many features of musical qualia, as well as of Husserl's notions of retention and protention. As before, readers should be aware that applications of such a formalization should be grounded in social, cognitive, and embodied reality, that no special ontological status is claimed for the abstractions involved, and that it is not intended as a

[18] The theory was introduced in Goguen (1977), but research has advanced beyond what is described there, and moreover, some presuppositions of that paper no longer seem acceptable.

grand general solution to all possible problems in the philosophy, psychology, sociology, etc., of music, let alone of consciousness.

Traditional Shannon information theory (Shannon & Weaver, 1964) has played a modest role in music theory, but has been rightly criticized for its inability to move beyond local features (such as so called *n*-grams) to larger grain structures, such as sonata form. More fundamentally, a theory that is based on probability necessarily makes some very dubious assumptions about the nature of music, such as that there are discrete atomic events, having fixed probabilities.[19] Complexity based information theories, along lines pioneered by Andrei Kolmogorov (1965), are more attractive, since they can potentially encompass hierarchical structures, i.e., nested whole/part hierarchies. However, they seem unable to take account of features of memory like those discussed in Section III.1.

A key concept of Goguen (1977) is that of an analysis or 'understanding' of a system *S* drawn from some given family or 'space' of systems. Such an *analysis* *A* is a network of components, which yield *S* when combined, where each component in *A* is either atomic, a combination of other lower level components in *A*, or else a transformation of some lower level component in *A*, where the atomic components, the modes of combination, and the allowed transformations are fixed for the given family of systems, each with a numerical 'weight' which reflects its cognitive difficulty. For music, the allowed components might be represented as functions from a temporal domain into a domain of musical notation; the set of such functions forms a 'space' called the *state space*.[20] The *complexity* *C*(*A*) of an analysis *A* is the weighted sum of the complexities of the components of *A*, which in turn are also such weighted sums, and so on hierarchically, down to some atomic[21] elements, noting that reuse of an existing component or subcomponent will in general be weighted much less heavily than the first use. These weights are not probabilities, not even so called 'subjective' probabilities, because cognitive difficulty is only partially determined by prior experience. Finally, the *structural complexity* of *S* is the non-negative real number denoted *H*(*S*), which is the minimum of the complexities *C*(*A*) of all analyses *A* of *S*. The result of analysis is not just this number, but more significantly, yields a simplest hierarchical structural analysis *A* of *S* (though this analysis need not be unique); this analysis reveals not only small grain structures, but also large grain structures, as well as how all these structures are inter-related. Note that *H*(*S*) is *not* a measure of aesthetic preference, like that of George David Birkhoff (1933).

Two unusual features of this theory are that components and transformations have weights, and that some components may be transformations of other

[19] Though this is not, of course, to say that probability cannot be used as a compositional technique, e.g., John Cage, Yannis Xenakis, Gyorgi Ligeti, and others have done so; but it is doubtful that most listeners attempt to infer those techniques from what they hear, either consciously or unconsciously.

[20] The space can be constrained by axioms that disallow some functions; also, multiple performers (or parts) can be handled by letting *S* take values in a product space of notational choices.

[21] These need not be atomic in the sense of having no component parts, but only in the sense of being treated as a whole; for example, the opening four notes of Beethoven's fifth symphony are atomic in this sense for many listeners.

components. In its application to music, the weight of a transformation should be determined by its cognitive difficulty. Thus, for classical music, a repeat of a (not too unwieldy) segment should have a very low additional complexity, and a transposition of it by a fifth or a fourth should have very little more, whereas more cognitively difficult transformations, such as retrograde inversion, should have a greater weight. Note also that this theory is not limited to standard musical notation; on the contrary, entirely different dimensions could be notated for a particular performance, such as musician biometrics (e.g., heart rate and posture), or audience acoustic energy, and of course spectral analyses or other less detailed analyses of timbre.

We are working to implement an algorithm to compute the minimum complexity and associated simplest structural analyses of temporal sequences, based on techniques of dynamic and backtrack programming. We found an early prototype to be very inefficient in both time and space. However, since human music listeners, as an aid to understanding music in real time, try to anticipate what might come next, based on what they have already heard, and on culture-specific conventions, it is natural to incorporate such features into a modified model, and implement it for experimentation. Let us call this model the *Anticipatory Model*. It will have a memory hierarchy, with sensory, short term, and long term components, where the latter includes templates for culturally preferred structures. The associated weights should correspond to the ease of retrieving information from the various layers of memory. For items in the sensory memory buffer, these weights should be very low, while items in short and long term memory should have greater weight. Although these modifications would lead to an algorithm that is much more efficient and closer to human listening, the resulting structural analyses would be unlikely to have minimum complexity; however, they should be close to minimum when the parameters and templates are a good match to a style of music. Methods for specifying the state space of possible hierarchical descriptions of music are described in Goguen (1977), and are a special case of the semiotic systems described in Section IV.2. A subtle technical point that we only mention here in passing, is to reconcile the set-based sheaf models of Goguen (1977) with the theory-based algebraic semiotics of Section IV.2; hidden algebra (Goguen, 2003) can be used for this purpose.

The Anticipatory Model can be related to the phenomenology of music listening through several hypotheses: The first issue, which we call the *Main Hypothesis*, is that our hierarchical analyses, using psychologically and culturally appropriate components and weights, are understandings of works for appropriate audiences, and that a minimum complexity analysis gives a 'best' such understanding, along with a precise structural analysis of the work in question. Second, the *Qualia Hypothesis* says that the weight of a unit corresponds (inversely) to its saliency, and the saliency of a unit gives its strength as a quale. This can explain some of the peculiar phenomenology of musical qualia discussed in previous sections. For example, it explains how the qualia of subphrases can be absorbed into the qualia of larger phrases: this occurs when new units of low weight are formed by incorporating prior material of originally higher weight. *Hypothesis S* says that a large-grain unit of low weight is one that is expected and remembered; a unit of relatively high weight is surprising, and hence is also remembered (though a very complex unit may be too difficult to remember well). This agrees with Meyer's (1956) view that anticipation plays a key role. The relation of these hypotheses to emotion is considered in Section VI.

The determination of saliency is of course an empirical issue, and will differ not only from one culture to another, but also from one style to another, and even from one listener to another. Given adequate saliency data, appropriate components and weights can be determined for a model, which could then be run and compared with the judgements of real listeners (it is of course necessary to carefully design experiments for this purpose). The flexibility to choose components and weights is an important feature of this approach, and distinguishes it from doomed modernist attempts to define universal aesthetic measures, such as that of George Birkhoff (1933). Just to be clear, the description of components is done using semiotic spaces, and the composition of a musical piece from its components is a blend of those components, in exactly the sense of structural blending that is described in Section IV.2. The cross-space mappings that result from blending are intra-musical metaphors, especially those that arise from transformations.

The Anticipatory Model captures aspects of Husserl's phenomenology of time. For example, it has versions of both retention and protention, and the right kind of relationship between them. It also implies Husserl's pithy observation that temporal objects (i.e., salient events or qualia) are characterized by both duration and unity. Since it is not useful to anticipate details very far into the future, because the number of choices grows very quickly, an implementation of protention, whether natural or artificial, needs a structure to accommodate multiple, relatively short projections, based on what is now being heard, with weights that increase with elapsed time; this is a good candidate for implementation by a neural net of competing Hebbian cell assemblies, in both the human and algorithmic instantiations, as well as robots (as in Tani, forthcoming), and it also avoids reliance on old style AI representation and planning.

The mathematical properties of the hierarchical complexity measure are very pleasing: it satisfies all the major equations and inequations of the classical Shannon information theory,[22] even though it greatly generalizes that notion, as well as generalizing Kolmogorov style complexity notions. This generalization justifies using such terms as 'entropy' or (under a different metaphor) 'temperature' for $H(S)$, although the term 'density' might be preferred by musicologists. Moreover, colimits in the sense of category theory (MacLane, 1971) are involved in the composition of hierarchical systems (Goguen, 1977), in the blending of conceptual spaces, and more generally, of semiotic systems (Goguen, 1999b).

The *conditional complexity function*, denoted $H(S'|S)$, intuitively measures the *additional* effort needed to understand S' given that S is already understood

[22] However, these relations will only be approximately satisfied for the Anticipatory Model.

(Goguen, 1977), or the *novelty* of S' relative to S; it provides a model for the cognitive distance[23] from S to S'. In the case of music where S',S are temporal series, S might be an intital segment of S'. Protention attempts to predict an extension S' of S out to some limit δ. Given a piece using some fixed elements, transformations, and weights, a *complexity profile* is determined for the piece, $\varphi(S,t) = H(S^t \mid S^{t-\delta})$, where S^t denotes an initial segment of S up to time t, and δ is a buffer size; intuitively, φ is intended to measure the cognitive effort required to understand the structure of the piece at each moment t. Sharp variations in $\varphi(S,t)$ will correspond to the boundaries of important structural units. For example, in an AABA form, there will be a sharp drop in complexity at the boundary between the first and second A unit, and a sharp rise at the boundary between the second A and the B unit. Of course, the exact values will depend on what material is encoded in the description S of the piece, for example, whether micro-tonal and micro-timbral inflections are included.

Among many other concepts that can be defined within this theory, a measure of how much one structure S' resembles another S, given by $r(S',S) = H(S'|S)/H(S)$, seems relevant for thinking about improvisation, where S',S are segments over the same temporal interval, produced by two different improvisers, since r measures the extent to which one musician is following, or is being influenced by, the other. This *resemblance measure* is *not* symmetric, and hence is closer to our intuition for this application than the usual statistical concept of correlation, which is symmetrical. Two other important concepts generalizing classical Shannon theory, are the *mutual information* of S' and S, defined by $I(S',S) = H(S') - H(S'|S)$, and the *joint information* of S' and S, denoted $H(S',S)$, defined to be the minimum complexity required to realize *both* S and S'. Mutual and joint information are both symmetric in their two arguments; see Goguen (1977) for more detail, including proofs of these and other equalities and inequalities familiar from the Shannon theory. Another interesting notion for exploration is the complexity difference between the anticipated and the actual continuation of a segment, since this measures the 'surprise' of the actual continuation.

We intend to use the Anticipatory Algorithm in some computational experiments, to validate the assumptions behind it on real musical examples. We will begin with simple examples, and then building on that experience, gradually move to more and more complex examples. We have already studied some simple melodies (e.g., nursery rhymes) in Goguen (1977), and will work our way up, with (for example) Charlie Parker solos as an intermediate step, towards contemporary group improvised music, some qualitative aspects of which are explored in work with David Borgo (Borgo & Goguen, to appear), as briefly discussed at the end of Section V. It would also be interesting to analyse some of the examples used by Meyer (1956). This experimental programme should raise interesting

[23] Strictly speaking, it provides a quasi-pseudo-metric, since $H(S'|S)$ is not symmetric, i.e., sometimes $H(S'|S) \neq H(S|S')$, and in general it also fails to satisfy the property $H(S'|S) = 0$ iff $S' = S$, although it does satisfy this when restricted to series of the same length, in which case it gives a quasi-metric, which can then be symmetrized to yield a proper metric, $d(S',S) = max\{H(S'|S), H(S|S')\}$.

challenges for the theory, and thus stimulate its further development. Some of those challenges will undoubtedly involve qualia.

Our complexity based approach can be extended to more directly address dynamic aspects of music, by viewing the space of pieces as a dynamical system,[24] with conditional complexity $H(S'|S)$ providing a notion of distance (see footnote 20) and with the complexity profile φ as a potential or energy function, so that notions like curvature, basin of attraction, and saddle point become meaningful. Here are some examples of dynamical systems concepts that correspond to musical concepts: a basin of attraction is a region of low energy; a direction of motion (given by a tangent vector to a piece) is similar to the notion of 'gesture' as used in musicology; complexity is similar to what is often called 'density' in music; and phase transitions correspond to significant changes in the texture of segments. Note that the Anticipatory Model should be used, since the complexity measures are used to extrapolate along a given path, and that one can apply the same ideas to projections of the state space onto some lower dimensional space; with an appropriate choice of coordinates, this could give an interesting phase space for some class of pieces.

V: The Social Life of Music

Many writers have addressed the social aspects of music, among whom one might particularly mention Theodor Adorno (2002); of course, music is irreducibly social, and there is little reason to belabour this point here. However, it seems worth raising two issues which further illuminate some previous discussion in this paper. The first is improvisation, which draws on an essay by an improviser (Ryoko Goguen) on a particular performance (at which this author was also present), given in Appendix A. The second issue is the evolution of musical notation, with some emphasis on the values that this reveals.

Improvisation challenges notions of music as pre-existing ideal form, as score, or as a set of performances. Every improvisation is unique, and is uniquely tied to the particular environment in which it occurred. Thus, for the improvisation discussed in Appendix A, the location in Vienna, the start of the Iraq invasion, the atmosphere of a university seminar, the audience of advanced music students, and the sophisticated hosts, all played important roles in what was performed, how it was performed, and how it was received. Even exactly the same acoustic energy in a different environment would have been a different event, e.g., consider a cafe, a night club, and a street corner; and no doubt, each such change of environment would also change the performance. When a similar seminar was given at a different university in Vienna a few days later, already the feeling of the war was different, the audience was different (there were many

[24] This refers to a class of mathematical models of complex systems having origins mainly in physics, but with applications to many areas, including multimedia (Andersen, 1998). We will use terminology from this area; e.g., see Alligood *et al.* (1996) for a precise but relatively readable exposition. Due to their complexity, further details of this approach are deferred to a future paper; moreover, realizing its full potential will require non-trivial additions, such as extending the hierarchical complexity theory to continuous systems.

undergraduate arts majors), the room was different (crowded), and so of course, the performance was different.[25]

This has profound implications for qualia: the qualitative feeling of music (or of anything else) is not just cognitive, it is also social. As anyone sufficiently experienced with improvisation knows, qualia arise in interaction with other musicians, the audience, the room (its particular acoustics, e.g., its resonant frequencies), the nature of the invitation to perform, the history of other performances in similar circumstances, and more, much more. As Ryoko wrote, 'improvisation is interconnection'. In the technical language of Section II.2, qualia are situated, and that situatedness is not just cognitive, or even embodied, it is enacted: Qualia are enacted in particular performances; they cannot be separated from the dynamics of those performances, and from everything that contributes to those dynamics. Following Vygotsky (1985), we would especially mention material mediation (e.g., instruments, scores, gestures by musicians, and sound itself), and cultural, historical development, including the stylistic expectations residing in long term memory, which will of course change as listening experience accumulates.

Turning to the second topic, the notation of Western classical music has an interesting evolution, with a clear progression towards exercising more control over performers. Early music notation did not even specify duration, let alone amplitude, whereas some recent notation attempts to specify various aspects of intonation, although this can be very difficult, as the subtle inflections of jazz musicians such as Miles Davis make especially (and very beautifully) clear. Also, recall our earlier mention of Nono's fermata.

Notation is never value neutral: it involves choices of what to notate, that is, of what is important; even the choice *to* notate involves the value of exercising certain forms of control over performers. The situation is similar for transcription, and even for analysis, because an analyst must make value-laden choices of what to analyse, how to analyse it, and how to report the results, among other things. For example, spectral analysis involves the value choice of leaving out performer interactions. However, this does not mean it is necessary to become hopelessly mired in a swamp of relativity. One can always speak in one's own voice, from one's one values, and one can also compare various forms of analysis, and use that to help infer their values. One approach is to expose some details that are ignored by some form of analyses, but that are important for 'alternative' forms of music (note the highly value-laden use of the term 'alternative'!). For example, one might use closely timed sequences of spectral analyses instead of transcription as a basis for examining some fine details of pitch, intonation, etc. Of course any discussion of such data is itself a form of transcription, which again necessarily involves value choices.

---

[25] A reader who has pondered Section IV.3 might wonder how audience, room acoustics, etc., could enter into the Anticipatory Model to affect its 'listening'. The answer is rather simple: an audience can be transcribed as if it were one of the musicians, and related to other time-varying parameters by appropriate components and weights.

Similar considerations apply to structure, which also encodes values, since deciding what counts as structure is a value-laden choice. For example, any preference between symmetry and asymmetry is value-laden, and even what counts as symmetry is culturally determined. The historical trend towards ever more precise notation, and the concomitant downgrading of improvisation within the classical tradition, attest to an ongoing devaluation of qualitative aspects of experience, in favour of more quantitative aspects, and this correlates with some of the philosophical movements discussed earlier in this paper. Qualia represent a kind of rebellion against all this, manifesting not only in philosophy, but also as a kind of social movement (e.g., Mogi, no date). But despite all this, it should certainly not be thought that qualia are incompatible with technical progress or with mathematical models; as suggested in Sections IV.2 and IV.3, such techniques can be used to model qualia, and to explore their properties in greater depth.

An interesting hypothesis is that good jazz improvisation involves forms of large grain structure that differ from those of classical music, and if so, we can hope for our minimum complexity algorithm to make these structures more explicit; there are also some interesting small grain structures to be explored. Of course, the very idea of looking for such structures involves values. A related idea is to identify patterns of interaction among improvising musicians. A research project on this could make dual use of video recordings and the structural resemblance measure r introduced in Section IV.3, to try to determine social and musical contexts where one improviser imitates, supports, or challenges another.

Application of the dynamical systems approach to free improvisation are being explored in collaboration with David Borgo (Borgo & Goguen, to appear). A preliminary observation is that improvisers do not behave like particles in physics: they rarely linger in low energy basins of attraction, and often try to avoid even getting near them; they sometimes 'defy gravity' (or 'defy entropy', depending on the choice of metaphor) and jump to a higher complexity; and they sometimes surf an 'edge of chaos' for a bit, before veering off in a new direction; see also Borgo (2002). No doubt the implicit drama and sense of freedom involved in this is part of the attraction of the best improvised music. It makes intuitive sense that the dynamic development of music should involve anticipation, time consciousness, qualia, and complexity in fundamental ways, and one might go so far as to suggest that theories that do not address these issues cannot be adequate.

VI: Conclusions

This paper has attempted to explore the qualitative aspects of experience using music as data, and to place this exploration in the context of some relevant philosophical, cognitive scientific, and mathematical theories. Our observations have supported certain theories and challenged others. Among those supported are Husserl's phenomenology of time, Vygotsky's cultural-historical approach, and

Meyer's anticipatory approach, while Chalmers' dualism, Brentano's thesis on intentionality, qualia realism, qualia atomism, Hume's pointilist time, and classical cognitivism have been disconfirmed at least in part. All these positions were discussed in the body of the paper, often briefly, and sometimes without the technical terminology. 'Qualia realism' asserts that qualia have real existence (or 'ontological status'), and 'qualia atomism' asserts that qualia are indecomposable.

Among the new ideas in this paper, one might wish to highlight the discussion of context in music, the definition of qualia that avoids dualism, the application of structural blending to music, the Anticipatory Model of music understanding, the Qualia and S Hypotheses about the structure of qualia, the emphasis on social and value issues in music, and the research projects suggested by the resemblance measure and the complexity-based dynamical systems model.

Cognitivism was also mentioned several times but not discussed in detail. Like many other theories, cognitivism arose as a rebellion against the overly restrictive worldview of some prior theory, in this case, behaviourism, which tried to study behaviour without invoking mind. Cognitivism in the broad sense of taking mind seriously, is admirable, but in fact, most cognitivist research takes a much more narrow view, in which cognition is considered computation, so that body, emotion, and society are neglected, and the representation of knowledge emerges as a central problem. In its classic form, now called 'good old fashioned AI' or 'GOFAI', knowledge is represented in symbolic logic, an approach which the logical positivists of the Vienna Circle would presumably have endorsed. The conspicuous failure of this approach, e.g., in the Japanese Fifth Generation project, has inspired a number of biologically motivated refinements, such as neural nets and so-called artificial life, which do not, however, abandon the computational model, nor do they solve the problem of representation, which can be more precisely formulated as the *symbol grounding problem*, posed, but not solved, by Stevan Harnad (1990): the issue is how the symbolic representations used in a computational model can come to refer to the real world.

While the information processing models of cognitivism appear adequate for many aspects of low level perception, their exclusion (or cursory treatment) of embodiment, emotion, and society render them unsatisfactory as a theory of what it means to be human (Dreyfus, 1992; Varela *et al.*, 1991). In particular, embodiment, emotion, and society are certainly important parts of how real humans can be living solutions to the symbol grounding problem. The pervasive influence of cognitivism is presumably one reason why qualia in general, and emotion in particular, have been so neglected by traditional philosophy of mind, AI, linguistics, and so on. We may hope that this is now beginning to change.

Our observations on musical qualia undermine (computational) cognitivism. Descartes' *Discourse on Method* (1956) and nearly all subsequent methodological guidelines for scientific research, suggest that elements of any reasonable kind should combine in ways not too dissimilar from how atoms combine to form molecules. But we have seen that musical qualia behave very differently from that ideal, so much so that it is difficult to imagine rules for a 'calculus of qualia' that could adequately describe how qualia combine. This is in part because qualia are temporal entities arising through the operation of a complex, heterogeneous system[26] that is largely unconscious, including modules that can be roughly described as buffers, memories, pattern recognizers, anticipators, and emotional feedback.[27] Although such descriptions using an information processing metaphor can certainly be helpful, the underlying complexity makes it impossible to do realistic simulations, and unreasonable to expect simple laws to hold for qualia. Indeed, reference to cultural norms, historical conditions and precedents, private emotional states, public reactions, and so on, are usually much more helpful in understanding music than speculations based on neural architecture. It is typical of emergent phenomena, i.e., of levels of complexity that can only be seen at a larger grain of description, that they do not fully reduce to lower levels; in this sense, they are *emergent*. For example, laws about valence in chemistry are difficult to reduce to the level of quantum mechanics. Because of such complexities, it seems worthwhile to explore the simpler, higher level models of Section IV. However, this does not mean that valuable insights cannot be had from models at the neural level, as illustrated by the possible cell assembly model for protention in Section IV.3. On the other hand, the dynamical systems theory of Section IV.3 models qualia, emotion, etc., at a more abstract emergent, global level.

Anticipation has been well explored in some areas of cognitive neuroscience, including efference copy in perception, and Daniel Dennett has even written that 'all brains are, in essence, anticipation machines' (Dennett, 1991). However, cognitive science has paid little attention to the kind of abstract anticipation involved in music, let alone to its connection with emotion, and this paper also has so far said relatively little about emotion, which is after all the essence of qualia. Meyer (1956) argues for a 'law of affect', that emotion in music 'is evoked when a tendency to respond is inhibited', or in a less behaviourist language, when an expectation is not met. However, this approach seems too simple, as is suggested by the numerous qualifications that Meyer is forced to invoke in order to apply this law to particular examples. We believe that the Qualia Hypothesis given in Section IV.3 is more precise, covers at least as many examples, and is more amenable to empirical test, though of course much work is needed to validate these beliefs. It seems possible that some such approach could provide a foundation for a future musicology that is both more precise and more adequate for contemporary forms of expression.

There is a clear evolutionary explanation for the role of emotion in helping organisms predict events in their environment: To promote survival, moderate curiosity and discovery should be rewarded, while uncertainty should arouse interest, but should become unpleasant when sufficiently strong. Let us call this *Hypothesis E*. Combined with the Qualia Hypothesis, it provides a rough guide to the kinds of emotion in music, and the circumstances of their production:

---

[26] This is typical of 'systems' produced by evolution, through the gradual accretion of new features on top of older structures; it also suggests that the music of a highly developed alien species would almost certainly be mutually unintelligible (and even ugly) to humans.

[27] Some interesting suggestions about the neural bases of qualia are given in Northoff (2003).

emotion arises from relations in the 'now' among retention, protention, and perception; the right balance of novelty and predictability will maintain interest and pleasure, while too little novelty will cause loss of interest, and too much will become unpleasant.[28]

The hypotheses in this paper have other implications, but to avoid diluting its focus, we mention only the following. They explain why music exhibits a continual development of new ways to create and manipulate listener expectations, as older ways become too familiar; indeed, it is possible to view the whole history of music in this light. They also explain the pleasure that musicians (and many other professionals) take in learning new skills and further developing old skills. Another implication for learning is that test-oriented teaching can be anti-productive, because it can inhibit emotional response, prevent exploration, and dull curiosity.

Consciousness has so far been mentioned mainly in relation to time and qualia. Section II.2 and Section III argued that enactment not only constructs objects-in-time, but also their contexts, and even time itself, through processes that involve retention, and protention or anticipation. Section IV.3 argued that qualia are determined by variations of saliency, or in the model, of weight, as an intrinsic part of these processes, which it therefore seems reasonable to call *semiosis*. Both Husserl's time construction and our qualia construction yield conscious events, and the former can be seen as implied by the latter, although it should be noted that much of what goes on is unconscious, including much of anticipation and saliency determination.

This suggests that *all* consciousness arises through sense-making processes involving anticipation, which produce qualia as sufficiently salient chunks. Let us call this the *C Hypothesis*; it provides a theory for the origin and structure of consciousness. If correct, it would help to explain why consciousness continues to seem so mysterious: it is because we have been looking at it through inappropriate, distorting lenses; for example, attempting to view qualia as objective facts, or to assign them some new ontological status, instead of seeing segmentation by saliency as an inevitable feature of our processes of enacted perception. It also implies that much research on consciousness has been misfocused on peripheral issues, thereby producing misleading results. In addition, it suggests that music is an ideal experimental medium for the study of consciousness, since it allows us see fine details in the production of qualia, is subject to experimental manipulation in a variety of ways, already has a rich literature and discipline of training, and is amenable to model construction at several levels.[29] The Main, Qualia, E and C Hypotheses help understand the structure of consciousness: its segments are qualia, hierarchically organized by their saliency, with emotional tone determined by their resonance with protention. It will be surprising if the future does not see a great deal more research on time, emotion and

[28] But it should be noted that much contemporary music is exploring gradations of this unpleasantness.

[29] Note the consistency of these points with the fourth person method of Section II.2.

consciousness using music as data, as well as research on music using concepts from cognitive science and consciousness studies.

Many writers have advanced ideas that are consistent with and/or similar to the C Hypothesis; we now briefly survey just a few of these. The role of time in consciousness was stressed by William James, who described the 'specious present' as having 'a certain breadth of its own on which we sit perched, and from which we look in two directions into time' (James, 1950); James thought this was about 12 seconds, in close agreement with Sams *et al.* (1993). James also wrote that the stream of consciousness is 'like a bird's life, made of an alternation of flights and perchings', a very fine description of the chunking of consciousness, and he considered the role of anticipation, using the term 'tendency'. Martin Heidegger's ready-to-hand (Heidegger, 1962) is also related. However, the combination of consciousness and anticipation has received relatively little scientific attention until recently. Ralph Ellis and Natika Newton (1998) advance a hypothesis related to ours, but do not consider time, qualia, or their structures. Moreover, Ellis and Newton, and many others, including Rodney Cotterill (2001), Rodolfo Llinás, and Gerald Edelman, limit their consideration of anticipation to sensory-motor systems, which excludes the case of music.

An insightful paper of Newton (2001) comes even closer, suggesting a naturalistic explanation for the emergence of consciousness, in which brain processes provide a physical basis for the mysterious and ineffable character of qualia, without claiming that they actually exist. Newton suggests that consciousness emerges to handle the novelty that results from blending incompatible components. However, her notion of blending is binding, whereas our notion is a precise mathematical formalization (Goguen *et al.*, 1978) of a structural generalization of the cognitive linguistic notion of blending.[30] Moreover, we do not agree with Newton (2001) that the blended items must be incompatible, claiming instead that more complex blends produce more conscious qualia. For us, ineffability arises because qualia have hierarchically structured parts with variable saliency, while temporal thickness results from the concurrent operation of perception, retention, and protention, whereas Newton attributes both ineffability and temporal thickness to the blending of incompatibles.

Although enthusiastic about anticipation, Dennett does little with it; moreover, his 'heterophenomenology' and his arguments against qualia distance him from consciousness almost as far as the behaviourists put themselves. Gibson's ecological perception is one early theory using anticipation in a serious way (Gibson, 1977; 1979). There is also work on anticipation in the semiotic tradition by Mihai Nadin (1991). In my opinion, the insights of Husserl and James are the most suggestive. Husserl achieves a stunning depth of analysis of the phenomenology of time, while James exhibits a remarkable breadth and clarity of vision, in both cases without benefit of the enormous recent advances in cognitive science. But it should also be noted that many of the same insights can be found centuries earlier in the Buddhist meditation literature. Our approach differs from all these

[30] But under the perhaps presumptive claim that structural blending explicates binding, our notion can be seen as an explication of hers.

in its grounding in the Main Hypothesis, with its hierarchical networks of weighted, shared, and transformed components, and in the precision that that model can confer on predictions that are made using the other hypotheses.

I wish to close this essay by extending a discussion about art and the sacred begun in Goguen (1999a). The present paper has argued that consciousness, qualia, and the phenomenal world of experience are produced by complex and largely unconscious processes, but it has not pointed out that this undermines belief in the existence of an independent unified 'self'. Our hypotheses do not imply that people do not exist, or that the appearance of a unified independent self does not exist, but rather that the unity and the independence have an illusory character. We are complex, dependent beings, continually recreated as 'conscious' through salient events, determined as such in a complicated process that is cultural and historical, as well as cognitive. Similarly, our experience of the world is 'manufactured' by this process, a complex and ever shifting mosaic of qualia of various textures and sizes; this does not imply that there is no 'real world', but rather that our access to it is achieved in a very complex and incomplete way. Similar insights were expressed nearly two thousand years ago by the Indian philosopher-sage Nagarjuna (1995), although of course using a different language, that of Mahayana Buddhism. More recent thinkers like Dogen (1992) and Keiji Nishitani (1982), among many others, have also expressed similar insights.

My meditation teacher, Chögyam Trungpa Rinpoche, said that the purpose of art is to show our non-existence in the world. It seems to me that close attention to music, and to how we hear it, can give precisely this insight. The experience can be vivid, clear, and deeply moving. Indeed, it can be an experience of the 'fourth moment' (*dus bzhi mnym pa chen po* in Tibetan), an experience of time suspended, of being not past, present, or future, but a limitless space of great equanimity that unifies and transcends all three, and in which both self and world disappear. This space is the abode of the sacred.

Acknowledgements

I thank Dr Ken Mogi of Sony for his suggestion to write up my observations on musical qualia, Dr Volkmar Klien and Prof Dieter Kaufmann of the Performing Arts University of Vienna, and Prof Robert Trappl of the University of Vienna, for their hospitality during a visit in which some of these ideas were given in preliminary form, Prof Mitsu Okada for inviting a lecture on this subject at Keio University, Profs David Borgo and George Lewis of UCSD, and Drs Erik Myin and Volkmar Klien for valuable comments and encouragement, Profs Chaya Czernowin and Chinary Ung of UCSD for putting up with a very early version in their class on metaphor and music, and Dr Jun Tani of the Brain Science Institute (Japan) for some stimulating conversations on dynamical systems and consciousness. Last but far from least, I thank my wife, Ryoko Amadee Goguen, for her help in performing this paper, and for immersing me in musical projects.

Appendix A: Improvisation Notes

The following gives a performer's view of one particular improvisation. It is used as data in the body of this paper.

> On 20 March 2003, the day the Iraq war began, I performed an improvisation at the University of Vienna (and again on 28 March, at the Performing Arts University of Vienna), in connection with lectures by my husband on some cognitive and philosophical aspects of music. Part of the lecture showed how the same 'middle A' could be perceived totally differently, depending on its context.
>
> I decided to use this same note, and some of those contexts, as a basis for improvisation, not forgetting Vienna, a city that experienced much pain as well as much great music in its history, and of course being very aware of the war, and thinking how everything is connected, the performer, the audience, the city, the war, the sadness and pain, the whole of history.
>
> Middle A is a beginning sound, and on a good piano (such as the Bosendorfer grand they gave me for practice) you can hear its many colours hanging in space, carrying the pain of numerous lives, from Mozart to Webern, and now poor Turkish immigrant workers, and Iraqi civilians. But you can also hear hope and love.
>
> Low A has an angry sound, an aggressive wish to control, a cynical view — but still with pain inside of it, and the possibility of understanding.
>
> High A is like a scream, a loved one lost in the war, frustration, need; or a whisper, even a caress.
>
> Every note has its overtones, and they are all connected, as are all of us, middle, high, low, hope, fear, pain, and love.
>
> Improvisation is interconnection.
>
> *Ryoko Amadee Goguen, 3 June 2003*

References

Adorno, Theodor (2002), *Essays on Music*, introduction & notes by Richard Leppert, trans. Susan H. Gillespie (University of California Press).

Aldwell, Edward and Schachter, Carl (1989), *Harmony and Voice Leading*, 2nd ed. (London: Thomson).

Alligood, Kathleen, Sauer, Tim and Yorke, James (1996), *Chaos: An introduction to dynamical systems* (Berlin: Springer, Textbooks in Mathematical Sciences).

Andersen, Peter Bogh (1998), 'Multimedia phase spaces', *Multimedia Tools and Applications*, **6**, pp. 207–37.

Assayag, Gerard, Feichtinger, Hans and Rodrigues, José-Francisco (2002), *Mathematics and Music: A Diderot Mathematical Forum* (Berlin: Springer).

Barthes, Roland (1968), *Elements of Semiology*, trans. Annette Lavers and Colin Smith (New York: Hill and Wang).

Barwise, Jon and Perry, John (1983), *Situations and Attitudes* (Cambridge, MA: MIT/Bradford).

Birkhoff, George David (1933), *Aesthetic Measure* (Cambridge, MA: Harvard University Press).

Borgo, David (2002), 'The orderly disorder of free improvisation', *Pacific Review of Ethnomusicology*, **10**.

Borgo, David and Goguen, Joseph (to appear), 'Sync or swarm: Group dynamics in musical free improvisation', Abstract to appear in Proceedings, Conference on Interdisciplinary Musicology, Graz, Austria.

Chalmers, David (1996), The Conscious Mind: In search of a fundamental theory (New York: Oxford University Press).

Churchland, Paul (1996), *The Engine of Reason, the Seat of the Soul* (Cambridge, MA: MIT Press).

Cotterill, Rodney (2001), 'Evolution, cognition and consciousness', *Journal of Consciousness Studies*, **8** (2), pp. 3–17.
Crane, Tim (2003), *The Mechanical Mind*, 2nd ed. (London: Routledge).
Crick, Francis (1994), *The Astonishing Hypothesis: The scientific search for the soul* (New York: Scribner & Sons).
Damasio, Antonio (1994), *Descartes' Error: Emotion, Reason and the Human Brain* (New York: Avon).
Damasio, Antonio (1999), *The Feeling of What Happens: Body, Emotion and the Making of Consciousness* (New York: Harcourt Brace).
Dennett, Daniel (1991), *Conscious Explained* (London: Penguin).
Dennett, Daniel (1988/1996), 'Quining qualia', in *Consciousness in Contemporary Science*, ed. Edoardo Bisiach and Anthony Marcel (Oxford: Oxford University Press).
Descartes, René (1956/1637), *Discourse on Method* (Englewood Cliffs, NJ: Prentice Hall).
Dogen (1992), *Shobogenzo: Zen Essays by Dogen* (University of Hawaii Press).
Dourish, Paul (2003), 'What we talk about when we talk about context', *Personal and Ubiquitous Computing*, Online edition.
Dreyfus, Hubert (1992), *What Computers Still Can't Do* (Cambridge, MA: MIT Press).
Ellis, Ralph and Newton, Natika (1998), 'Three paradoxes of phenomenal consciousness: Bridging the explanatory gap', *Journal of Consciousness Studies*, **5** (4), pp. 419–42.
Fauconnier, Gilles and Turner, Mark (1998), 'Conceptual integration networks', *Cognitive Science*, **22** (2), pp. 133–87.
Fauconnier, Gilles and Turner, Mark (2002), *The Way We Think* (New York: Basic Books).
Garfinkel, Harold (1967), *Studies in Ethnomethodology* (Englewood Cliffs, NJ: Prentice-Hall).
Gibson, James (1977), 'The theory of affordances', *in Perceiving, Acting and Knowing: Toward an Ecological Psychology*, ed. Robert Shaw and John Bransford (Hillsdale, NJ: Erlbaum).
Gibson, James (1979), *An Ecological Approach to Visual Perception* (Boston, MA: Houghton Mifflin).
Goguen, Joseph (1977), 'Complexity of hierarchically organized systems and the structure of musical experiences', *International Journal of General Systems*, **3** (4), pp. 237–51.
Goguen, Joseph (1996), 'Semiotic morphisms', Available on the web at www.cs.ucsd.edu/users/goguen/papers/smm.html. Early version in Proc., Conf. Intelligent Systems: A Semiotic Perspective, Vol. II, ed. J. Albus, A. Meystel and R. Quintero, Nat. Inst. Science & Technology, (Gaithersberg MD, 20-23 October 1996) pages 26-31. See also UCSD Dept. Computer Science & Eng. Report CS97-553, 1997.
Goguen, Joseph (1999a), 'Introduction to special issue, Art and the Brain, Part 1', *Journal of Consciousness Studies*, **6** (6–7), pp. 5–14.
Goguen, Joseph (1999b), 'An introduction to algebraic semiotics, with applications to user interface design', in *Computation for Metaphors, Analogy and Agents*, ed. Chrystopher Nehaniv, (Springer; Lecture Notes in Artificial Intelligence, Volume 1562).
Goguen, Joseph (2000), 'What is art? Introduction to special issue, Art and the Brain, Part 2', *Journal of Consciousness Studies*, **7** (8–9), pp. 7–15.
Goguen, Joseph (2003), 'Semiotic morphisms, representations, and blending for interface design', in *Proceedings, AMAST Workshop on Algebraic Methods in Language Processing*, pp. 1–15. AMAST Press, 2003. Conference held in Verona, Italy, 25-27 August, 2003.
Goguen, Joseph and Harrell, Fox (2003), 'Information visualization and semiotic morphisms', in *Visual Representations and Interpretations*, ed. Grant Malcolm (Elsevier). Proceedings of a workshop held in Liverpool, UK.
Goguen, Joseph and Harrell, Fox (in preparation), 'Foundations for active multimedia narrative: Semiotic spaces and structural blending'.
Goguen, Joseph and Linde, Charlotte (1984), 'Optimal structures for multi-media instruction', Technical report, SRI International, 1984. To OAEce of Naval Research, Psychological Sciences Division.
Goguen, Joseph and Malcolm, Grant (1996), *Algebraic Semantics of Imperative Programs* (Cambridge, MA: MIT Press).
Goguen, Joseph, Roçu, Grigore & Lin, Kai (2003), 'Conditional circular coinductive rewriting', in *Recent Trends in Algebraic Development Techniques,* 16th International Workshop, WADT'02. Springer, Lecture Notes in Computer Science. Selected papers from a workshop held in Frauenchiemsee, Germany, 24-27 October 2002.
Goguen, Joseph, Thatcher, James & Wagner, Eric (1978), 'An initial algebra approach to the specification, correctness and implementation of abstract data types', in *Current Trends in Programming Methodology, IV*, ed. Raymond Yeh (Englewood Cliffs, NJ: Prentice-Hall).
Goodman, Nelson (1968), *Languages of Art: An Approach to a Theory of Symbols* (Indianapolis, IN: Bobbs-Merrill).
Grady, Joseph, Oakley, Todd & Coulson, Seanna (1999), 'Blending and metaphor', in *Metaphor in Cognitive Linguistics*, ed. Raymond Gibbs and Gerard Steen (Amsterdam: John Benjamins).
Hanslick, Eduard (1986), *On the Musically Beautiful*, ed. Geoffrey Payzant (Hackett).

Harnad, Stevan (1990), 'The symbol grounding problem', *Physica D*, **42**, pp. 335–46.
Heidegger, Martin (1962/1927), *Being and Time*, trans. John Macquarrie and Edward Robinson (Oxford: Blackwell).
Hume, David (1986/1740), *A Treatise of Human Nature* (New York: Viking).
Husserl, Edmund (1964), *Phenomenology of Internal Time-Consciousness* (Indiana University Press).
James, William (1950/1890), *Principles of Psychology* (New York: Dover).
Kivy, Peter (1980), *The Corded Shell: Reflections on Musical Expression* (Princeton, NJ: Princeton University Press).
Kolmogorov, Andrei (1965), 'Three approaches to the quantitative definition of information', *Problems of Information Transmission*, **1**, pp. 1–11.
Lakoff, George (1987), *Women, Fire and Other Dangerous Things: What categories reveal about the mind* (University of Chicago Press).
Lakoff, George & Johnson, Mark (1980), *Metaphors We Live By* (University of Chicago Press).
MacLane, Saunders (1971), *Categories for the Working Mathematician* (Berline: Springer).
Meyer, Leonard (1956), *Emotion and Meaning in Music* (University of Chicago Press).
Mogi, Ken (no date), 'Qualia manifesto', http://www.qualia-manifesto.com/.
Nadin, Mihai (1991), *Mind: Anticipation and Chaos* (Belser).
Nagarjuna (1995), *Mulamadhyamikakaraka*, trans. Jay Garfield (Oxford: Oxford University Press).
Newton, Natika (2001), 'Emergence and the uniqueness of consciousness', *Journal of Consciousness Studies*, **8** (9–10), pp. 47–59.
Nishitani, Keiji (1982), *Religion and Nothingness* (University of California).
Northoff, Georg (2003), 'Qualia and ventral prefrontal cortical function: "Neurophenomenological" hypothesis, *Journal of Consciousness Studies*, **10** (8), pp. 14–48.
Peirce, Charles Saunders (1965), *Collected Papers* (Harvard, 1965). In 6 volumes; see especially Volume 2: Elements of Logic.
Plato (1993), *The Republic* (London: Everyman).
Ramachandran, Vilayaner S. & Hirstein, William (1999), 'The science of art: A neurological theory of aesthetic experience', *Journal of Consciousness Studies*, **6** (6–7), pp. 15–51.
Sama, Mikko, Hari, Riitta, Rif, J. & Knuutila, J. (1993), 'The human auditory sensory memory trace persists about 10 sec: Neuromagnetic evidence', *Journal of Cognitive Neuroscience*, **5**, pp. 363–70.
Saussure, Ferdinand de (1976), *Course in General Linguistics*, trans. Roy Harris (London: Duckworth).
Shannon, Claude & Weaver, Warren (1964), *The Mathematical Theory of Communication* (University of Illinois Press).
Suchman, Lucy (1987), *Plans and Situated Actions: The Problem of Human–Machine Communication* (Cambridge: Cambridge University Press).
Sudnow, David (1979), *Ways of the Hand* (Bantam; Reprinted by Harvard).
Tani, Jun (forthcoming), 'The dynamical systems accounts for phenomenology of immanent time: An interpretation from a robotics synthetic study', *Journal of Consciousness Studies*.
Taylor, Richard (2000), 'The use of science to investigate Jackson Pollock's drip paintings', *Journal of Consciousness Studies*, **7** (8–9), pp. 137–50.
Turner, Mark (1997), *The Literary Mind* (Oxford: Oxford University Press).
Varela, Francisco (1996), 'Neurophenomenology: A methodological remedy for the hard problem', *Journal of Consciousness Studies*, **3** (4), pp. 330–49.
Varela, Francisco (1999), 'Present-time consciousness', *Journal of Consciousness Studies*, **6** (2–3), pp. 111–40.
Varela, Francisco, Thompson, Evan & Rosch, Eleanor (1991), *The Embodied Mind* (Cambridge, MA: MIT Press).
Vygotsky, Lev (1985), *Mind in Society* (Cambridge, MA: Harvard University Press).
Whitehead, Alfred North (1985/1929), *Process and Reality* (New York: Free Press).
Widmer, Gerhard (2003), 'Discovering simple rules in complex data: A meta-learning algorithm and some surprising musical discoveries', *Artificial Intelligence*, **146** (2), pp. 129–48.
Wittgenstein, Ludwig (1922), *Tractatus Logico-Philosophicus*, trans. D.F. Pears and B.F. McGuinness, with an Introduction by Bertrand Russell (London: Routledge and Kegan Paul).
Zbikowski, Lawrence (2002), *Conceptualizing Music* (Oxford).
Zeki, Semir (1999), 'Art and the brain', *Journal of Consciousness Studies*, **6** (6–7), pp. 76–51.

Amy Ione

Klee and Kandinsky

Polyphonic Painting, Chromatic Chords and Synaesthesia

As an artist I admittedly scrutinize all of the theories related to the arts closely. I do this for a number of reasons. The obvious one is that I have a deeply felt personal relationship with the subject matter. Less obvious is my experience in general. My early research was motivated by a desire to discover the historical circumstances that led to the difficulty in fitting visual art (as I knew it in my studio) into the discussions I encountered. Generally, it seemed that the dominant framework trivialized what I considered the most important aspects of the creative process. Over time I concluded that developing an interdisciplinary approach offered the best option for expanding views, although it is not an easy task. Establishing areas of commonality across a range of disciplines must somehow accommodate the ways in which each has developed a research agenda that seems to serve its core needs. In consciousness studies, for example, we have a field that relies heavily on scientific research and humanistic methodologies when building the philosophical models scholars use to structure theories. This methodology is not only removed from the nuts and bolts of art, it is also easily manipulated in discourse on art due to the ease with which we can fit aspects of art (*e.g.*, aesthetics) into the philosophical framework.[1] Clearly this approach fits nicely with philosophically defined concepts such as meaning, emotion, and other elusive modes. In addition, using the well-honed categories aids in bracketing themes such as metaphor, interpretation, subjectivity, language and history. Nonetheless, in reading through the studies, I repeatedly conclude that the voices of practitioners need to be included to a greater degree.

Correspondence:
Amy Ione, The Diatrope Institute, PO Box 6813, Santa Rosa, CA 95406, USA.
Email: ione@diatrope.com

[1] Consciousness studies are generally framed in terms of science and the humanities, assuming that the arts are simply a limb of the humanities. This point of view draws significantly from C.P. Snow's *Two Cultures* presentation. Some of the problems with including art in Snow's scheme are developed by Victoria in 'Towards a Third Culture: Being in Between' (2000) and my upcoming book *Visualizing Innovation*.

Journal of Consciousness Studies, **11**, No. 3–4, 2004, pp. 148–58

It is with these thoughts in mind that this paper turns to the practices of two artists, Paul Klee and Vassily Kandinsky. These men, who appear quite similar at first glance, brought differing approaches and philosophical dispositions to their studios, writings, and teaching pursuits. Case studies that delineate their differences allow us to, albeit briefly, engage with diverging viewpoints even while we seek confluence. Thus the summaries below, while not at all representative of the totality of art, do nonetheless allow some engagement with nuanced information. Also, in an effort to relate these two men to my overall research concerns, a truncated survey of neuroscientific/consciousness themes related to the work of the artists discussed is included to round out the discussion.

Klee and Kandinsky

All of us can recall the sense of exhilaration that often accompanies encountering an artistic masterpiece we previously knew only from secondary sources. If our first hearing of Beethoven's Fifth or our first visual exchange with a Cézanne painting came after developing an acquaintance with the work through descriptive accounts, we were likely reminded of the degree to which explanations suffer when compared with the artwork itself. Regardless of how skilfully our metaphors express the rhythm, tonality, colour, and texture, exposure to the authentic creation suggests the contrived representation is aptly termed a shadow or pale imitation. Invariably a translation fails to capture the way visual art connects with us in space and music pulsates in time. Even a non-verbal syntax, like the relatively recent phenomenon of musical notation, reminds us that a symbolic text can convey a compositional arrangement, but in this form the sensory vitality of the music is rigidified and silenced.

Equally fascinating are the many artists who agree that their creations defy explanation, leaving the impression that successful work is somewhat magical from their perspective as well. Projects in which an artist successfully merges sensory modalities are perhaps more intense and harder to explain in discrete terms. The variables we must address are particularly evident when we look at the work and stories of those who choose to experiment in this way. For example, Vassily Kandinsky (1866–1944) and Paul Klee (1879–1940), both painters and trained musicians, were drawn to the ways one can manipulate abstract possibilities in both art and music. Yet, although each effectively brought musicality to his painted work, when looking at the motivations of these two colleagues we find significant points of divergence.

Apparently Klee and Kandinsky first met, briefly, in Franz Stuck's painting class in the Munich Academy in the summer of 1900 (Roskill, 1992). They met again in 1911 and their professional friendship further strengthened after Klee joined the Blue Rider group (founded by Kandinsky and the painter Franz Marc) in 1912. Later the bonds between the two deepened when Klee accepted an appointment at the Bauhaus in 1921 and Kandinsky joined him in 1922. Working side-by-side for many years, both painters articulated their projects in terms of the Bauhaus aspiration to unify all of the arts, a goal they shared even before their appointments. Indeed some claim that the resemblance between their work in the early 1920s is so close that an untrained eye might well confuse the two (Haftman, 1967). Perhaps more intriguing are the distinct variations between them that clarify on examination, despite the evidence that they often articulated similar principles. According to Roskill, 'Klee and Kandinsky . . . [were] like a musical partnership . . . even while their "styles" of performance and commentary remained entirely different in cast.'[2] (Roskill, 1992, p. xvi)

In particular, Klee's approach was based on personally felt impulses and was quite process-oriented. His hope was to 'one day . . . be able to improvise freely on the keyboard of colours: the rows of watercolours in my paint box' (Düchting, 1997, p. 17). His urge to work colour as one might sound led to an experimental practice often discussed in terms of his efforts to find innovative ways to group chords and express resonance. Kandinsky, by contrast, aspired to develop a vocabulary that would point toward universals. He saw art as a medium of the mystical and, to him, 'Colour is the keyboard, the eyes are the hammers, the soul is the piano with many strings. The artist is the hand which plays, touching one key or another, to cause vibrations in the soul.' (Kandinsky, 1986, p. 25) Haftman succinctly summarizes the psychological premises that defined each process, writing, 'Kandinsky took hold of the world but remained outside it. Klee sank himself in the world.' (Haftman, 1967).

Delving into their compositions, writings, and histories further supports this contrast. Paul Klee worked from a seed he felt within himself and endeavoured to make something precious to him, and previously invisible to others, visible. To his mind, compositional elements were tools he could use to engage all that he felt intuitively and internally. This was evident when he taught his students that 'Not form, but forming, not form as final appearance, but form in the process of becoming, as genesis.' (Haftman, 1967, p. 86). Playful, sardonic, and child-like, his wide-ranging variations delineate how freely he accommodated each work as it was shaped. We see this in the wiry forms in Klee's early graphic work (*e.g.,* his 1903 *Virgin in a tree*, and the 1914 *Instrument for New Music*), the subtle tonality of his polyphonic images (*e.g., Dynamic–Polyphonic*, 1931), done with coloured chalk on paper), and the many fantasies he presents in a secret language to illustrate the degree to which he continually strived, and succeeded, in his quest to say something novel. Whether using line variations to suggest rhythm or capturing a chromatic tonality, Klee aimed to feel the pulse of his piece and to slowly nurture it along in tune to a tempo we feel through looking at it.

Kandinsky, on the other hand, adopted a top-down approach that was echoed in his frequent use of the word *Gesetzmässigkeit* (loosely translated as law-governed character). His best known book, *Concerning the Spiritual in Art*, (originally published in 1911 as *Über das Geistige in der Kunst*), and later pieces demonstrate this. The work also illustrates his efforts to present his art in terms of

[2] Vassily Kandinsky's wife, Nina, noted that although they worked as colleagues for close to thirty years, Kandinsky preserved a certain distance in his relationship with Klee, preferring the formal mode of address *Sie* to the familiar *Du*.

spiritual science.[3] This tract, and his other theoretical expositions, are quite unlike Klee's writings, where we find records of soul-searching and documentation of his experiments (Roskill, 1992). Kandinsky's allegiance to universalism, and his attraction to mysticism, theosophy, and other occult systems was evident in the classroom, his publications, and compositionally. When lecturing his students, Kandinsky, unlike Klee, would proceed quite deliberately. Grouping a few objects together, he would abstract from them a logical structure of lines and particles of colour. Then he would analyse this structure in terms of the pictorial means — point, line, surface, space and so on (Haftman, 1967, p. 82). Basically, to Klee's mind, the kind of structure Kandinsky was seeking to articulate through his logical, calm, and carefully constructed analysis was an intellectualised short-cut that lost sight of personal dynamism. Klee's advice to his students conveys his distaste of an analysis of structure in terms of pictorial means. He said: 'To paint well is simply this: to put the right colour in the right place.' (Kudielka, 2002, p. 32). In the *Fugue in Red*, for example, we see how he stabilizes the beat of the colours on the flat surface, evoking musicality through subtle coloration.

Even in musical terms, the contrasts are striking. Indeed, their musical tastes too show foundational disagreements. Kandinsky's equated his work with Schönberg's twelve-tone music, which made him realize that the concept of tonal harmony was undergoing a radical change, and that dissonance was becoming a means of expression on par with consonance (Maur, 1999). Kandkinsky endeavoured to join this view of music with his own move toward abstraction and transcendence. As Kandinsky explains in *Concerning the Spiritual in Art* (1911), it is his view that 'The spiritual life, to which art belongs and of which she is one of the mightiest elements, is a complicated but definite and easily definable movement forward and upwards . . . [The Artist] sees and points the way.' (Kandinsky, 1986, p. 4). Later, in *Point and Line to Plane* (1926) he elaborates on how the artist points the way to others (Kandinsky, 1979). Having asked what is to replace the objects of traditional art, Kandinsky declares it is the task of a science of art to reveal the compositional laws inherent in abstract forms, enabling the artist to discard fidelity to merely 'external' nature. His words carry his view that 'The coming period demands a more exact and objective way to make collective work in the science of art possible.' (Kandinsky, 1979, p. 76).

Klee, on the other hand, was convinced that the modern music of his day, which Kandinsky applauded, was too academic and overly dictated by educational theory. For this reason Klee focused on developing an abstract, visually based language based on historical musical models. His move to create cross-disciplinary harmonies clearly diverged from those of his colleague, who was not seeking innovation so much as fulfilment of his desire to blend the arts into an all-inclusive spiritually felt meshing of sensations. Moreover, Kandinsky's systematisation of a tonal harmony that coincided with his

[3] A compelling overview of Kandinsky's interest in the spiritual and how this influenced his practices is offered by Ringbom in 'Transcending the Visible: The Generation of Abstract Painters' (1987).

elevation of an objective, mystical science outside of nature represented precisely the kinds of academic equation Klee reviled. Klee believed that musical development had already passed its prime, going downhill after Mozart. He acknowledged that he deliberately chose painting over music in the belief that innovative possibilities were emerging in visual abstraction, while music was going in the wrong direction. His animated expressions show he nonetheless adeptly made his choice in a way that combined both modalities. Inserting a musical quality, Klee's artwork is distinct from both the art and music of earlier epochs. Beyond a doubt, it is very much of his time. Indeed, his special way of tuning the visual to the musical articulated how ably he put together projects that aligned with his personal sensitivities more than a communal style. His accomplishments are particularly evident in the overlapping qualities he used to combine qualities of both art forms, perhaps most clearly articulated in the structures he derived to refine his variations of themes, something which he noticed above all in the polyphonic fugue (Düchting, 1997, p. 14).

Klee, Kandinsky, and Consciousness

Equally striking is the way each artist intersects with the cognitive neuroscience and consciousness studies literature. Topics that stand out include the relationship between science and spirituality as well as unresolved issues such as emergence and binding. Perhaps the most pronounced distinction comes through when we compare Kandinsky's urge to depict transcendence with Klee's view that 'For the artist communication with nature remains the most essential condition. The artist is human; himself nature; part of nature within natural space.' (Klee, 1969/1925, p. 7). Clearly Klee's embrace of personal process differs from Kandinsky's aim to build 'a spiritual pyramid which would some day reach to heaven' (Kandinsky, 1986, p. 20). Nuances that distinguish them further clarify the distance between a science of art grounded in the mystical (Kandinsky) and a practice that relies on experimentation (Klee).

Kandinsky's aspiration to give form to universal tenets using the 'scientific method' comes up frequently in consciousness debates. His legacy also offers one example of the weak empirical foundations often used in these arguments. This artist's efforts to formulate 'objective' statements that he saw in terms of a science of art, although systematic, are not scientifically convincing. As Roskill points out, in pressing for the existence of a pictorial logic grounded in scientific laws, while at the same time rejecting the positivistic tenor of latter-day science, Kandinsky's argument slips and slides: it breaks up into opposites and alternatives pursuing logic along a flexibly shifting thread, but also giving space to digressions that seem based on free association between one topic and another (Roskill, 1992, p. 40). Given this, it is difficult to interpret Kandinsky's laws as we would a laboratory science, which in part explains why scientists have often considered the techniques he speaks about as metaphorical at best and (more often) closer to the metaphysical and mystical.[4] Still, since Kandinsky often talked of his experiences with synaesthesia, we can endeavour to position this aspect of his experience in terms of current scientific research and philosophical debates (Ione & Tyler, 2003; 2004).

The specific condition we term synaesthesia occurs when an individual receives a stimulus in one sense modality and experiences a sensation in another. Generally, philosophical interpretations have built on what Aristotle termed '*Sensus Communis*', a theoretical position many continue to reference in some form when seeking to update theories about sensory unity.[5] For example, twenty-five years ago, Lawrence E. Marks begins his book *The Unity of the Senses: Interrelations among the Modalities* with a summary of his theoretical position, writing,

> What is 'the unity of the senses?' Simply stated, it is the *thesis* that the senses have a lot in common. . . . The unity of the senses is perhaps a *theory*, but even more importantly is a way of looking at sensory functioning: It is a viewpoint that pulls together a host of phenomena. . . . My goal is to assemble all of its parts, to show how the unity of the senses expresses itself in perception, in phenomenology, in psychophysics, in neurophysiology. (Marks, 1978, p. ix) *[italics added]*

More recently, Richard E. Cytowic's *Synaesthesia: A Union of the Senses* (2002)[6] updates Marks' theory and also pairs synaesthesia with art. He writes that 'Both synaesthesia and the artistic experience are ineffable, and both indescribable by language.' (Cytowic, 2002, p. 319). Furthermore, according to Cytowic, 'when we say that art speaks to the depths of our souls — it speaks to

[4] A particularly problematic aspect of his argument is that it is based on the unscientific assumption that artists are seers who glimpse a higher truth and reveal it to others through the pieces that they create. See *Nature Exposed to our Method of Questioning* for an analysis of the problems inherent in this argument (Ione, 2002)

[5] Aristotle introduced this term in the first part of *On Memory and Reminiscence* and thus we can date the philosophical legacy in the West back to him. He explained the idea saying that 'Why we cannot exercise the intellect on any object absolutely apart from the continuous, or apply it even to non-temporal things unless in connexion with time, is another question. Now, one must cognize magnitude and motion by means of the same faculty by which one cognizes time (i.e. by that which is also the faculty of memory), and the presentation (involved in such cognition) is an affection of the *sensus communis*; whence this follows, viz. that the cognition of these objects (magnitude, motion time) is effected by the (said *sensus communis*, i.e. the) primary faculty of perception. Accordingly, memory (not merely of sensible, but) even of intellectual objects involves a presentation: hence we may conclude that it belongs to the faculty of intelligence only incidentally, while directly and essentially it belongs to the primary faculty of sense-perception'. This line of thought has been continually updated as the philosophical tradition refined its concepts. For example, Immanuel Kant writes in his *Critique of Judgment*: 'we must [here] take *sensus communis* to mean the idea of a sense *shared* [by all of us], i.e., a power to judge that in reflecting takes account (*a priori*), in our thought, of everyone else's way of presenting [something], in order *as it were* to compare our own judgment with human reason in general. . . Now, we do this as follows: we compare our judgment not so much with the actual as rather with the merely possible judgments of others, and [thus] put ourselves in the position of everyone else. . .' (Immanuel Kant, *Critique of Judgment*, trans. Werner Pluhar, p160; Ak. 293–4). Harry T. Hunt again revisits these ideas in *On the Nature of Consciousness* (1995). Hunt, too, expands the theoretical focus, seeing the idea in terms of symbolic cognition, Romantic imagination, aesthetics, and consciousness.

[6] This revised edition of his 1989 publication with the same title speaks to Marks' abstraction theory directly.

that greater formless part of ourselves of which we have no awareness' (Cytowic, 2002, p. 306). These broad statements are hardly built upon a scientific foundation. They do, however, equate nicely with Kandinsky's urge to place artistic sensitivity in a transcendent realm that we cannot speak about directly. Ironically, in making these blanket assumptions Cytowic open a space for placing synaesthesia in terms of the all-embracing mysticism Kandinsky elevated. Whether or not this is an explicit intention, views that are founded on theories outside of our awareness are arguably unarguable.[7]

V.S. Ramachandran, one of the most exciting researchers working on synaesthesia (Ramachandran & Hubbard, 2000; 2001), offers some comments that suggest interpreters should assert more care when drawing conclusions about synaesthesia. As he explains, 'you can't use one mystery in science to explain another mystery'(Romano, 2002) and that 'synaesthesia is just metaphor [it] doesn't explain anything because we have no idea how metaphors are represented in the brain. . . research has shown there is a neural basis for synaesthesia and provided an experimental foothold' (Romano, 2002). To my knowledge Ramachandran and other researchers have not yet developed experiments that are refined enough to probe whether a deeper understanding of the artist's brain could point to information that goes beyond establishing a neural basis for synaesthesia.

Indeed it seems likely that artistic experiments might have much to say about binding or brain plasticity given the many who have stated it is possible to develop and/or increase cross-modal awareness through working toward this end in one's studio. For example, Jack Ox is an intermedia artist who has been experimenting for over twenty years with how to combine different media into one. She claims that now it is easy and natural for her to *see* sonic forms (Ox, 1999, p. 7). Kandinsky likewise claimed he saw colours (he refers to 'my colours' when explaining his experience of a Wagner opera).[8] Yet, although he claimed he was a synaesthete, some now say Kandinsky was not a 'natural' so much as one who developed his abilities through associative techniques aimed at enhancing sensory exchange, much like one might develop relative pitch. While we can't test him, pencilled notes in his books that spoke of exercises one could do to enhance the experiences and offer some support of this idea.[9] Even the titles of his works (*e.g., Improvisations, Impressions, and Compositions*) evoke music and accentuate his desire to bring the essence of cross-modal experience to a wider audience.

---

[7] *Nature Exposed to our Method of Questioning* (2002) offers a broad overview of the many implicit assumptions that elevate spirituality in discussions of philosophy, art, and science.

[8] Kandinsky described the impact of an 1896 performance of Richard Wagner's Lohengrin in Moscow, saying: 'The violins, the deep tones of the basses, and especially the wind instruments at that time embodied for me all the power of that pre-nocturnal hour. I saw all my *colours* in my mind; they stood before my eyes. Wild, almost crazy lines were sketched in front of me' (Kandinsky, 1913, p. 364 [italics added]).

[9] This ideas are further developed in 'Is Kandinsky a Synaesthete?' and 'Synaesthesia: is F-Sharp Colored Violet?' (Ione & Tyler, 2003; 2004).

Klee's techniques, on the other hand, stimulate thoughts about psychophysically designed experiments, along the lines pioneered by J.J. Gibson (Gibson, 1950; 1987). Some may argue that Gibson's work is now somewhat peripheral to research highlighting cognitive operations (Zeki, 2001). A counter argument would be that his interest in the world we see is relevant to visual arts precisely because the artist establishes an environmental relationship with the artwork while constructing it. Klee, who never aspired to call his approach science, talks about his far-reaching experiments with colour and form without attempting to adopt an empirical facade. His words instead suggest he revised his motifs as he constructed them, continually adjusting elements in order to tease out intense visual reactions. The abstract, subtle relationships that resulted, as such, are hard to characterize but do, nonetheless, evoke complex chords, rhythms, and tonal variations.[10] Placing these modalities in terms of higher cognition and symbolic language seems to rigidify the objects he made more than it allows us to recognize their musical vitality. To side-step the degree to which he formed an active relationship with each developing work would bc particularly naïve in light of what we know of his teaching method, as discussed above. To be sure, his work appears deceptively simple at first glance. What makes the originals striking is that the imagery is so infused with the delicate rhythms and intricate counterpoint of musical composition that the symbolic language becomes secondary. Our experience of Klee's virtuosity confirms he achieved his goal of playing colour like a 'chromatic keyboard'.[11] Clearly, working on his own terms, Klee became one of the most original technicians and innovators among the earlier abstract expressionist artists of the twentieth century. Reviewing his motifs, moreover, we find that they demonstrate that Klee continually re-examined his personal themes and re-evaluated his forms as he derived his visual elements. His *oeuvre* seems to suggest a mind capable of seemingly limitless invention.

---

[10] Artists who do representational work demonstrate yet another reason to inject psychophysical research into the mix. For example, it is generally agreed that Edward Degas had a condition called retinopathy. Michael Marmor's *Degas Through His Own Eye* (2002) shows how this artist's visual acuity changed as he matured. Marmor, an ophthalmologist, convincingly refutes Degas' personal conviction that the differences in vision are of no importance to the artist. As he explains, despite Degas' assertion that inner vision determined the nature of an artist's work, his decreasing visual acuity resulted in precisely the kind of crudeness in composition clinically associated with retinopathy. This is particularly evident when we compare the flawless rendering of his early work with the grotesque figures he painted at the end of his life. One mature painting Marmor discusses at length is *Madame Alexis Rouart and Her Children*. Despite many modeling sessions, their faces look deformed in the finished painting. Marmor uses computer simulations to hypothesize that they images might have looked quite correct to the painter.

[11] Also striking is the way his small compositions rarely attempt to resolve large issues. The tension between simplicity and complexity further belies their size and makes them difficult to interpret. Ranging from small watercolors to linear, geometric, and mosaic-like motifs in his career, Klee's work eventually culminated in a simplified, flatly painted and broadly drawn series of gouaches and oils done between 1935 and 1940. This style came about when he suffered from a progressive skin and muscular disease. In summary, the translation of motifs taken from nature into free, rhythmical linear structures and tonal values is based on the principle of rhythm: a vision the artist distilled from his knowledge of the rudiments of music.

Conclusion

Placing these artists into an art and consciousness framework is a tricky proposition and far beyond the scope of this short paper. In concluding, however, it seems imperative to note that the vast range of perspectives on art suggest that the kind of universalism many consciousness thinkers desire must somehow be squared with the pluralistic, cultural activity that has led others to suggest that a theoretical construct might not be an achievable or even a desirable goal. For example, in *But is it art?: An Introduction to Art Theory,* Cynthia Freeland writes 'My strategy here is to highlight the rich diversity of art, in order to convey the difficulty of coming up with suitable theories.' (Freeland, 2001, p. xvii). Similarly, in *the Art Question*, Nigel Warburton writes:

> The most plausible hypothesis is that 'art' is indefinable not just at the exhibited level, but at the relational non-exhibited level, too. There is no simple argument that will lead irresistibly to this conclusion, but the inadequacies of a range of existing definitions, together with the ever-changing nature of art, make this conclusion likely (Warburton, 2002, p. 121).[12]

This is not to say that studies in cognitive neuroscience/consciousness do not add to our understanding of art. I believe they add immensely. Moreover, in my view, including information about brain processing the range of viewpoints is an important step.[13] It aids in formulating questions that have the potential to foster a closer relationship with art (as well as consciousness). Questions we might raise include: Are we interested in Art only as an aesthetic modality in terms defined by the philosophical tradition? When speaking of cognitive operations, do we benefit more from examining the arts individually or in tandem? Is it possible for reductive examinations of cognitive operations to mesh with the experiential and contextual environment in which art is produced/appreciated? Are discussions that adopt axiomatic assumptions about what art IS weighed down by their initial definitions? In other words, there remain many avenues through which we can approach the subject. More succinctly, one approach might assert unequivocally that art IS 'a higher cognitive process, a fully human kind of symbolic language'.[14] Another, and I see myself in this category, rejects the inference that we know precisely what art is and what we need to explain.[15] As I have explained in earlier publications (Ione, 1999; 2000a,b; 2001; 2003a; 2003b,c;

[12] A good reference for the range of views is *Theories of Art Today* (Carroll, 2000), a collection of articles by contemporary philosophers of art (Dickie, Danto, Davies, Stecker). This publication offers a survey of the major voices in regard to art theory. As a whole this book demonstrates that it seems premature to conclude that there is some agreement on what we mean by art and aesthetics in the contemporary world. The *Art in Theory* series (Harrison & Wood, 1993; Harrison, Wood & Gaiger, 1998; 2001) also offers arguments detailing major themes from 1648–1990.

[13] The two issues on art and the brain published by the *Journal of Consciousness Studies* demonstrate this well. Also of interest from a consciousness perspective are Robert Solso's *Cognition and the Visual Arts* (1994) and *The Psychology of Art and the Evolution of the Conscious Brain* (2003), Margaret Livingstone's *Vision and Art: The Psychology of Seeing* (2002), and Semir Zeki's *Inner Visions: An Exploration of Art and the Brain* (1999).

[14] This comment was included in an anonymous review of an earlier version of this paper.

[15] Footnotes 12 and 13 support the view that there is no consensus on how we should characterize art

Ione & Tyler, 2003), I do not see that the lack of a precise definition precludes establishing points of conjunction that will aid in our understanding of both art and cognitive neuroscience. Instead, looking directly at the work artists do, particularly closely paired contemporaries like Klee and Kandinsky, reveals there is evidence to support the idea that a number of approaches to art exist. This essay does not pretend to comprehensively examine or resolve the theoretical issues related to them. Nor is it a detailed response to the long-standing debates on the question of whether we should view the arts as distinct or harmonious. It does, however, aim to offer information that can aid in building a richer relationship with the complexity of art. Surveying how Paul Klee and Vassily Kandinsky, two trained musicians, related visual art and music also illustrates how foundations might overlap and display conceptual variations nonetheless.[16]

References

Carroll, N. (2000), *Theories of Art Today* (Madison, WI: University of Wisconsin Press).

Cytowic, R.E. (2002), *Synesthesia: A Union of the Senses* (Cambridge, MA: MIT).

Düchting, H. (1997), *Paul Klee: Painting Music* (Munich: Prestel).

Freeland, C. (2001), *But Is It Art?: An Introduction to Art Theory* (Oxford: Oxford University Press).

Gibson, J.J. (1950), *The Perception of the Visual World* (Boston, MA: Houghton Miflin).

Gibson, J.J. (1987), *The Ecological Approach to Visual Perception* (Mahwah, NJ: Lawrence Erlbaum Associates).

Haftman, W. (1967), *The Mind and Work of Paul Klee* (New York: Praeger).

Harrison, C. & Wood, P. (1993), *Art in Theory: 1900–1990. An Anthology of Changing Ideas* (Oxford: Blackwell Publishers).

Harrison, C., Wood, P. & Gaiger, J. (1998), *Art in Theory: 1815–1900. An Anthology of Changing Ideas* (Oxford: Blackwell Publishers).

Harrison, C., Wood, P. & Gaiger, J. (2001), *Art in Theory: 1648–1815. An Anthology of Changing Ideas* (Oxford: Blackwell Publishers).

Hunt, H.T. (1995), *On the Nature of Consciousness: Cognitive, Phenomenological, and Transpersonal Perspectives* (New Haven and London: Yale University Press).

Ione, A. (1999), 'An inquiry into Paul Cezanne: The role of the artist in studies of perception and consciousness', *Journal of Consciousness Studies*, **7** (8–9), pp. 57–74.

Ione, A. (2000a), 'Connecting the cerebral cortex with the artist's eyes, mind and culture', *Journal of Consciousness Studies*, **7**, pp. 21–27.

Ione, A. (2000b), 'Science: Method, myth, metaphor?', *Alexandria*, **5**, pp. 353–91.

Ione, A. (2001), 'Innovation in art and science: A response to Semir Zeki', *Trends in Cognitive Science*, **5** (4), p. 140.

Ione, A. (2002), *Nature Exposed to Our Method of Questioning* (Berkeley: Diatrope Press).

Ione, A. (2003a), 'Book review: A scientist's vision of art: A review of Margaret Livingstone's "Vision and Art: The Biology of Seeing"', *PSYCHE*, **9**.

Ione, A. (2003b), 'Book review: The judgement of the eye: "The Metamorphoses of Geometry — One of the Sources of Visual Perception and Consciousness" (by Jurgen Weber, Springer, 2002)', *Leonardo Reviews*.

Ione, A. (2003c), 'Examining Semir Zeki's "Neural concept formation and art: Dante, Michelangelo, Wagner"', *Journal of Consciousness Studies*, **10** (2), pp. 58–66.

Ione, A. (forthcoming), *Visualizing Innovation: Art, Science, Technology, and Visual Studies* (Amsterdam & New York: Rodopi).

Ione, A., & Tyler, C.W. (2003), 'Is Kandinsky a synesthete?' *Journal of the History of the Neurosciences*, **12**, pp. 223–6.

Ione, A., & Tyler, C.W. (2004), 'Synesthesia: Is F-sharp colored violet?' *Journal of the History of the Neurosciences* (in press).

Kandinsky, V. (1913/1982), in *Kandinsky: Complete Writings on Art*, ed. Vergo, K.C.L.a.P. (London: Faber & Faber).

Kandinsky, V. (1979), *Point and Line to Plane* (New York: Dover Publications).

Kandinsky, V. (1986), *Concerning the Spiritual in Art* (New York: Dover Publications).

Kant, I. (1929), *Critique of Pure Reason* (New York: St. Martin's Press).

[16] Special thanks to C.W. Tyler for his thoughtful input as this paper developed.

Klee, P. (1969/1925), *Pedagogical Sketchbook* (New York: Frederick A. Praeger).
Kudielka, R. (2002), in *Paul Klee: The Nature of Creation (Exhibition Catalog)*, eds. Kudielka, R., & B. Riley (London: Hayward Gallery).
Livingstone, M. (2002), *Vision and Art: The Biology of Seeing* (New York: Harry N. Abrams).
Marks, L.E. (1978), *The Unity of the Senses: Interrelations among the Modalities* (New York: Academic Press).
Marmor, M.F. (2002), *Degas through His Own Eyes: Visual Disability and the Late Style of Degas* (Paris: Somogy editions d'art).
Maur, K.V. (1999), *The Sound of Painting: Music in Modern Art* (Munich: Prestel).
Ox, J. (1999), 'Color me synesthesia', *Leonardo*, **32**, pp. 7–8.
Ramachandran, V.S., & Hubbard, E.M. (2000), 'Psychophysical investigations into the neural basis of synaesthesia', *Proceedings of the Royal Society of London*, **B**, pp. 979–83.
Ramachandran, V.S., & Hubbard, E.M. (2001), 'Synaesthesia: a window into perception, thought and language', *Journal of Consciousness Studies*, **8**, pp. 3–34.
Ringbom, S. (1987), 'Transcending the visible: The generation of abstract painters', in *The Spiritual in Art: Abstract Painting 1890–1985*, ed. M. Tuchman (New York: Abbeville Press).
Romano, C.J. (2002), 'The mind's eye: Neuroscience, synesthesia, and art', *Neurology Reviews.com*, **10**.
Roskill, M. (1992), *Klee, Kandinsky, and the Thought of Their Time* (Urbana and Chicago, IL: University of Illinois Press).
Snow, C.P. (1959), *Two Cultures* (Cambridge: Cambridge University Press).
Snow, C.P. (1964), *Two Cultures and the Scientific Revolution* (Cambridge: Cambridge University Press).
Solso, R. L. (1994), *Cognition and the Visual Arts* (Cambridge, MA and London, England: A Bradford Book)
Solso, R.L. (2003), *The Psychology of Art and the Evolution of the Conscious Brain* (Cambridge, MA: MIT Press).
Vesna, V. (2000), 'Towards a third culture: Being in between', *Leonardo*, **34**, pp. 121–5.
Warburton, N. (2002), *The Art Question* (London and New York: Routledge)
Zeki, S. (1999), *Inner Visions: An Exploration of Art and the Brain* (Oxford: Oxford University Press).
Zeki, S. (2001), 'Closet reductionist', *Trends in Cognitive Science*, **5**, pp. 45–6.

Vijay Iyer

Improvisation, Temporality and Embodied Experience

This journal's well-intentioned consideration of the arts has turned out to be quite the Pandora's box. As soon as we broach the subject of aesthetics, we are already in the realm of ideology; as soon as we impose the frame of scientific inquiry upon any subject, we invoke another kind of ideology. The previous issues in this series have depicted the unfolding of an ideological clash of cultures between sciences and the humanities, enough to make C.P. Snow blush. For the time being, this is an unavoidable condition; yet the more we remain aware of it, the further we may push our insights.

In my previous work (Iyer, 1998; 2002; 2004), I have brought the dual frameworks of embodied and situated cognition to bear on music. The fundamental claim is that music perception and cognition are embodied, situated activities. This means that they depend crucially on the physical constraints and enabling of our sensorimotor apparatus, and also on the ecological and sociocultural environment in which our music-listening and -producing capacities come into being. I have argued that rhythm perception and production involve a complex, whole-body experience, and that much musical structure incorporates an awareness of the embodied, situated role of the participant.

The claim that music perception and cognition are embodied activities also means that they are actively constructed by the listener, rather than passively transferred from performer to listener. This active nature of music perception highlights the role of culture and context. For example, the discernment of entities such as pulse and meter from a piece of music is not a perceptual inevitability; rather, it depends on the person's culturally contingent listening strategies (Iyer, 1998, pp. 83–104). In addition, I have argued that rhythmic expression is often directly related to the role of the body in making music, and to certain cultural aesthetics that privilege this role. In particular, certain varieties of subtle microrhythmic variation — which I have called expressive microtiming, in reference to the body of literature on expressive timing — are shown to display

Correspondence:
Vijay Iyer, 606 West 116th Street #2, New York, NY 10027, USA. *Email: vijay@vijay-iyer.com*

systematic structure, which often carries an encoded sonic trace of the culturally situated music-making body (for a detailed explanation, see Iyer, 2002).

In the course of this work, I have drawn heavily from African American and non-Western musical forms that are familiar to me as a musician and composer. Generally, when considering issues in music cognition, we too often gravitate to the well-trodden examples from pre-1900 European classical tonal music, and eschew nearly every other form of music, including all non-Western music, any contemporary or popular work, or any works that might be categorized as 'experimental'. Arguments for the relevance of ethnomusicology to music perception, while beyond the scope of this paper, should be obvious. After all, how can one make assertions about cognitive universals of music without studying the music of more than one culture?

In the case of the sciences' general avoidance of experimental music, the tacit assumption is that such work is not concerned with the fundamentals of perception. But often it is precisely through artistic experimentation that we reach new awareness of our perceptual and cognitive processes. The works of Seurat, Monet, and even Picasso, experimental in their time, are well-cited examples in the visual arts; Noë's (2000) work on Serra and Smith provides a rare example of late-twentieth-century artists considered from the point of view of cognition. But how often does one look to African American experimental composer–improvisors such as Thelonious Monk, Cecil Taylor, or John Coltrane in terms of the implications of their discoveries for music perception? (Lewis (1996; 1998; 2001–02) convincingly describes the music referred to as jazz as a tradition of experimental practice, in light of which the artists mentioned here could certainly be characterized as such.) For that matter, when do scientists consider twentieth-century European composers such as Ligeti, Varèse, or even Debussy for their perceptual insights?

In this paper I focus specifically on improvisational music, and on what it can tell us about consciousness and cognition. Building upon the notion of cognition as embodied action, I would like to propose an understanding of certain improvisational music as quintessentially *experiential*, in that it leads us to re-experience our own practice of perception.

Time and Temporal Situatedness

A fundamental consequence of physical embodiment and environmental situatedness is the fact that *things take time*. Temporality must ground our conception of physically embodied cognition. Smithers (1996) draws a useful distinction between processes that occur 'in time' and those that exist 'over time'. The distinction is similar to that between process-oriented activity, such as speech or walking, and product-oriented activity, such as writing a novel or composing a symphony.

In-time processes are *embedded* in time; not only does the time taken matter, but in fact it contributes to the overall structure. The speed of a typical walking gait relates to physical attributes like leg mass and size, and shoulder–hip torsional moment; this is why we cannot walk one-tenth or ten times as fast as we do. Similarly, the rate at which we speak exploits the natural timescales of lingual and mandibular motion as well as respiration. Accordingly, we learn (or more likely we are hardwired) to process speech at precisely such a rate. Recorded speech played at slower or faster speeds rapidly becomes unintelligible, even if the pitch is held constant. The perceived flow of conversation, while quite flexible, is sensitive to the slowdown caused by an extra few seconds taken to think of a word or recall a name.

Over-time processes, by contrast, are merely *contained* in time; the fact that they take time is of no fundamental consequence to the result. Most of what we call computation occurs over time. The fact that all computing machines were originally considered computationally equivalent regardless of speed suggests that time was not a concern in the original theory of computation, and that the temporality of a computational process was theoretically immaterial. Though computational theory is more nuanced today, 'real-time' computer applications make use of the speed of modern microprocessors, performing computations so fast that the user doesn't notice how much time is taken. However, this is not what the mind does when immersed in a dynamic, real-time environment; rather, it exploits both the constraints and the allowances of the natural timescales of the body and the brain as a total physical system. In other words, Smithers (1996) claims, *cognition chiefly involves in-time processes*. Furthermore, this claim is not limited simply to cognitive processes that require interpersonal interaction; it pertains to all thought, perception, and action.

The Temporality of Musical Performance

In intersubjective activities, such as speech or music making, one remains aware of a sense of mutual embodiment. This sense brings about the presupposition of 'shared time' between the listener and the performer. This sense is a crucial aspect of the temporality of performance. The experience of listening to music is qualitatively different from that of reading a book. The experience of music requires the listener's 'co-performance' within a shared temporal domain (Schutz, 1964). While the essentially solitary act of reading a book also takes time, the specific amount of time is of little consequence. (Literary notions of co-performance, such as Roland Barthes' idea of 'writerly texts' (1975), do not fundamentally incorporate the temporality of experience.) The notion of musical co-performance is made literal in musical contexts primarily meant for dance; the participatory act of marking time with rhythmic bodily activity physicalizes the sense of shared time, and could be viewed as embodied listening.

The performance situation itself might be understood as a context-framing device. In his study of music of a certain community in South Africa, ethnomusicologist J. Blacking wrote, '. . . Venda music is distinguished from non-music by the creation of a special world of time. The chief function of music is to involve people in shared experiences within the framework of their cultural experience' (Blacking, 1973, p. 48). There is no doubt that this is true to some degree in all musical performance, and we can take this concept further in the case of improvised music. The experience of listening to music that is understood to be improvised differs significantly from listening knowingly to composed music. The main source of drama in improvised music is the sheer fact of the shared sense of time: the sense that the improvisor is working, creating, generating musical material, in the same time in which we are co-performing as listeners. As listeners to any music, we experience a kind of *empathy* for the performer, an awareness of physicality and an understanding of the effort required to create music. This empathy is one facet of our listening strategies in any context. In improvisational music, this embodied empathy extends to an awareness of the performers' coincident physical and mental exertion, of their 'in-the-moment' (i.e., in-time) *process* of creative activity and interactivity. Thus improvisation heightens the role of embodiment in musical performance.

Time framed by improvisation is a special kind of time that is flexible in extent, and in fact carries the implied possibility of endlessness, similar to that pointed out in Shore (1996) in the case of baseball games. Instances like Paul Gonsalves's 27 choruses (over 6 minutes) of blues on Ellington's 'Diminuendo and Crescendo in Blue' (Ellington, [1956] 1990) and Coltrane's sixteen-minute take on 'Chasin' the Trane' (Coltrane, [1961] 1998) — significantly, both live recordings — attest to the power that the improvisor wields as framer of time, deciding both the extent and the content of the shared epoch.

Temporal Situatedness and Musical Form

Accordingly, improvisational music requires a different concept of musical form from composed music; improvisational musical form must be described in terms of temporal situatedness. It is enlightening to consider the concept of form in the classical improvised music of India:

> Syntactical forms are virtually unknown in the music of India. Instead we hear long, cyclical, chain structures and a general progression of organic growth that reveals the guidance of quite different formal models and metaphor. The tactics of form go hand-in-hand with the prevailing models of structure: hierarchical and syntactical forms are naturally implemented by such tactics as contrast, parallelism, preparation, rise, transition, and the like; serial forms [as in Indian music], however, tend to be modular, decorative, incremental, progressive, and open-ended. The Indian version of musical structure tends to emphasize variation of the module: by permutation of its elements, by inflation and deflation of patterns, by pattern superimpositions, and by progressive organic development (Rowell, 1988).

Improvisational African and African American music can share many of these traits, particularly in the long-term organization of material. The major role of improvisation in many oral musical traditions, combined with the important function of groove, make possible alternative notions of musical form that do not conform to the recursive hierarchies of tonal-music grammars. A teleological concept of form, in which the meaning of music is taken to be its large-scale structure, maybe replaced with an alternative, modular approach, in which the structural content of music is located in the free play of smaller constituent units.

Such notions of musical structure appear in many African and African American musics. Instead of long-range hierarchical form, the focus is on fine-grained rhythmic detail, the dialogic interplay of various musical elements, and superpositional rhythmic hierarchy. Thus, large-scale musical form *emerges* from an improvisatory treatment of these short-range musical ingredients — that is, from the in-time manipulation of simple, modular components.

A prime example is vocalist/bandleader James Brown's frequent practice of 'takin(g) it to the bridge' (Brown, 1991). A typical composition might consist of two different musical spaces or grooves, the transitions between which are cued musically by the vocalist. Hence each section may be arbitrarily long, since all that delineates it is an improvised cue to the next section. Before the performance of the piece, Brown and his band may not know exactly what will happen when; rather, they know what the raw materials are and how to manipulate them during performed time. They are skilled at reacting to environmental cues, individually and collectively, in real time.

As another example, jazz drummer E.W. Wainwright (private communica tion, 1997) described to me a practice of creating large-scale temporal form out of a relatively open-ended musical environment, as it was done by John Coltrane's legendary quartet in the early 1960s (cf. the title track to Coltrane, 1993). In such pieces, the group would improvise in 4/4 time, using a certain pitch organization as a loose framework, such as a mode or a pedal point. Eventually, formal small-section boundaries would emerge by the systematic doubling of the musical period. As was told to Wainwright by Elvin Jones (the quartet's drummer and Wainwright's teacher), the group would initially accent the beginning of every four bars, using intensity as well as rhythmic, melodic, and harmonic parameters. As the piece unfolded, they would expand the period to eight bars, then sixteen, and so on. The larger the period became, the greater heights the intensity and dissonant tension could reach, and the more effective the unified release at the beginning of the next period. As Jones told Wainwright, this practice emerged organically over the course of hundreds of improvised performances, never having been discussed verbally by any band members. These two examples suggest that aspects of musical form can stem from the collective experience of shared, lived time, and from the ways in which musical variation is executed 'in time'.

Perception of Musical Motion

Musical motion is often discussed as a structural abstraction in pitch space, involving the play of forms against one another. A typical view is evident in the following quote from noted composer-theorist Roger Sessions. 'The gestures which music embodies are, after all, invisible gestures; one may almost define them as consisting of movement in the abstract, movement which exists in time but not in space, movement, in fact, which gives time its meaning and its significance for us' (Sessions, 1950, p. 20, quoted in Shove & Repp, 1995, p. 58).

A more grounded approach is taken by Friberg *et al.* (1999; 2000), who investigate the psychological associations of music with certain rhythmic gaits and other locomotive phenomena. But a review of the concept of musical motion by Shove and Repp (1995) highlights the important and overlooked fact that musical motion is, first and foremost, *audible human motion*. To amplify this view, Shove and Repp make use of Handel's (1990, p. 181) three levels of event awareness: the raw psychophysical perception of tones, the perception of abstract qualities of the tones apart from their source, and lastly the apprehension of environmental objects that give rise to the sound event. At this third level, 'the listener does not merely hear the *sound* of a galloping horse or bowing violinist; rather, the listener hears a horse *galloping* and a violinist bowing' (Shove & Repp, 1995, p. 59) In this event-based cognitive framework, the source of perceived musical movement is the human performer, as is abundantly clear to the listener attending to music in performance (Shove & Repp, 1995, p. 60). We connect the perception of musical motion to human motion; from this perspective, music consists of the sound of concerted human action.

Experientialist Music

With the preceding ideas in mind, I wish to pick up the argument laid out by Noë (2000), who discusses the possibility of self-reflexive moments that disrupt the *transparency* of experience, by which he means the invisibility of the process of perception itself. As Noë outlines, when we attempt to perceive the process of perception, we instead perceive the object of perception; the 'experience' of perceptual experience, being mediated through the senses, cannot itself be perceived by the senses. Noë points out that perceptual experience is best understood as a 'temporally extended process of exploration of the environment on the part of an embodied animal' (2000, p. 128) — that is, as *perceptually guided action*. Therefore, 'to investigate experience we need to turn our gaze not inward, but rather to the activity itself in which this temporally extended process consists, to the things we do as we explore the world' (*ibid*).

Noë suggests that certain artists' work foregrounds the actual *experience* of perception (as opposed to the object of perception), thereby interrupting the transparency of experience. He describes the massive sculptural works of Richard Serra as *environmental* in nature, overwhelming in *scale*, *complex* enough to lack a perspicuous vantage, and *particular* in their uniqueness (i.e., site-specific and not reproducible). Noë asserts that these traits demand a process of experiential exploration, as opposed to a passive, transparent, instantaneous perception. In this way, they provide an occasion for the self-reflexive experience of perceiving one's own process of perception.

Encapsulating the embodied process of being in the world, Noë describes experience as a 'temporally extended pattern of exploratory activity'. This could be a definition of improvisation: the real-time interaction with the structure of one's environment. As with improvisation, it is not a passive interaction, for the perceiver/improvisor is engaged in sensorimotor activity, skilfully probing the world at will. This process of embodied action situates the perceiver within the environment; so the perceiver must interact with her embodied self as well. Noë's choice of the word 'pattern' suggests that the activity is either learned, or grounded in some repeatable behaviour.

In this way, we may understand *musical* improvisation as the in-time, temporally extended exploratory interaction with the structure of one's acoustic, musical-formal, cultural, embodied, and situated environment. Musical interaction is not a passive interaction either, because it also *generates* structure — it has its own sonic trace, which becomes part of the same interactive environment, and is perceived as contributing to and altering this environment. This view of musical improvisation has implications for the study of consciousness, as the following examples may illuminate. Noë's notions of scale, complexity, uniqueness, and environment are addressed in these examples. What I wish to stress is the way in which these improvisative performances foreground their *in-time* status, drawing attention to the *experiential* aspect of real-time music-making.

Cecil Taylor

The above concepts came to life in my experience as a performer with Cecil Taylor in 1995. A fearsomely virtuosic pianist–improvisor–composer, Taylor has irreversibly impacted contemporary music with his rich and nuanced musical vision. Taylor's exacting pianistic approach is characterized by a fluid, relaxed, yet powerful technique that could be described as athletic. His performances are rather reminiscent of high-level martial arts: a physical behaviour that is intuitive, improvisational, and interactive, yet at the same time muscular, deeply structured, and surgically precise (Taylor, 1975; 2002b).

The occasion was the performance of his 'creative orchestra' music, which forty west-coast musicians studied and interpreted under his guidance. (A smaller but similar ensemble can be heard on Taylor, 2002a.) Taylor's approach spoke volumes about improvised music as a collective activity. Composition in an improvising context can take on a variety of forms — perhaps some thematic material as a point of departure, or perhaps some music-generative methods or processual cues. Early on, when we were repeatedly questioning him about the role of the written material, he said, 'This [written material] is the formal content of the piece; what I want is for all the players to bring their individual languages to the interpretation and execution of the piece'. Taylor desired that we create a collective embodiment of his material by filtering it through our individual 'languages,' framing the music as discourse, individual sound as personal narrative.

In our week of daily rehearsals with Mr. Taylor, the earlier sessions led us to believe that he was a stickler for detail. I recall that we spent the first three-hour rehearsal on one postage-stamp-sized corner of one of his scores; he would continually repeat and rework the material bit by bit, singing or conducting a certain phrase for us, or asking us to permute the written pitches in a certain way. But towards the end of the week, his requirements grew less stringent, his guidance less direct; he would simply set us in motion and leave the room for a while. I realized that somehow he had taught us his language — his sense of phrasing and repetition, his attention to detail, the way he rigorously reworks and dissects a turn of phrase. Once this had happened, we were free to bring our own ideas to this context — to embody his language. When he returned to the rehearsal room, he would find that we had made something out of his cryptic scores. Evidently, Taylor's aesthetic privileges the sound of personalities interacting over conventional concepts of form. Because of the heightened role that group interactivity played, it felt at times as though we had formed not just an orchestra but a small musical civilization.

Indeed, our group experienced in microcosm the conflict, strife, and tension that a society experiences in macrocosm. Much of this was enacted on a musical level in the performance on October 26, 1995. For example, when some musicians reached the stage, they abandoned their allegiance to the unwritten, brittle orchestral aesthetic that had been developed over the course of rehearsals, choosing instead to yield to the temptation to play non-stop with furious intensity. This behaviour raised the issue of (physical) power: clearly, a tenor saxophonist can play with enough force to drown out a section of six violinists, and a drummer can bury a pianist's efforts with ease. It was found that the louder instrumentalists possessed the privilege to control the intensity level directly, while the softer instrumentalists were forced to defer to such control. (Fellow musician Matthew Goodheart (1996) has observed the added role played by the self-serving musical choices made by certain individuals who wanted to get noticed by the legendary pianist for possible career advancement.)

Also, in the absence of a more dictatorial leader figure or a hard and fast text to which to adhere, we found ourselves in frequent disagreement as to what was 'supposed' to be happening or what to do next. Different factions formed to conduct their own unified small-group activities, allowing for the emergence of pockets of apparent order in the sonic chaos. The resultant performances (which included Taylor himself) featured truly sublime flashes of fortuitous beauty and moments of brilliantly focused small-group improvisation, amidst often-inscrutable orchestral noise.

What about this musical instance could be characterized as 'experiential'? Noë's notions of *environment*, *scale*, *complexity*, and *uniqueness* were each specifically addressed in this performance. In keeping with Taylor's directions, as the audience entered, musicians also entered the stage from the wings and the hall's aisles, bringing their chairs and music stands onstage while chanting and moving in geometric patterns. The musicians were engaging in a performative ritual of 'constructing' the performing environment; this act drew attention to this environment's constructedness, and incorporated the environment into the performance itself. Effectively for the audience, it was unclear at what point in space or time the performance had begun; it was somehow fused with the concert-hall *environment* itself, and with the spectator's entrance into the space. Such performative rituals preface many of Taylor's solo and group concerts; he never takes the setting or occasion for granted, nor does he allow the audience to do so.

The audience members witnessed musical structure emerging in real time as extreme polyphony. From a distance, the overall sound may have seemed vast, dense and unfathomable, fulfilling Noë's requirement of overwhelming *scale*. But with closer attention, they saw small subgroups of musicians visibly discussing strategies, arriving at collective decisions, and acting on them; they observed individual musicians in the aggregate occasionally electing to foreground themselves by performing soloistically, and they saw and heard the real-time response of other members of the ensemble to such acts. The audience was left to contend with these intra-group dynamics and come to their own conclusions about the proceedings. An individual audience member could zero in on small regions of activity, but no single listener ever possessing one privileged listening perspective. This is the musical correlate to experiential *complexity*, in that there is no perspicuous vantage from which to perceive the entire event, and no particular ordered set of perceptions for the listener to follow passively in order to apprehend the ideal 'work'. Lastly, the performance was specific to that time and place; it is non-repeatable in any except the most general sense, and so it displays the required trait of *uniqueness*.

Throughout this performance, our experience of ensemble-as-social-group highlighted the sense of music as the sound of human action, and the sense of improvisation as an embodied, situated activity. The performance consisted of our enacted, sonorous experience of negotiating the improvisative process. We were an orchestra with our experiential apparatus exposed.

Roscoe Mitchell

Recently I had the privilege of working in multi-instrumentalist/composer/improvisor Roscoe Mitchell's ensemble. A pioneer in experimental music, Mitchell is a founding member of the celebrated Art Ensemble of Chicago ([1972] 1991; [1975] 1998; see also Lewis 1998) and the hugely influential collective of African American composer–performers known as the Association for the Advancement of Creative Musicians (Lewis, 2001–02). He is noted for his novel approaches to form, texture, and timbre, unusual instrumentations, and interesting use of constraints in compositions and improvisations.

Mitchell's work on various wind instruments frequently finds him exploring the most liminal behaviours of these instruments (e.g. Mitchell, 1978; 2003). He might construct an entire solo improvisation by passing air through the alto saxophone in various fingering configurations so as not to generate an actual tone; the sporadic pitches that arise from this process provide a dramatic emergent form that keeps the listener transfixed. Or he might circular-breathe through the horn for several minutes, allowing the resultant variation in air pressure to impose a periodic timbral surge on his sound. Or he might find a note on the soprano saxophone that squeaks or cracks, and then work through turning that squeaking into a formal element right before your ears, constructing a masterful solo piece from this odd, 'impure' sound emanating from the horn. On these occasions we witness an intrepid sonic explorer in poignant performative dialogue with his instrument, creating music out of the experiential process of making sound. These performances and the act of listening to them are inherently non-repeatable, predicated as they are on the process of mutual discovery.

Mitchell's ensemble music covers a wide range of instrumentations, stylistic points of reference, and degrees of complexity, and they vary from fully notated to entirely improvised to anywhere in between. In some of Mitchell's ensemble pieces (e.g., Mitchell, 1986), he has the musicians improvise independent, focused streams of musical activity, without self-consciously interacting with the other individual musicians. This would seem at first to go against the standard view of 'jazz' as a highly interactive, dialogic medium. But in fact Mitchell is privileging that very dialogue, insisting on a transparent counterpoint among the various melodic streams. He knows that this dynamic cannot be forced, so his directive is to listen closely without 'following' or imitating one another. Musical counterpoint can occur in unexpected ways, and in this case it unfolds spontaneously from the juxtaposed sonorous actions of the participants. Having performed such pieces with Mitchell, I can attest to the rich variety and specificity of dynamics, textures, and emergent forms that arise from such deceptively simple principles.

At one point in the course of a weeklong studio recording project (Mitchell, 2002), he guided his nine-piece group improvisationally through the sculpting of an introduction to one of his notated pieces, entitled 'this' and based on a poem by e. e. cummings. A certain utterance he made in the process shed light on his creative perspective. Exploring the available options, he asked percussionist Vincent Davis to tap on a wood block, and then to hit a gong. Then he asked guitarist Spencer Barefield about the sympathetic strings on his acoustic guitar, and had him strum them by way of demonstration. Next, he asked percussionist Gerald Cleaver to try a few tremolo dyads on the marimba, first with hard mallets, then with soft ones. He asked to hear these sounds again, one by one, and then in sequence, presumably to compare them, I thought. Then, casually, Mitchell said, 'All right, may I please hear *that much music* again?'

This request hit me hard, because it hadn't dawned on me that what was happening during this process even *was* music; I had unconsciously dismissed it all as pre-compositional timbral exploration. But Mitchell *knew* we had crossed the line into music: a series of human sound events, intentional sonic gestures in organized succession. Of course it was music; how could I have thought otherwise?

In that instant, I learned something profound and difficult to explain. It struck me how the rawest sonic materials and the most primal human acts can be heard as compelling, even beautiful music. I saw that music need not be understood simply as the execution of pre-ordained gestures, and that it can be viewed as a *process of inquiry*, a *path of action*, an exploratory, in-time sonorous exploration/construction of the world — a description that sounds a lot like Noë's description of perceptual experience. It struck me, therefore, that perhaps humans are always making music — that counterpoint and form necessarily emerge from the sound of experiential, perceptually guided human action in time and space.

It was also made clear in this exchange that music can be viewed as a consequence of active listening; it is, at some level, *through* informed listening that music is constructed. Placing the skilful listener in such an active role explodes the category of experiences that we call listening to music, because it allows the listener the improvisatory freedom to frame any moment or any experience as a musical one. *The virtuosic improvisor is always listening; the virtuosic listener is always improvising.*

Challenging the boundary in this way between music and non-music, Mitchell's perspective suggests a listener-centred, bottom-up in/version of Noë's characterization. In this view, it is within the improvising listener's power to re-construct music from sounds in her *environment*, and to reclassify perceptual experiences of arbitrary *scale*, *complexity*, and *uniqueness*, actively reframing the tumult of everyday action as music. The listener is empowered to *constitute* music, self-consciously and actively, from guided sensory input. This view underscores an *essential identity between perceptual experience and improvisation*.

This standpoint, indicated by Mitchell's comment, resonates with Taylor's own all-encompassing view of music as a way of life, as he articulated in an interview:

> It seems to me what music *is*, is everything that you do. . . . [H]opefully everything that I try to do in this situation has the same kind of *control over the senses* that the making of, you know, the *particular* art of music is. So to read, or dance, you know, to converse, is all a part of the making of music. So that, you know, when one walks down the street, and one looks, if there is a fuchsia-coloured awning sticking out on the thirtieth floor, one says, *oh wow*. So that to *me* what it is, *is everything one does* (Mann, 1981, transcribed by author).

It is important to situate this perspective on musical improvisation, in many ways common to Mitchell and Taylor, in the context of African American expressive culture. African American history has at its foundation a proximity to terror and violence imposed from without (Gilroy, 1993). African American expressive culture should therefore be viewed in part as a set of tactics for survival in these conditions. Here improvisation takes on a symbolic weight; in this context, the phrase 'improvised music' suggests not simply that the notes and rhythms are extemporized, but moreover that one is working from a subaltern standpoint of dispossession, in a setting where sheer survival cannot be taken for granted, improvising music using whatever is at hand — even one's own raw sensory input. Hence, it has been suggested that we consider blackness as inherently improvisational, as even at some level synonymous with improvisation (Moten, 2003). (Within the scope of this essay, I cannot possibly do justice to such a vast, complex, and charged topic; for more extensive discussions, a partial list of sources would include Baker, 1984; Baraka, 1963; Benston, 2000; Gilroy, 1993; Moten, 2003; Monson, 2003; Small [1987] 1998.)

I say all this in part to stress that *any* perspective on music and improvisation is necessarily situated in culture, and any discussion of music perception or perceptual experience must account for the cultural situatedness of the very practice of perception.

On Electronic Music

Music production and music perception are interrelated, embodied activities. Until very recently in the history of humankind, with few exceptions (such as birdsong or wind chimes), the music that humans perceive and respond to has always been human music. Before the last century of technological developments, music was almost always generated by human bodies. This is why the class of events that we recognize as music occur in the timescales of human activity — seconds, minutes, hours — and not in microseconds or decades. Music and humanity have arisen in tandem, the former out of the bodily activity of the latter, and so music necessarily bears rhythmic traces of our embodiment: pulse, phrase, gesture, ornament. We bob our heads or tap our feet to pulsations in the tactus range, and we breathe or sway along with the phrasing of a singer, and we listen to rapid rhythmic filigree as if it were speech (Iyer, 2002).

More than a century after the invention of recording technology, we have become accustomed to recorded, disembodied, and electronically generated music. But still, music tends to bear these same traces of embodiment. Pulse-heavy electronic dance music often makes sonic references to the stomping of feet and to sexually suggestive slapping of skin. It is indeed rather telling that today, the most widespread uses of electronic music are in contexts meant for dance; the least humanly embodied music is ironically that which is *most* dependent on our physical engagement with it. It has emerged as a cheaper or less taxing alternative to human music making. One can re-create the pulsating texture of dance music without the physical exertion previously required to do so. The idea of a drum loop encapsulates this possibility; one can loop a danceable drum pattern indefinitely through digital means, thereby creating a whole new notion of temporality in music that lies outside of human action, but still denotes it.

Often, popular electronic music plays in the grey area between bodily presence and electronic impossibility. Much of the electronica of the most recent decade (e.g., Squarepusher, 1997; 2002) displays this playful ambiguity. A sampled 'beat' — i.e., a brief recording of a human drummer — is sliced into small temporal units. These units are played back in rearranged orders, sped up or slowed down, multiply triggered, and otherwise manipulated electronically. Because the original sampled recording bears the microrhythmic traces of embodiment, the result sounds something like a human drummer improvising with often amusing flourishes and ample metric ambiguity. Momentarily regular, almost human-sounding pseudo-drumming devolves into inhumanly rapid sequences of rhythmic attacks, fast enough to resemble digital noise. Such electronic manipulation of familiar musical sounds serves to problematize the listener's image of a human drummer. These manipulations are typically carried out 'out of time' in the studio, in a fashion similar to composition, but the object of these manipulations is a human performance that took place 'in time'. Hence this approach is able to alternately engage and confound our sense of embodied empathy, constructing and deconstructing our mental image of the person behind the sounds.

Also displaying the play of embodiment in contemporary urban music is the hip-hop DJ, who treats the turntables as a kind of improvisational percussion meta-instrument (e.g., X-ecutioners, 1997). Using strategically chosen segments of a vinyl record, the DJ moves the record back and forth with one hand, while creating amplitude envelopes with a fader on a mixer in the other hand. The sound generated is of two general types: one is a percussive scratch derived from rapid motion of the record, and the other is a recognizable, meaningful fragment of recorded music or sound. The latter stroke type often hides the sophisticated, impeccably timed physical gestures involved in their creation, as these gestures are unrelated to the sonic material. The scratch sound, however, bears a direct sonic resemblance to the physical motion involved. There is an interesting continuum between these two general types, and that continuum is navigated improvisationally. A fragment of recorded sound can be manipulated percussively in real time, in a manner that temporarily overrides its referential content, causing it to refer instead to the physical materiality of the vinyl-record medium, and more importantly to the 'in-time' embodiment, dexterity and skill of its manipulator.

These twin art forms each create a sustained interruption of the transparency of perception. The listener experiences the disruption/breakage of the physical act of performance, as recorded fragments of human musical acts undergo ironic, physically impossible manipulations (the root *manus* meaning *hand* revealing the counter-embodiment of the manipulator). This is the subtext of the term 'broken beat', itself an ironic re-tensing of 'break beat': the perceptual experience of this music consists of the *recognition of the act of breaking music with the hands* — the metamusical sound of broken music, of hands breaking the body's beats, of one body taking action upon the sonorous actions of another.

Concluding Remarks

The understanding of music as sonorous human action occurring 'in time' is fundamental to our experience of music. It arises as a consequence of embodiment, and it is an aspect of music-making that is largely taken for granted. The experimental musical improvisations that I have described draw attention to this facet of music, helping us realize the inherent musicality of human activity, and the sense of drama we derive from music as sonorous embodied action embedded in time. The examples of Taylor and Mitchell illustrate some ways in which musical improvisation can foreground its own process, playing the role of experience itself, reminding the listener of one's own act of experiencing it.

Taylor's and Mitchell's approaches share with, say, the X-ecutioners' turntable music, a grounding in the improvisational practices that emerged from

African American experimental forms of the late-twentieth century— and they are perspectives too often neglected by the research community. These are the sorts of perspectives that we need when trying to understand the musical mind, or the science of art, or the relationship of the arts to cognition. We need to maintain as full as possible an understanding of the arts, and to do so we must remain engaged with as many forms of artistic inquiry as we are able. As Ione (2000) notes with respect to Cézanne, many artists knowingly spend long periods of time on the frontiers of their own perception and cognition, dwelling in that self-reflexive experiential domain where one engages in careful phenomenological reflection on sensory experience (Noë, 2002, p. 75). What they find there often stretches our conventional notions of beauty, aesthetics, and even the fundamentals of expression; precisely because of this, their work has much to teach us about consciousness.

References

Art Ensemble of Chicago ([1972] 1991), *Live at Mandel Hall* (compact discs) (Chicago: Delmark Records).

Art Ensemble of Chicago ([1975] 1998), *Fanfare for the Warriors* (compact disc) (New York: Koch Jazz).

Baker, H. (1983), *Blues, Ideology, and African American Literature: A Vernacular Theory* (Chicago: University of Chicago Press).

Baraka, Amiri (Leroi Jones) (1963), *Blues People* (New York: HarperCollins).

Barthes, R. (1975), *S/Z*. Trans. Richard Miller (London: Cape Publishers).

Benston, K. (2000), *Performing blackness: Enactments of African-American modernism* (New York: Routledge).

Blacking, J. (1973), *How Musical is Man?* (Seattle: University of Washington Press).

Brown, James (1991), *Star Time* (compact discs) Compilation of original releases 1956–1984 (New York: PolyGram Records).

Coltrane, John (1993), *Transition* (compact disc). Reissue of original 1970 release, recorded 1965 (New York: GRP Records).

Coltrane, John (1998), *The Complete 1961 Village Vanguard Recordings* (compact discs). Reissue of original recordings (New York: GRP Records).

Ellington, Duke ([1956] 1990), *At Newport* (compact disc) (New York: Columbia Records).

Friberg, A., & Sundberg, J. (1999), 'Does music performance allude to locomotion? A model of final ritardandi derived from measurements of stopping runners', *Journal of the Acoustical Society of America*, **105** (3), pp. 1469–84.

Friberg, A., Sundberg, J., & Frydén, L. (2000), 'Music from motion: Sound level envelopes of tones expressing human locomotion', *Journal of New Music Research*, **29** (3), pp. 199–210.

Gibson, J.J. (1979), *The Ecological Approach to Visual Perception* (Boston, MA: Houghton Mifflin).

Gilroy, P. (1993), *The Black Atlantic: Modernity and double consciousness* (Cambridge, MA: Harvard University Press).

Goodheart, M. (1996), 'Freedom and individuality in themusic of Cecil Taylor', Master's thesis, Mills College, Oakland, California.

Handel, S. (1990), *Listening* (Cambridge, MA: MIT Press).

Ione, Amy (2000), 'An inquiry into Paul Cézanne: The role ofthe artist in studies of perception and consciousness', *Journal of Consciousness Studies* **7**, (8–9), pp. 57–74.

Iyer, V. (1998), *Microstructures of Feel,Macrostructures of Sound: Embodied Cognition in West African and African-American Musics*. Ph.D. Dissertation, University of California, Berkeley. Available onlineat http://cnmat.cnmat.berkeley.edu/People/~vijay/

Iyer, V. (2002), 'Embodied mind, situated cognition,and expressive microtiming in African-American music',*Music Perception* **19** (3), pp. 387–414.

Iyer, V. (2004), 'Exploding the narrative injazz improvisation', in *New Essays in Jazz Studies.*, ed. O'Meally, R., Edwards, B. & Griffin, F. (New York: Columbia University Press).
Lewis, G. (1996), 'Improvised music since 1950: Afrological and Eurological forms', *Black Music Research Journal,* **16** (1), pp. 91–119.
Lewis, G. (1998), 'Singing Omar's song: A (re)construction of Great Black Music', *Lenox Avenue*, **4**, pp. 69–92.
Lewis, G. (2001–02), 'Experimental music in black and white: The AACM in New York, 1970–1985', *Current Musicology* **71–73**, pp. 100–57.
Mann, R. (1981), *Imagine the Sound* (documentaryfeature film) (Janus Films).
Mitchell, R. (1978), *L-R-G, The Maze, S II Examples* (compact disc) (Whitehall, MI: Nessa Records).
Mitchell, R. (1986), *The Flow of Things* (compact disc) (Milan: Black Saint Records).
Mitchell, R. (2002), *Song for my Sister* (compact disc) (New York: Pi Recordings).
Mitchell, R. (2003), *Solo 3* (compact disc) (New York: Mutable Music).
Monson, I. (ed. 2003), *The African Diaspora: A Musicalperspective* (New York: Routledge).
Moten, F. (2003), *In the break: The aesthetics of the blackradical tradition* (Minneapolis: University of Minnesota Press).
Noë, A. (2000), 'Experience and experiment in art', *Journal of Consciousness Studies* **7** (8–9), pp. 123–35.
Noë, A. (2002), 'On what we see', *Pacific Philosophical Quarterly* **83**, pp. 57–80.
Rowell, L. (1988), 'The idea of music in India and theAncient West', *Acta Philosophica Fennica* **43**, pp. 323–42.
Schutz, A. (1964), 'Making music together', in *Collected Papers II: Studies in Social Theory* (The Hague: Martinus Nijhoff).
Sessions, R. 1950. *The Musical Experience of Composer, Performer, Listener* (Princeton: Princeton University Press).
Shore, B. (1996), *Culture in Mind: Cognition, Culture, and the Problem of Meaning* (New York: Oxford University Press).
Shove, P. & Repp, B. (1995), 'Musical motion and performance:theoretical and empirical perspectives', in *The Practice of Performance*, ed. J. Rink (Cambridge, UK: CambridgeUniversity Press).
Small, C. ([1987] 1998), *Music of the Common Tongue: Survival and Celebration in African American music* (Hanover, NH: Wesleyan University Press).
Smithers, T. (1996), 'On What Embodiment Might Have to do with Cognition', in *Embodied Cognition and Action: Papers from the 1996 AAAI Fall Symposium (Technical ReportFS-96-02)* , ed. M. Mataric (Menlo Park, CA: AAAI Press), pp. 113–16.
Squarepusher (1997), *Big Loada* (compact disc) (Sheffield, UK: Warp Records).
Squarepusher (2002), *Do You Know Squarepusher?* (compact disc) (London: Warp Records).
Taylor, Cecil. (1975), *Silent Tongues* (LP record) (Germany: Black Lion Records).
Taylor, Cecil. (2002a), *The Light of the Corona* (compact disc) (Berlin: FMP Records).
Taylor, Cecil. (2002b), *The Willisau Concert* (compact disc) (Zürich: Intakt Records).
X-ecutioners (1997), *X-pressions* (compact disc) (San Francisco: Asphodel Records).

David Borgo

The Play of Meaning and the Meaning of Play in Jazz

Trumpeter Don Cherry was fond of saying that 'there is nothing more serious than fun'.[1] And philosopher Hans Georg Gadamer (1993, p.102) seems to echo his words when he writes: 'Seriousness is not merely something that calls us away from play; rather, seriousness in playing is necessary to make the play wholly play'.[2] Individuals, communities and cultures the world over delight in the play of musical sound *and* debate its play of meanings. For specialists, musical discussion often hinges on cryptic symbols and impenetrable codes, but for everyone, understanding music relies on basic cognitive and social processes. By *musicking* together — to borrow Christopher Smalls' (1998) evocative phrase for taking part in any way in musical activity — we bond with one another and create shared meanings.[3] We also define or express ourselves within and against a musical community and a historical and cultural tradition.

The world of jazz as a tradition provides a rich context for investigating the relationship between formal musical syntax, social interactive processes and cognitive and cultural understandings. In this essay I explore original jazz performances by John Coltrane (*A Love Supreme*) and Sonny Rollins (*Freedom Suite*) and recent reinterpretations by other artists for insight into the cognitive and social processes through which musical meanings are negotiated and renegotiated. My analysis draws on work in cognitive science with categorization and conceptual mapping and on the notion of signifyin(g) first proposed by Henry Louis Gates (1988) for African American cultural studies.

Correspondence:
David Borgo, Music Department, University of California at san Diego, 9500 Gilman Dr., La Jolla, CA 92093-0326, USA. *Email: dborgo@ucsd.edu*

[1] Quoted to me in an interview with Adam Rudolph, a percussionist and former collaborator with Cherry.

[2] See Sutton-Smith (1974) for an introduction to anthropological perspectives on play.

[3] In *Keeping Together in Time*, William H. McNeil (1995) argues that coordinated rhythmic activity is fundamental to life in society. And music, from marching bands to dance clubs, certainly plays an important role in organizing this coordinated rhythmic activity.

Journal of Consciousness Studies, **11**, No. 3–4, 2004, pp. 174–90

A Love Extreme: Defining and Categorizing Music

Categorization is a central part of human cognition, and it dramatically affects how we attend to our environment and which details we recognize, store and later recall. How and what we categorize also invariably affects other important debates over cultural, historical and artistic value. Considerable research in cognitive science demonstrates that the 'basic' level of human understanding operates at the middle level of taxonomy, optimising efficiency and information (e.g., Rosch, 1978). A child first learns to categorize things like 'table', or 'cat' before the more specific level of 'coffee table' or 'Himalayan Persian cat' or the more general level of 'furniture' or 'pets'. And when I am asked by a stranger to describe what is in my case when I am travelling, I normally respond with 'saxophone' rather than 'musical instrument' or 'Selmer Balanced Action tenor saxophone', optimising information with efficiency.

This cognitive economy can be achieved in several ways. One can determine membership based on formal, necessary and sufficient conditions. For example, the category of birds would seemingly involve the necessary and sufficient conditions of feathers, beaks and winged flight. Obviously an approach focused on a limited set of prevalent features may inappropriately include, or exclude, members. For example, a categorization of fish focused exclusively on the necessary and sufficient conditions of natural environment and means of locomotion would include whales and dolphins despite the fact that their mode of respiration and means of reproduction makes them mammals. Alternatively, one can invoke prototypes as a way to describe the most typical member of a given category. A wren or robin, for instance, is often perceived as a more typical bird than say a penguin or emu. Finally, models of categorization are inherently conditioned by individual and cultural values and goals, which can change, often dramatically, over time.

In many jazz circles, performers, listeners, critics and scholars debate not only the merits of specific performances, but also the very naming of the music and which approaches and sounds can be considered as 'authentic' jazz. Definitions of jazz range from those focused on necessary and sufficient conditions — such as 'acoustic music' that 'swings' and features 'improvisation' — to those that accept and even emphasize the fluid and hazy boundaries of graded membership (e.g., Latin jazz, Turkish jazz, classical jazz, electronic jazz, and so on). Our definitions of jazz, or at least the processes we use to categorize potential instances of the music, significantly affect how we hear and evaluate both newer and prototypically canonical work. Referring to 'textbook' definitions of music in general, Zbikowski (2002, p.48) writes 'although such debates appear to be about music, they are in fact about how to define the categories through which we organize our understanding of music'.[4]

---

[4] Of course the category of 'music' itself varies between individuals, cultures and historical time periods. Ethnomusicologists often point out that not all cultures have a term that translates to Western notions of 'music', both accepting more and less into their conceptualizations. And contemporary Western musicians have challenged listeners to hear any sound as musical (for instance, John Cage,

The specific sounds and dynamic structures of musical performance can also exploit and challenge our ability to categorize. Each musical gesture or utterance, on first or subsequent encounter, is heard in relationship to our individual musical history and acculturated musical sensibilities. The mere mention of the title to John Coltrane's album *A Love Supreme*, for instance, invokes a whole host of responses to jazz aficionados. For many, the title brings immediately to mind the four-note motive — A-Love-Su-Preme — that serves to unify the composed and improvised parts of Coltrane's suite.[5] Others may instead hear in their 'mind's ear' the opening stroke on the Chinese gong and the introductory 'benediction' of Coltrane's horn. And for Los Angeles residents and National Public Radio listeners, the mention of *A Love Supreme* may even bring to mind the KCRW program titled *Which Way LA?*, which uses Coltrane's memorable introduction as its opening theme. Jazz performers may be triggered to reflect on their own experiences either practicing along with the recording in private, or trying their hands at playing the spiritually charged music with a group at a jam session or in concert. Avid fans may connect to the first time they heard the suite or to the context of a particularly memorable encounter with the recording. A select few may even have been fortunate enough to hear the only known live performance of *A Love Supreme* by Coltrane's group in Antibes, France in 1965. Regular jazz concert-goers may also be able to recall experiences hearing all — or more likely part — of the suite performed live by groups led by Elvin Jones, McCoy Tyner, Alice Coltrane, or perhaps John McLaughlin and Carlos Santana, or others. And those listeners newer to jazz may actually know the recent recorded version of *A Love Supreme* by Branford Marsalis' quartet rather than the original recording.

All of this is to say that *A Love Supreme* invokes at least as many meanings as there have been individual listeners to the now-famous work. And yet it also, increasingly so, has a shared canonical meaning to historians, performers and fans alike — a meaning that appears to transcend its historically situated original incarnation. Ashley Kahn's (2002a) recent book focuses explicitly on Coltrane's best-known work. And it does much both to provide specific historic detail on the production and reception of the album *and* to preserve and further the sense that *A Love Supreme* holds a transcendent place in the recorded work of Coltrane and in the history of recorded jazz. According to Kahn (2002b) *A Love Supreme* has become Coltrane's 'career-defining, genre-defying classic'. In exploring the specifics of categorization, one might ask how this 'classic' work evolves and what the impact of such a prototype continues to be on the listening and performing jazz community.

The music on the original release was recorded direct to two-track stereo in less than four hours (the evening of December 9, 1964) and in album order, and,

although his role as a 'composer' and the performance of his works as 'compositions' conform to our conceptual models for music and music making.

[5] Lewis Porter (1985) uses this perceived structural unity to argue for Coltrane's uncanny ability to improvise with 'extraordinary compositional clarity . . . to get the most out of his restricted selection of materials' (pp. 600 and 607). His emphasis and specific language, however, reflect the general bias for compositional study and European conceptions of musical structure and coherence in the music academy.

in the case of the third and fourth parts, in one seamless take.[6] Its quick release in February of 1965 benefited from both commercial and cultural factors. ABC–Paramount, Impulse's parent company, offered strong support to the album's release, riding the industry-wide wave sparked by the success of the 'British Invasion.' And Coltrane's profoundly spiritual music and message — delivered most clearly in the album's liner notes and 'recited' by Coltrane's horn in 'Psalm,' the fourth part of the suite — struck a chord with both civil rights activists and the burgeoning counterculture (Kahn 2002a, pp.150–65).

Coltrane, however, only performed *A Love Supreme* once in concert, and the existing recording confirms that the suite was improvised over only the barest of preconceived sketches. The ontological identity of *A Love Supreme* as a conceptual model may then be construed as somewhat fluid. Conceivably a new version of the work need only reference these basic underlying materials to ensure membership in the category. Even off-the-cuff quotations of the 'A-Love-Su-Preme' motive on bandstands and at jam sessions around the world — frequently in extremely diverse contexts — can evoke the original work to listeners and other musicians without fail. And yet the definitive studio recording is so well known and well regarded by millions of listeners that any attempt to revisit its structure, or any departure from its original form and content is suspect. Not only is the 'A-Love-Su-Preme' motive well known, but the exact instrumentation and personnel on the album, and each musician's approach to improvisation and exact improvised solos are intimately familiar to countless listeners. An 'authentic' approach to this work focused on these 'necessary and sufficient' conditions would require a drummer who 'sounds like' Elvin Jones, a piano player who plays like McCoy Tyner, a bass player who can imitate Jimmy Garrison's individual touch, and a saxophonist who can reference Coltrane's sound and style and his specific approach to developing the four-part suite.

So how have performers dealt with *A Love Supreme*? Countless saxophonists who have been influenced by Coltrane's music have, of course, offered posthumous tributes, but usually with the conspicuous absence of this 'career-defining classic'. Musicians who play instruments not featured on the original recording seem more willing to take on Coltrane's signature suite. Electric guitarists John McLaughlin and Carlos Santana recorded a popular version of *A Love Supreme* (actually only Part 1 — 'Acknowledgement') in 1973, which adds Latin percussion, fiery riffs and electronic distortion to produce a very different group sound and approach. And more recently, trombonist Conrad Herwig and trumpeter Ray Vega have offered Latinized versions of Coltrane's best-known work as well. And perhaps the most unconventional contemporary interpretation of Coltrane's memorable music is by bagpiper Rufus Harley.

[6] On the following day in the studio, Coltrane invited saxophonist Archie Shepp and bassist Dr. Art Davis to expand the group to a sextet but none of this material made the original release. It seems that the sextet only recorded 'Part I — Acknowledgement' that day. The two surviving takes were released for the first time on a 2-CD Deluxe Set by Impulse in 2002 and provide an interesting example of how unreleased material, when later released, can provoke similar ontological comparisons as those discussed in this article. See Kahn (2002a, Ch. 2) for a nice discussion of this session and for commentary from involved musicians and listeners.

Even those musicians intimately associated with John and the original sessions have only touched on his suite lightly. His widow, Alice Coltrane, was first to record a portion of the suite in 1971 (again, only 'Acknowledgement'), but she used a drum-less group featuring her organ and harp playing and Leroy Jenkins' violin. Drummer Elvin Jones, in revisiting his original work on the album, has perhaps stayed closest to the 'classic' quartet arrangement and approach. As Jones stated, 'I always live in the hope that someday all of John Coltrane's compositions will be played as a matter of course. It shouldn't be anything exceptional for musicians to play this music' (quoted in Kahn, 2002a, p.207). Starting in 1978, Jones added two parts of the suite ('Acknowledgement' and 'Resolution') to the repertoire of his groups, despite the misgivings of some of his sidemen including Frank Foster, a tenor saxophonist, who later expressed, 'I wish I had stuck to my guns and said, "No, Elvin, I can't do this"'. Even saxophonist Ravi Coltrane (John's son) admits,

> when you go to a gig, and somebody wants to play *Resolution*, it might be fun, but to me, it's sacred as a whole. *A Love Supreme* is not just a tune or a record, it's an offering to God, and not just an idle offering. It's really music for a different purpose, not to be hip or cool, or even nostalgic (quoted in Kahn, 2002a, p. 206).

Despite these frequent warnings and misgivings, several contemporary jazz musicians have taken on this rather marked challenge in John Coltrane's repertoire. Starting in 1992, trumpeter Wynton Marsalis has occasionally performed the entire suite in a quartet setting (often with Elvin Jones on drums) and in February of 2002 he led the Lincoln Center's fifteen-piece jazz orchestra in an arranged reading of the work. Saxophonist Branford Marsalis recorded a truncated version of the suite for the compilation album *Red, Hot & Cool* and more recently revisited the work with his quartet on the album *Footsteps of our Fathers*. Saxophonist David Murray has also recently recorded 'Part I — Acknowledgment' on his album titled *Octet Plays Trane*.

For his rendition, Branford Marsalis used not only the 'classic' quartet instrumentation, but also the same rhythmic structure and transition approach for each part of the suite and the same order of solos. While the improvised portions of the suite clearly differ (and represent the experienced style of each of the band members), they differ in a way that keeps the original in mind for the well-versed listener. From the opening gesture of 'Acknowledgement' — which maintains the gong-like statement and the rubato saxophone introduction — to the spiritually evocative recitation of 'Psalm' it is possible to hear Marsalis' performance as a conscious and continual reference to, and reframing of, the original. Coltrane's opening call of the 'benediction' is a forceful ascending phrase, so Marsalis enters with a stately phrase utilizing the intervals of the primary 'A-Love-Su-Preme' motive but in descent. And the recurring 'Thank You Lord' cadence of the original 'Psalm' relies on a descending minor 3rd or perfect 5th interval, while Marsalis' version seems to imply more often than not an ascending resolution to tonic from the minor 7th just below. It is at this level of micro-improvisational detail that Marsalis' recording exploits and challenges, in subtle ways. His approach seems also to imply that an 'authentic' performance of Coltrane's suite must include many of the 'necessary and sufficient conditions' discussed above.[7]

In contrast, David Murray's recording adds two trumpets, a trombone, and an alto sax to the original foursome. Although Murray plays the original's opening 'benediction' figure rather literally and his bass player, Jaribu Shahid, plays the four-note unifying motive throughout the performance, it is also clear from the opening gestures that the expanded instrumentation allows Murray additional possibilities of improvised and arranged polyphony. The four other horns quickly enter into a densely improvised texture to frame Murray's 'benediction', and background figures appear and reappear throughout the performance to frame each of the solo statements. Murray's drummer, Mark Johnson, also performs a rather different rhythmic interpretation than the original, offering a more funk-based groove throughout.

On the original recording of 'Acknowledgment,' Coltrane uses the four-note motive as the building block of his improvisation. At one point (starting at 4:54) he plays the figure 37 times in succession, transposing the melodic fragment through all twelve chromatic keys with, in the words of Ashley Kahn (2002a, p.102), 'exhaustive precision and apparent randomness'. Murray's tenor saxophone solo, by contrast, uses extreme glissandos and vocalized screams that, at times, blur exact pitches in a style more reminiscent of Coltrane's later work. The various individual soloists in Murray's octet also depart in significant ways from the motivic, developmental approach to modal improvisation pioneered by Coltrane. Murray's reliance on the central 'A-Love-Su-Preme' motive in the bass ensures that informed listeners are continually aware of the original conceptual model, but the instrumentation, rhythm, arrangement and soloing styles heard on his recording depart significantly from the model established by Coltrane and his colleagues. In the liner notes to the album, Murray acknowledges:

> I admired his songs, his arrangements, his technique, the tempos he chose. But to do this recording, I did not want to just copy him. The writing, the playing, had to have my signature.... I had to get a signature sound before I could embrace someone like Coltrane.

A Love Supreme, both in its original form and as it has been reified and refashioned, invites us to rethink the ways in which we discuss and categorize music, performance and cognition. The ontological identity of the music is intimately bound into a complex network of experiences for listeners and performers so that the notions of perception, conception and action — often treated as separate cognitive processes — appear to emerge from a single experiential blend. From its inception, Coltrane's suite connected strongly with its socio-political moment *and* was received as a work of universal and timeless significance. *A Love Supreme* represented both genre-defying music and, perhaps ironically, the most

[7] His comments during a 'Before & After' ('blindfold') test conducted by *Jazz Times* magazine (December 2002) when Murray's octet performance was heard also appear to support this contention.

prototypical jazz of its time. Its status as a revered recording made it something to which subsequent generations of musicians would aspire and something from which they just as often would recoil. Depending on one's perspective and ideologies, Coltrane's work exemplified the 'prototypical' approach for music without preconceptions and boundaries or the 'necessary and sufficient' conditions that describe competent and compelling modern jazz.

Performed with only the barest of compositional sketches, the elastic and dynamic form of *A Love Supreme* challenges the all-too-frequent notion that music is best represented as an abstract and symbolic code and in a disembodied and ahistorical fashion. Events, rather than objects and their names, appear to form the basis for the process of categorization and conceptualisation (Rosch, 1999). Our models of categorization are also inherently conditioned by individual and cultural values and goals, which can change, often dramatically, over time. In the case of Coltrane, his immense spiritual and emotional resonance in the jazz community made certain of his performances 'off-limits' to all but those who were most intimately connected to the man and his music or to those daring enough to depart in significant and marked ways from the originals. But perceptions and categorizations can change. An untouchable part of the revered canon can, over time, become a decidedly more impersonal historical milestone. And yet, at any given moment, the range of artistic conceptions and interpretations will vary widely. While Elvin Jones' dream may have become a partial reality — it *is* less exceptional to play even Coltrane's most spiritually evocative work like *A Love Supreme* — the status of Coltrane as a canonical 'forefather' may always mark in complex ways any tributes to his work and significance.

Sweet Freedom: Musical Syntax and Cross-domain Mapping

In listening to music, we rely on syntactic conventions to understand the local patterns specific to the immediate performance we are hearing and to relate those patterns to previously encountered musical structures. In other words, musical syntax describes at the same time the structure specific to an individual work and the structures shared between musical 'works' that give rise to a musical tradition or genre.

Cross-domain mapping is a general cognitive process through which we structure an unfamiliar or abstract domain in terms of a more familiar or concrete one. Recent work in cognitive linguistics has offered substantial evidence that cross-domain mappings are not simply manifestations of literary creativity, such as figures of speech, but rather are pervasive in everyday discourse and integral to the very process of cognition and consciousness.[8] Cross-domain mappings do not simply 'represent' one domain in terms of another. They are grounded in our

[8] In *The Literary Mind*, Mark Turner (1996) asserts that simple stories are basic to human communication and cognition. And Antonio Damasio (1999), in *The Feeling of What Happens*, offers considerable empirical evidence and neurophysiological detail to support the idea that 'simple stories' are fundamental not only to human communication and cognition, but also to consciousness itself.

bodily experiences and perceptions and create precise, inference-preserving mappings between the structures of both domains (Lakoff & Johnson, 1980).

Because of the rather abstract and transient nature of musical sound, cross-domain mapping plays an important role in musical discourse. Our musical vocabularies are filled with conceptual metaphors: pitches are high or low; sounds are close or distant; textures are dense or sparse. We cross modalities with other senses: sounds can be light, bright, clear, or dark; harmonies can be sweet or tart; textures can be sharp, rough, or smooth. To quote Larry Zbikowski (1998, n.p.)

> Although we speak of 'musical space' (and locate tones within it), this space does not correspond, in a rational way, to physical space; although we speak of 'musical motion', the motion is at best apparent, and not real. The concepts of space and motion are extended to music through metaphorical transference as a way to account for certain aspects of our experience of music. These metaphors are not an addition to musical understanding, but are in fact basic to it.

Zbikowski analyses the conceptual metaphor *pitch relationships as relationships in vertical space*. After a century of ethnomusicological inquiry, it is clear that this metaphor is not valid in every culture or even in every time period in the West. The Balinese have 'large' and 'small' pitches to correspond to the size of their gongs and metallophones. And in Ancient Greece, pitches were conceived of as 'sharp' or 'heavy'. Why has the conceptual metaphor of *pitch relationships as relationships in vertical space* become the dominant one in the contemporary Western World? It does not correspond to the physical layout of all, or even most western instruments: e.g., to go up in pitch on a cello or stand-up bass you must go further down the neck of the instrument. But it does correspond well to the system of notation that has permitted the preservation and visualization of musical works for several centuries. As Zbikowski (2002, p. 72) notes, 'The cross-domain mappings employed by any theory of music are thus more than simple curiosities, they are actually key to understanding music as a rich cultural product that both constructs and is constructed by cultural experience'.

Framing jazz in terms of the cultural experiences it constructs and is constructed by is no easy task. Jazz music has exhibited, to loosely borrow W.E.B. Du Bois' well-known phrase, something of a double-consciousness. Much of the impetus for past and present scholarship in jazz studies has been to gain a more nuanced understanding of the ways in which African and European values, resources and imperatives have combined and continue to recombine in this music. From the earliest meetings of downtown Creoles of Color and uptown Negroes in turn-of-the-century New Orleans, jazz has been a multi-cultural music. Over the years (and particularly since the 1960s) many jazz artists have looked to freer, more avant-garde modes of improvisation and interaction and away from traditional Western conceptions of tonality, metred time, and, by connection, the hegemony of musical notation and the role of the composer in music. Not only did many practitioners of the jazz avant-garde dispense with the use of standard notation; in many cases, this freer approach to improvising and the often highly complex resulting sounds and textures defied the very act of notating music. How, they might ask, can a dynamic, temporal art ever be reduced to a static, two-dimensional representation?[9]

Unhinged from the process and products of standard music notation, this type of music, or better 'musicking', encourages different cross-domain mappings and different ways of engaging with musical sound and meaning, while at the same time not completely dispensing with those mappings that are already established. One conceptual metaphor that remains in use today for describing this type of adventurous jazz playing is 'outside' (Such, 1993). The continuum from 'inside' to 'outside' playing creates a cross-domain relationship between our embodied sense of interactions with containers or structures and the music's allegiance to traditional Western musical values and practices. Musical dimensions in which a music or musician may travel 'outside' include tonality, metered time, instrumental timbre, articulation and others.

For example, jazz historians often describe John Coltrane's music developing from his more 'inside' playing of the 1950s to the final 'outside' explorations shortly before his death in 1967. The music of Coltrane's quartet circa *A Love Supreme* — with its minimal compositional details and heavily improvised, polyrhythmic and polytonal character — marks, for many, the beginnings of Coltrane's final artistic phase and his desire to move further 'outside' of accepted jazz conventions. Elvin Jones' drumming was pushing 'outside' of the confines of standard 4/4 metric time by layering multiple contrasting rhythms over and across the underlying musical meter. McCoy Tyner's harmonic accompaniment was exploring 'closely' and 'distantly' related keys (note the existing conceptual metaphor for the spatial dimension of harmony). And Coltrane was superimposing yet more harmonic implications and, with his explorations of the extreme registers and timbres of the saxophone, seemed to be finding sounds 'beyond' the instrument's traditional sonic palette (see Borgo, 2003b).

Most commentators have also connected these and similarly impassioned sounds with the larger social, cultural and political climate of the times. For example, *Freedom Suite*, a 19-minute, three-movement, integrated work by Sonny Rollins, has been called jazz music's first explicit instrumental protest piece. Duke Ellington and others had made culturally and politically aware instrumental music prior to this time, but Rollins' 1958 album came shortly after the Little Rock school integration incident (about which Louis Armstrong had made some of his first public criticisms of government policy) and the album also included a short note by the saxophonist making his message explicit:

> America is deeply rooted in Negro culture: its colloquialisms; its humour, its music. How ironic that the Negro, who more than any other people can claim America's culture as his own, is being persecuted and repressed; that the Negro, who has exemplified the humanities in his very existence, is being rewarded with inhumanity.

---

[9] Jazz music has, of course, since at least 1917, relied on the 'temporally frozen' sounds of recordings to document and disseminate much of its history and performance practice. And avant-garde jazz musicians have, at times, devised innovative notational strategies for documenting and disseminating their work.

Sparked most directly by his first-hand experience of housing discrimination in New York, Rollins later said, 'At the time it struck me. . . . Here I had all these reviews, newspaper articles and pictures . . . what did it all mean if you were still a nigger, so to speak? This is the reason I wrote the suite' (Bowden, 2002). Although it appeared before the Civil Rights Movement reached critical mass nationally, the album's original release on Orrin Keepnews' Riverside label did cause a minor sensation. Less than a month after it hit the shelves, Keepnews repackaged the LP with the title *Shadow Waltz*, the name of another track on the recording, and wrote a new set of liner notes that pulled back slightly from Rollins' original statement. Although Rollins' protest suite is often given less treatment by historians than similarly intentioned, but later work by artists such as Charles Mingus, Max Roach, John Coltrane, and Archie Shepp, the fact that his words were effectively censored speaks to their importance and perceived radicalism at the time.

Like Coltrane's *A Love Supreme*, Rollins' *Freedom Suite* has received only limited treatment by other artists. Its original cultural context placed it firmly in a time and place that other artists perhaps felt unwilling or unprepared to revisit. A quick search of the database at allmusic.com produced only one additional reference to the work prior to 2002, a nine-minute rendition by pianist Walter Bishop Jr. in 1972. In 2002, however, two next-generation saxophonists recorded Rollins' suite, providing rather different interpretations and a point of discussion for the flexibility of approaches to performing and interpreting musical syntax in jazz.

First, a quick discussion of the original work as performed by Rollins. Filling one side of an LP, Rollins and his piano-less trio present the three movements of the work in a seamless fashion with a fourth theme serving as an interlude both before and after the second movement. A central melody, presented at the outset, reappears at various times in the composed and improvised sections and eventually concludes the work, providing a singular, unifying feeling to the whole. The first movement involves a rhythmically playful romp alternating between pedal point sections in G major and walking-type bass lines which briefly 'side-slip' to a distantly related key. The pronounced rhythmic interplay between all three musicians, and especially the drumming of Max Roach, lends an open and freer feeling to what is still a rather structured eight-bar form.[10] The interlude leading to movement two is in a boisterous 6/8 time with a propulsive bass line provided by Oscar Pettiford. There are no improvised solos on the brief interlude, and only a short cadenza-like line by Rollins at the end that appears unaltered in both presentations. Movement two is something of a conventional ballad, but in a somewhat unconventional move, all three musicians, including Roach on drums, take solos. At the ballad's end, the principle theme is quoted and the interlude reappears. The final movement is an up-tempo reworking of the central thematic material and provokes some of the most heated playing by Rollins and some of

[10] The rhythmic complexity of the performance causes author Eric Nisensen (2000, p. 128) to misidentify the alternating sections as contrasting 4/4 with 3/4.

the most involved interactions between all three. The suite ends with a final statement of the concluding phrase of the initial melody and a decisive cadence.[11]

In addition to *A Love Supreme,* Branford Marsalis recorded a complete version of Rollins' best-known suite on his album *Footsteps of our Fathers.* Similarly, Marsalis also adopts the same instrumentation as the original, removing his regular piano player, Joey Calderazzo, to form a core trio. He also maintains the same three-part structure and produces a recording only slightly longer than the original. In the only departure from the original's formal arrangement, Marsalis uses the interlude between the first and second movements only, opting for an extended drum solo to bridge to the final section. The solo order and use of conversational passages between the instruments is unchanged from Rollins' performance. Marsalis does adopt a more modern vocabulary at times, reflecting different sensibilities towards dissonance or 'outside' playing, but interestingly, during the ballad, his solo harks back to the sweetness of Ben Webster's approach as much as it does to Rollins' more brittle and idiosyncratic style. By continually evoking the original to knowledgeable listeners, Marsalis' trio plays with the specific grammar or micro-syntax of *Freedom Suite*, and makes few alterations to the overall form or rhetoric of the work. Although Rollins' original recording in 1958 only hinted at the musical freedoms that would quickly follow, Marsalis' approach in 2002 remains well 'inside' the original's frame.

By contrast, saxophonist David S. Ware, who studied privately with Rollins in the 1970s, recorded a version of *Freedom Suite* in 2002 that honours the spirit and basic structure while exploring additional territory only hinted at in the original. The most immediate difference is in instrumentation. Ware adds pianist Matthew Shipp to the original trio format, perhaps preferring not to disrupt his working quartet, but also necessitating a significant reworking of the suite. In the late 1950s, artists such as Sonny Rollins were experimenting with piano-less formats to free up the harmonic structure of their performances and remove any strong reference to Western tonality and tempered pitch. But over forty years later, the list of progressive piano stylists has grown long and impressive. Shipp's presence and musical sensibilities immediately take this performance in new directions.

The differences appear at both the macro and micro level of development. On the macro level, Ware and his quartet frequently opt to forego strict, metered time in favour of the open yet propulsive rhythmic delivery now common to freer improvisational jazz settings. And although he adopts most of Rollins' original melodic material, he frequently delivers it in rubato fashion and launches solos far less tied to predetermined chordal structures. Ware's most notable alteration to the overall arrangement of the suite is expanding the interlude material — described in its original form by author Eric Nisensen (2000, p.128) as 'ominous', 'driving', dark' and 'intense' — into a tumultuous, extended groove

[11] On a slightly more technical note, it is worth mentioning that the key centres for the three movements move progressively upward, from concert G to A-flat to B-flat. The final statement of the theme in this new key provides not only a sense of closure to the suite, but also a sense that we have taken a journey and arrived at a 'higher' place.

described by *Wire* contributor Bill Shoemaker (2002) as 'more pile driving than dancing'. Ware also treats the ballad — which in its original can't help but be heard as slightly dated or nostalgic to contemporary ears — to a passionate, rubato delivery more akin to the modal and spiritual explorations of Coltrane and his admirers.

Even on the micro level, subtle differences mark a more contemporary interpretation of the work. To start, Ware takes apart the unifying theme of the suite and expands on the 'openness' of the drum and bass sections, a 'freedom' which was only implied on the original recording, and he launches his solo on the first movement from the unresolved, 'side-slip' portion of the melody, foregoing the strong resolution of the original and Marsalis' versions. Shipp doesn't play during Ware's solo, but when he is ready to enter (3:45) he restates the theme before beginning his own piano improvisations. He, too, starts his solo at a surprising place, landing on a sharply dissonant cluster just as the theme is about to resolve.

Rollins' third movement, now Ware's fourth with the expansion of the interlude, is also presented with a truncated melody that stays close to the unifying theme of the suite but also propels the improvisations into more 'outside' territory. And the brief cadenza-like moment of the interlude from the original version is seized upon by Ware as a moment to, according to Shoemaker (2002), 'reel in the loose ends of the past fifty years' tenor saxophone vocabulary'. In brief, Ware's interpretation expands greatly on the rhythmic, harmonic, and melodic 'freedoms' at play in the original recording. His performance goes well 'outside' of the model established by Rollins, and yet it does not result in a formless music devoid of rules or structures. Instead, his group negotiates between existing codes and their pleasurable dismantling, to borrow a definition of improvisation offered by Corbett (1995, p. 237).[12]

This negotiation resonates well with contemporary models of the way we think. The work of Fauconnier and Turner (2002), for instance, builds on the idea of cross-domain mapping to provide a more nuanced picture of the ways in which new meanings and understandings can arise from the blended input of several conceptual frames. The basic processes of blending include composition, completion and elaboration. Composition projects the content from each of the inputs into the blended space, completion fills out the pattern in the blend by referencing information in long-term memory, and elaboration involves extending or applying the now fully formed blend into new domains or new situations (see also Grady *et al.* 1999). At each of these stages of the blend, new content and new meanings may develop that were not available from either of the input spaces. Blends can be created 'on the fly' with only fleeting significance, or they may become established in conventions of thought and, in turn, allow for other distinct blends to emerge.

Each of the performances discussed here establishes a conceptual blend on the level of musical structure by referencing existing musical constructs and by extending or augmenting those mental and sonic spaces in performance.

[12] For related work see Borgo (2002 and in press).

Conceptual blends may also emerge on hearing each of these new recordings and by drawing on one's familiarity (or non-familiarity) with the original and on one's lifetime of musical and cultural experience. And blends of this type may undergo significant elaboration or may trigger additional conceptual blends in 'non-musical' domains as well.

Freedom, for instance, has been, and will continue to be, interpreted in countless ways depending on individual, cultural and historical circumstance (see Borgo, 2003a). Rollins' original recording is connected socio-politically to the Civil Rights Movement and it evoked for many listeners, both then and now, conceptual blends between its sonic domain and its cultural and historical moment. Although there are no liner notes to accompany Ware's recent disc, his musical approach (and perhaps also the red, white and blue artwork on the cover) has sparked some comment on contemporary social and political concerns. In his *All Music Guide* review, Thom Jurek (2002) hints that the album's 'layers of meaning are particularly evocative at the turn of the twenty first century, where the very meaning of freedom is hotly debated in all cultures'. And Marshall Bowden (2002) writes 'one is also tempted to remember the story of Rollins' censorship upon the release of the original album and see a parallel with the possible erosion of civil liberties in the wake of 9/11'.

Perhaps the most compelling aspect of musical performance is its ability to engage listeners on a variety of levels, from syntax to semantics to social awareness, all embedded within an evolving historical, cultural and individual consciousness. In responding to an interview question about his choice to record *Freedom Suite*, David S. Ware stated: 'This is a perfect opportunity to show the link between me and Sonny, an opportune time to show how one generation is built upon another and how the relationships work in the whole stream of music that's called jazz' (Bowden, 2002). Ware's remarks remind us that we need better and more appropriate tools to discuss the ways in which tradition and expectation are referenced in musical performance and cognition. And we need to be aware of the variety of culture-specific ways in which these performances and processes are framed and valued.

Signifyin(g): The Play of Meaning in Jazz Performance

Signifyin(g), the term most often used to describe the semantic play commonly encountered in African American language and music, is a culture-specific example of what Mikhail Bakhtin (1984) refers to as double-voiced discourse. Henry Louis Gates (1988) has published the most extensive work on signifyin(g) and several music scholars have applied his insight to discussions of jazz. Gates describes signifyin(g) as a mediating strategy for discourse, rooted in pan-African discursive mythologies, involving aspects of repetition and revision to create double meaning, indirectedness, and subtle humour.

Gates differentiates his usage of signifyin(g) from the Saussurian sense of a fixed sign by emphasizing the dialogic interactiveness of performance and the mutability and ambiguity of meaning found in African American arts in general.

As Gates (1988, p. 54) writes: 'One does not signify something; rather, one signifies in some way'. Margaret Drewal (1992, p. 4) also comments on the nature of signifyin(g) as a verb:

> What is especially interesting to me is that Afro-Americans take the concepts of signifiers and signifieds (objects–persons, places, things) and turn them into a verb 'signify', simultaneously turning the static equation between two related 'things' into a double-voiced process. 'To signify' is to revise that which is received, altering the way the past is read, thereby redefining one's relation to it.

Signfyin(g) represents an engagement with preceding texts so as to 'create a space' for one's own, both enabling a new text and in important ways reshaping our conception of the tradition in which these texts occur. In jazz scholarship, this dynamic approach to reference and revision has been commented on in several ways. John Murphy (1990) explores the process of interaction among jazz improvisers, repositioning Harold Bloom's rather Eurocentric idea of the 'anxiety of influence' to better reflect the 'joy of influence' heard as jazz musicians reference one another's work through musical tribute and quotation, and, more generally, through the process of apprenticeship. Ingrid Monson (1996) highlights in her analysis of Coltrane's performance of 'My Favorite Things' the sense of parody or irony that can accompany a jazz musician's choice to rework popular material. Gary Tomlinson (1991) offers an insightful account of the ideologies of canon formation and a cogent critique of the mistreatment of Miles Davis' fusion period by most jazz historians. And Robert Walser (1995) focused the lens of signifyin(g) theory on a detailed analysis of Davis' famous recording of 'My Funny Valentine', reminding jazz listeners and scholars that musical creativity need not be limited by abstractions such as notes.

Most signifyin(g) scholarship in jazz has relied on the idea that the first conceptual model is recognized as 'authoritative' but the validity is then granted to the second, authorial model through the rejection of the first. With 'My Favorite Things', for instance, Coltrane rejects Richard Rodgers' show-tune model for the song, the 'authentic' version of the work, and 'signifies' with a new, 'authoritative' performance. And yet the signifyin(g) relationship is decidedly more complex and subtle than that. As Walser (1995, p. 173) points out in his analysis of 'My Funny Valentine', 'as a performer, Davis is signifyin' on all of the versions of the song he has heard; but for his audience, Davis is signifyin' on all of the versions each listener has heard. What is played is played up against Davis's intertextual experience, and what is heard is heard up against the listener's experiences.'

What are we to make, then, of the recent moves by saxophonists Marsalis, Murray and Ware to engage with the 'authoritative' work of Coltrane and Rollins? Marshall Bowden (2002) implies that *Freedom Suite* and *A Love Supreme* have become 'a real yardstick' for anyone playing the tenor saxophone. But if signifyin(g) means nothing more than referencing a tradition, then it is so commonplace in jazz, and in fact in all music, as to signify nothing. Can we hear these newer versions of 'classic' works as something more than mere technical exercises or matter-of-fact tributes celebrating the 'joy of influence'?

To hear these reinterpretations as signifyin(g) on the original involves a complex matrix of cultural knowledge. If that matrix of knowledge is not in place, we are left with only the more routine process of referencing a traditional model or simply with unmediated authorial discourse. For signifyin(g) to signify something more than a most general kind of musical reference, it must hinge on musical, historical and cultural tensions between the voices at play. As Zbikowski (2002, p. 241) points out, 'signifyin(g) becomes interesting when tensions between the models become obvious — that is, when tensions become as important as the models themselves'. Can we also hear these tensions as both reflecting and shaping the various ideologies and cultural understandings that inform the production, consumption, and critical discourses of jazz?

Krin Gabbard (1995) has argued that canon formation may be inescapable if jazz is to claim its place within the academy, and yet we must be continually aware that the process of canon formation is a discourse of power, reinforcing the values of the canonizers. Canon formation entails not only choosing those individuals to be included or excluded, but also how we value and approach the work of those who have been included. Branford Marsalis' approach to the classic work of Rollins and Coltrane puts him in dialogue with their authoritative versions. While leaving the overall form and presentation of the work the same, he and his band mates signify on the details of the original performances. Their performances are heard in constant 'dialogue' with the original voices. David Murray adopts several of the defining features of Coltrane's signature work, but recasts them with different instrumentation, rhythm, arrangement and style. Both saxophonists stressed their approach to referencing the specific 'musical' aspects of Coltrane's composition. Marsalis asserts, 'If you take off the name, if you take away the fact that it's a tribute to God, then it becomes this great body of work, a great piece of music'. And Murray maintains, 'It's like any other music out there' (quoted in Kahn, 2002a, p. 203).

David S. Ware's recording of *Freedom Suite* offers a different and possibly more radical approach to signifyin(g). His performance, embedded in the present, seems both to look to the future and to ask listeners to reassess the past. Celebrating Ware's disc, Ben Schulman (2002) writes that 'The record stands as a true testament to the fact that our most musical of musics indeed still thrives when applied by those who truly understand its structure, intent, history, and most of all, possibilities'. Yet Bill Shoemaker (2002), in praising the same performance, worries briefly that 'Ware puts the original in an arguably ambivalent light, dating Rollins' sensibilities'.

Ware's freewheeling approach to the suite does seem to highlight the fact that, despite its provocative title and message, Rollins' original performance departed in only limited musical ways from the standard practices of the hard bop era. Not long after its initial release, Rollins took the first of his celebrated 'sabbaticals' from the jazz scene, at least in part to explore the variety of sounds and approaches that were circulating in the nascent free jazz community removed from the pressures of the commercial music industry. As Bowden (2002) comments: 'I don't doubt that the piece might have leaned much more towards free jazz had Rollins recorded it a couple of years later'.

And yet Rollins' work, beyond any formalist treatment of its musical details, *was* a cry of protest against America's treatment of African Americans and Shoemaker correctly assesses that 'Ware's diamond-yielding force serves the spirit, if not the letter of Rollins' suite'. Ware does, it would seem, call the 'authority' of the original into question at the same time that he heeds the original's aesthetic and cultural impetus. With signifyin(g), meaning is not something that is fixed, but something that is created by the performer and listener in a dynamic, cultural context. Great jazz — past, present, and future — draws on a robust tradition and, in turn, must signify in some way on that tradition, calling even cherished notions and works into question. The 'prototype' for 'authentic' jazz may actually be that which departs from the specific qualities of previous work, albeit in culturally organized and sanctioned ways.

Jazz music, after roughly a century of development and dissemination, is at a point in which a few of its most influential artists and 'works' have been granted the inviolable status of master and masterpiece. Gary Tomlinson (1991, p. 243) believes

> Difficulties arise not in our inevitable making of personal canons but rather in our move to empower them by uniting with others who hold fundamentally similar personal canons. . . . It is a shift away from dialogue . . . by which we might sustain a healthy flux of impermanent and intersubjective canons.

Juxtaposing different performances or interpretations of the same musical work, regardless of genre, will create a point of comparison and the potential for new meanings to arise. Signifyin(g), however, offers a culture-specific example of musical and conceptual blending; one which involves playful comment *and* criticism, calling the original work into question and potentially inverting or subverting the status quo. Contemporary cognitive science has probed the ways in which our embodied experiences shape both our preconceptual and conceptual understandings. Conceptual structures can and do organize how we learn, discuss and engage with musical sound. They are frequently grounded in our shared bodily experiences and can be extremely precise in their application, while at the same time they remain flexible enough to allow for considerable cultural variation. Music performance, and indeed all aspects of cultural performance, relies on a strong link to community and tradition. Jazz music has hinged on and heralded resistant social formations for over a century, and it continues to provide a rich context for investigating the relationship between musical syntax, social interactive processes, and cognitive and cultural understandings.

References: Discs

Coltrane, A. (1998), *World Galaxy*, Impulse (JPN Import) CD TCL0631294.
Coltrane, J. (2002), *A Love Supreme (Deluxe Edition),* Impulse CD 314 589 945-2.
Harley, R. (1998), *Brotherly Love,* Tartan Pride CD 9801.
Herwig, C. (1996), *The Latin Side of John Coltrane*, Astor Place Records CD 4003.
Marsalis, B. (2002), *Footsteps of our Fathers*, Marsalis Music 613301.
McLaughlin, J., Santana C. (1990), *Love, Devotion, and Surrender*, Sony CD 32034.
Murray, D. (2000), *Octet Plays Trane*, Justin Time CD 131-2.
Rollins, S. (1991), *Freedom Suite*, Original Jazz Classics CD 67.
Ware, D. S. (2002), *The Freedom Suite*, AUM Fidelity CD 023.
Vega, R. (2002), *Pa'lante*, Palmetto Records CD 2079.

References: Books and Articles

Bakhtin, M. (1984), *Problems of Dostoevsky's Poetics*, trans. Caryl Emerson (Minneapolis: University of Minnesota Press).

Borgo, D. (in press), 'The chaotic self, or the embodiment of Evan Parker', in *Playing Changes: New Jazz Studies*, ed. Robert Walser (Duke University Press).

Borgo, D. (2003a), 'Negotiating freedom: Values and practices in contemporary improvised music', *Black Music Research Journal*, **23** (1)..

Borgo, D. (2003b), 'Between worlds: The embodied and ecstatic sounds of jazz', *The Open Space*, **5**.

Borgo, D. (2002), 'Synergy and surrealestate: The orderly-disorder of free improvisation,' *Pacific Review of Ethnomusicology*, **10**.

Bowden, M. (2002), 'Freedom Suite Revisited,' *Pop Matters*, (popmatters.com/music/reviews/w/waredavid-freedom)

Corbett, J. (1995), 'Ephemera underscored: Writing around free improvisation', in *Jazz Among the Discourses*, ed. Krin Gabbard (Durham: Duke University Press).

Damasio, A. (1999), *The Feeling of What Happens: Body and Emotion in the Making of Consciousness* (New York: Harcourt Brace).

Drewal, M.T. (1992), *Yoruba Ritual: Performers, Play, Agency* (Bloomington: Indiana University Press).

Fauconnier, G., Turner, M. (2002), *The Way We Think: Conceptual Blending and the Mind's Hidden Complexities* (New York: Basic Books).

Gabbard, K. (1995), 'The Jazz Canon and its Consequences', in *Jazz Among the Discourses* (Duke University Press).

Gadamer, H.G. (1993), *Truth and Method* (New York: Continuum Publishing).

Gates, H.L. Jr. (1988), *The Signifying Monkey: A Theory of Afro-American Literary Criticism* (New York: Oxford University Press).

Jurek, T. (2002), Review of David S. Ware's *Freedom Suite*, *All Music Guide* (allmusic.com)

Kahn, A. (2002a), *A Love Supreme: The Story of John Coltrane's Signature Album* (New York: Penguin Books).

Kahn, A. (2002b), liner notes to *A Love Supreme: Deluxe Edition* (2-CD, Impulse Records).

Lakoff, G. and Johnson, M. (1980), *Metaphors We Live By* (Chicago: University of Chicago Press).

McNeil, W.H. (1995), *Keeping Together in Time: Dance and Drill in Human History* (Cambridge, MA: Harvard University Press).

Monson, I. (1996), *Sayin' Something* (Chicago: University of Chicago Press).

Murphy, J. (1990), 'Jazz Improvisation: The Joy of Influence', *The Black Perspective in Music*, **18** (1), p. 2.

Nisensen, E. (2000), *Open Sky: Sonny Rollins and His World of Improvisation* (Da Capo Press).

Porter, L. (1985), 'John Coltrane's *A Love Supreme*: Jazz Improvisation as Composition', *Journal of the American Musicological Society*, **38**, p. 3.

Rosch, E. (1978), 'Principles of categorization', in *Cognition and Categorization* (Hillsdale, NJ: Lawrence Erlbaum Associates).

Rosch, E. (1999), 'Reclaiming concepts', *Journal of Consciousness Studies*, **6** (11–12), pp. 61–77.

Schulman, B. (2002), Review of David S. Ware's *Freedom Suite*, *Action Man Magazine* (www.aumfidelity.com).

Shoemaker, B. (2002), Review of David S. Ware's *Freedom Suite*, *Wire* (October).

Smalls, C. (1998), *Musicking: The Meanings of Performing and Listening* (Hanover, NH: Wesleyan University Press).

Such, D. (1993), *Avant-Garde Musicians Performing 'Out There'* (Iowa City: University of Iowa Press).

Sutton-Smith, B. (1974), 'Toward an Anthropology of Play', *The Association for the Anthropological Study of Play Newsletter* 1.

Tomlinson, G. (1991), 'Cultural dialogics and jazz: A white historian signifies', *Black Music Research*, **11**, p. 2.

Turner, M. (1996), *The Literary Mind* (New York: Oxford University Press).

Walser, R. (1995), '"Out of notes": Signification, interpretation, and the problem of Miles Davis', in *Jazz Among the Discourses*, ed. Krin Gabbard, (Durham: Duke University Press),

Zbikowski, L. (2002), *Conceptualizing Music: Cognitive Structure, Theory, and Analysis* (New York: Oxford University Press).

Zbikowski, L. (1998), 'Metaphor and music theory: Perspectives from cognitive science', *Music Theory Online*, **4**, p. 1.

Annual Subscription Rates (for 12 monthly issues)
Individuals: $99/£62
Institutions: $296/£185
Includes accelerated delivery (UK & USA), surface mail rest of world.
Orders to : Imprint Academic, PO Box 200, Exeter EX5 5YX, UK.
Tel: +44 1392 841600; Fax: 841478; Email: sandra@imprint.co.uk.
Cheques (£ or $US 'Imprint Academic'); VISA/AMEX/MASTERCARD

STYLE SHEET AND GUIDE TO AUTHORS

JCS is aimed at an educated multi-disciplinary readership. Authors should not assume prior knowledge in a subject speciality and should provide background information for their research. The use of technical terms should be avoided or made explicit. Where technical details are essential (for example in laboratory experiments), include them in footnotes or appendices, leaving the text accessible to the non-specialist reader. The same principle should also apply to non-essential mathematics.

Articles should not normally exceed 9,000 words (including footnotes). A short 150 word summary should accompany each submission. In general authors should adhere to the usages and conventions in Fowler's *Modern English Usage* which should be consulted for all questions not covered in these notes.

Footnote numbering should be consecutive superscript throughout the article. References to books and articles should be by way of author (date) or (author, date). Multiple publications from the same year should be labelled (Skinner, 1966a, b, c . . .). A single bibliography at the end should be compiled alphabetically observing the following conventions:

1 **References to complete books** should take the following form:
Dennett, D.C. (1998), *Brainchildren* (Cambridge, MA: MIT Press).

2 **References to chapters in books** should take the following form:
Wilkes, K. (1995), 'Losing consciousness', in *Conscious Experience*, ed. T. Metzinger (Paderborn: Schöningh).

3 **References to articles** should take the following form:
Humphrey, N. (2000), 'How to solve the mind–body problem', *Journal of Consciousness Studies*, **7** (4), pp. 5–20.

SUBMISSION OF MANUSCRIPTS BY EMAIL

Authors are encouraged to email their wordprocessor files (retaining italics, accents, superscripts, footnotes etc.) or PDF files. We cannot currently review LaTex files. Send all submissions to **anthony@imprint.co.uk**.

Where it is necessary to send contributions by normal mail, they should be clearly typed in double spacing. One hard copy should be submitted, plus a copy of the article on disk. This will enable us to email it to editors and reviewers and speed up the review process. Please state what machine and wordprocessing program was used to prepare the text.